2004

It Sounded Good
When We Started

It Sounded Good When We Started

A Project Manager's Guide to Working with People on Projects

Dwayne Phillips

Roy O'Bryan

A JOHN WILEY & SONS, INC., PUBLICATION

Published by John Wiley & Sons, Inc., Hoboken, New Jersey.
Published simultaneously in Canada.

For general information on our other products and services please contact our Customer Care Department within the U.S. at 877-762-2974, outside the U.S. at 317-572-3993 or fax 317-572-4002.

Wiley also publishes its books in a variety of electronic formats. Some content that appears in print, however, may not be available in electronic format.

Library of Congress Cataloging-in-Publication Data is available.

ISBN 0-471-48586-1

Printed in the United States of America.

10 9 8 7 6 5 4 3

Contents

Part 8

Preface

We enjoy working with people on projects. This is what the two of us have done for most of our professional lives (some 60 plus years between the two of us). Projects fascinate and challenge us because they comprise people trying to work together to do something they could not do individually, given limited resources. This book contains some of our experiences working with people on projects and in other situations. It contains some of our trials and triumphs and many of our mistakes.

The intended audience of this book includes anyone who works with people on projects and in many other circumstances. We think this is a large audience because our view of projects encompasses most people. Project managers are one obvious group who may benefit from our experiences. The same is true of people who want to be project managers one day. This book may help them avoid many of the problems we have encountered. We feel this book contains items for almost everyone else regardless of their title, type of employment, or whether or not they work on projects. We have found that most people have the ability to shape their relationships with other people, and this act of shaping represents a large part of this book.

The two of us have been working with people on projects for many years. Roy began doing this professionally in 1960, whereas Dwayne began in 1980. Our paths crossed in 1998 when we were thrown together on a project that we call Delphi in this book. This project sounded like a good idea when we started. Everything you could want on a project was in place. A study contract preceded a second contract that built a prototype. These two contracts led to an initial production contract—Delphi. The requirements were set, funding was in place, and the people were ready. The, project, however, was full of problems. These problems were so plentiful and severe that we almost cancelled the project. We persevered, worked with the people, finished the project, and delivered a product that the users are using happily every day. Such an ending, rare given the circumstances, was quite satisfying.

We enjoyed working with the people on this project so much that we decided to share our experiences in a book. The two of us came to this book project from different backgrounds. Roy is known as a good storyteller. He has the talent for filling the time spent in airports, hotel lobbies, and while watching system testing by telling stories of the many places he has been and the many things he has done (boxing, automobile racing, hunting in Africa, etc.). Dwayne is a writer of sorts, having published several books and many articles. Roy transformed our experiences into chapter titles and themes, and Dwayne typed most of the words. Hereafter, we use forms of the word "we" to describe the two of us. Unless specified, the word "I" refers to Dwayne.

Each chapter in the book has three basic sections. The first section contains stories from our past. Most of the stories are about problems we had on projects. We tend to remember problems more than successes. Also, problems tend to provide more opportunities for learning. Our project had plenty of problems, so we learned much during our three years together.

The second section of each chapter contains warning signs of coming trouble. These are things that we noticed at the time, but did not understand what they meant. After the trouble occurred, we remembered what preceded the trouble and the warning signs. For example, one warning sign is when we visit a builder, ask to see the printout of the schedule, and hear, "We tried to print it yesterday, but there's something wrong with the plotter and the software." Red lights should flash and sirens should wail (see Chapter 9 for some reasons why).

The third section of each chapter contains preventative measures. These are things we can do to create an environment in which problems do not seem to grow as readily. This sounds like a section for the project managers of the world. Nevertheless, as we stated earlier, we find that anyone on a project can contribute to a good environment.

The book is a collection of independent chapters. We urge the reader to read Chapters 1 and 2, as they define terms that we use throughout. After that, browse the table of contents and read what interests you most. We have tried to group the chapters with other chapters having a similar theme. The eight parts of this book hold these little groups. As stated earlier, Part 1 contains two chapters that introduce terms we use throughout the book.

Part 2, Chapters 3 through 5, is about things that happen at the start of a project. These include the proposal, staffing-up, and starting the project short-handed. Part 3, Chapters 6 through 10, discusses some basics of project management. These include planning, requirements, design, tracking a schedule, and risk mitigation. Part 4, Chapters 11 through 14, is about working with people, including a discussion of the project manager, communicating with people, people making decisions, and rewarding people. Part 5, Chapters 15 through 17, is about when people do not pull together the way we wish, including digging yourself into a hole, not reviewing products created by others, and not providing adequate supervision. Part 6, Chapters 18 and 19, is about misusing others and ourselves. Chapter 18 discusses having more confidence than experience, and Chapter 19 discusses assuming what talents people bring to a project. Part 7, Chapters 20 through 22, is about big issues such as using the right people, using the right approach, and doing the right thing. These include discussions of hiring a large corporation for a small project, outsourcing, and building the wrong product. Part 8, Chapters 23 through 25, closes the book with the subject of fooling ourselves. This includes the topics of knowing what we know, not breathing properly, and thinking we are out of the woods before the project is completed.

We hope you enjoy reading this book. We further hope that you can avoid many of the problems we have experienced. Sometimes, we like to have a difficult situation because it teaches us things and gives us a nice story to tell. We would rather have not lived through many of the stories we tell in this book. They took a terrible toll on the lives of people on projects and their loved ones at home.

This book does not contain "the most important things we have ever learned about people working on projects." It is more like a collection of some of the things we have seen. We suppose there is much more we could tell, but we had to stop writing sometime. Maybe we will write more another day.

We appreciate our families for their love and support while we were writing this book. Families comprise wonderful people, and our lives with our families are the greatest project we ever undertake. Dwayne thanks Karen, his wife since a hot July day in Louisiana in 1983. Dwayne also thanks his three sons Seth, Nathan, and Adam. Roy thanks Lynda, his wife since the hottest day in Seattle in July 1962. Roy also thanks his family; Kim, Fred, and grandson of two months Joshua; Stacey and Kevin; Ty and new daughter Tyra, honeymooning in Ireland.

A special thanks to Kim for making a quick pass through the manuscript between feedings to catch any major grammatical blunders before we sent the book to the publisher.

Roy O'Bryan
Dwayne Phillips

Fairfax County, Virginia
May 2003

Part 1

The first two chapters set the stage for the rest of this book. The first chapter introduces the people, process, and product of the Delphi project. Delphi is the subject of most of this book, so we urge you to learn the terms we will use throughout. The second chapter discusses the project room. This is a public place in which to put all the information related to the project. We recommend that all projects have and use a project room.

Chapter 1

It Sounded Good When We Started. By Dwayne Phillips and Roy O'Bryan
ISBN 0-471-48586-1 © 2004 by the Institute of Electrical and Electronics Engineers.

It Sounded Good
When We Started

In November of 1998, I* boarded a United Airlines flight to Los Angeles from Dulles Airport near Washington, DC. I would be spending my 40th birthday listening to a contractor describe the achievements, or lack thereof, made during the previous month on a project. My managers had asked me to go on this trip because I was the software specialist in our office and they anticipated that the contractor would soon be entering the phase for upgrading the software on a system. They were wrong, as this upgrade would not occur for several years. Nevertheless, my managers would soon volunteer me to be the lead on the project, and I would be taking these monthly and sometimes twice-monthly flights to the West Coast to monitor progress.

Accompanying me on this and many of the trips was Roy O'Bryan. He had retired from government service and was working for a company that provided technical assistance on this and other projects. He was the "experienced" one. He had worked four years on the project that preceded this one and had been working on this project since its start-up, almost a year before I arrived on the scene. What neither of us knew or anticipated at this point, was that this project was neither going to be like its predecessor, nor like any that we had experienced previously.

This project, which we shall call "Delphi," was not going well. A big problem was that people in our East Coast office thought the project was on firm ground. There had been a few problems in the first few months, but "the contractor had taken the appropriate action, fixed the problems, and all would be well from here on." That would not be the case. We experienced

---

*Throughout this book, "we" refers to both authors; "I" refers to Dwayne Phillips.

It Sounded Good When We Started. By Dwayne Phillips and Roy O'Bryan
ISBN 0-471-48586-1 © 2004 by the Institute of Electrical and Electronics Engineers.

months of discovering problems, denying them, concentrating on short-term fixes, and punishing innocent bystanders before we faced the facts. We had been suckered into dispensing Band-Aids to fix systemic problems and had failed miserably when it came to endemic diagnosis. Initially, we spent far too much time on the dance floor before we decided to go up to the balcony to really see what was happening. The efforts of a few smart and courageous people brought Delphi around. To some of the bystanders, the project was a failure, but to users—the real stakeholders—it was successful and remains so today.

Delphi was not supposed to have all these problems, denial, and tribulations. It was to be a great project that went smoothly and produced an excellent product on time and on budget. In other words, it sounded good when we started.

There is an old adage about teaching old dogs new tricks. Roy and I had more years than we wish to admit running projects. We thought that we were pretty savvy when it came to the various aspects of project management, but during the three-plus years of working on Delphi we experienced much and learned even more. There was a lot of grief, but somewhere in midst of all our pain there was irony and some humor. Roy, being somewhat perceptive, recorded this wit as one-liners on 3 × 5 cards. Periodically, we would shuffle through the cards, muse about the one-liners as prospective chapters titles, and facetiously opined that the Delphi experience—what we had learned and had experienced—could fill the pages of a book. At some point in the spring of 2001, the thoughts could no longer be contained and I started writing. The one-liners became topics, and the topics became the titles of chapters. As we wrote, other chapter titles came to mind.

This chapter sets the stage for the rest of the book. We define terms here so that we do not have to repeat them throughout the rest of the chapters.

THE PRODUCT

The product of Delphi was a system with both hardware and software. The hardware portion was mostly analog circuitry. Our desire to make the system as small and light as possible drove us to use technologies that were difficult to handle physically. Assembly workers did much of their work using microscopes. They touched the parts with machines instead of their hands. These technologies are common when people need to build small, high-performance analog systems.

The software portion was split between an embedded processor in the system and its controller. About half of the software ran on an embedded processor in the system. This controlled the flow of signals through the system. Most of the system comprised analog circuitry, with the control portions being digital. We admired the people who worked on the software, as it was complex and difficult to write and maintain. It was conceived when object-oriented design was relatively new, DOS was the standard operating system, and a 30 MHz embedded processor was really fast. By the time Delphi was delivered, object-oriented design was an accepted development methodology, Pentium processors were in their third generation, and Windows dominated the operating environments.

The system's controller was a laptop computer. This software was also difficult to maintain, as we were using laptop computers from the early 1990s (later chapters explain why). The programmers had to squeeze the software into limited memory and make it perform efficiently to meet the timing requirements of real-time control.

Delphi produced nine systems. Because tiny analog circuits were a major part of the project, each system had challenges of its own. We never reached the end of a learning curve where the engineers could turn their backs while assemblers built and tested the systems.

THE PEOPLE

There were close to 100 people involved with Delphi. These people were divided into three major groups. First were the users. These people needed the systems to do their jobs. They stated the requirements of the product during the early 1990s. The users took several trips a year with us to the West Coast to monitor progress. They also tested the systems by using them in their environment.

The second group was the builders. These people worked for the contractor who built the systems. They toiled long hours and weekends to deliver systems that the users needed. There were several groups of people working for the builder. One group was the engineers who designed, integrated, and tested the system. Another group was the programmers who wrote, tested, and maintained the software. A less appreciated but equally important group was the assembly workers. These people sat in front of microscopes and machines and assembled the tiny components into a system.

We worked in the group we will call "the buyer." Our job was to take the user's requirements to the builder and monitor the builder's progress. We managed the contract between our organization and the builder. If we had done Delphi in the 1960s, we would have built the product ourselves, but in the 1990s, like today, we worked with someone else to build the product.

These three groups—the users, builders, and buyers—had managers. The managers of the users and buyers funded the project. The builder's managers represented their company to our managers. It would be easy to blame all the problems we experienced with Delphi on the managers. That, however, would not be the truth. The managers on the user and buyer sides listened to our concerns and gathered the funds we needed to complete the project. The managers on the builder side put the necessary people on the project and did not quit when business logic showed otherwise.

We had a fine collection of individuals working on Delphi. There were some days when some people lashed out at others from fatigue and frustration. Some people quit the project and moved elsewhere. Despite the troubles and trials of Delphi, most of the people stayed with it for most of the project. The most satisfying part of this project was watching people come to work everyday and push against a mass of thousands of interlaced problems until that mass went away.

Throughout this book are the names of many people. We changed the names to protect the privacy of the people who worked on Delphi.

THE PROCESS

Delphi was a government project. I was an employee of the U.S. Federal government (still am), as were the users. We encourage readers to keep reading even if they don't work for or with the government. The challenges and lessons of Delphi apply to almost any human endeavor.

Delphi was part of a larger program involving the users, buyer, and builder. This program started in the early 1990s. The builder won a competitive contract from the buyer. They ran a four-year, $40M project in which they delivered two prototype systems. I was not involved with that project, but Roy was. Those systems were so expensive because the builder had to invent much of the hardware and develop all the software algorithms. The users took the systems into their environment and used them. Their experiences produced a new set of requirements.

Shortly after finishing this first contract, the buyer awarded the builder the Delphi contract to build more systems. The builder would not have to invent things as they had to on the first project. Instead, "all they would have to do" was produce nine more systems and include a few enhancements so these systems would meet all the user's requirements. At least that is all that most people felt the builder would have to do. Delphi proved otherwise.

OTHER THINGS

Delphi involved many other things that made the project both possible and difficult. We had a small mountain of documents, including requirements, high-level designs, low-level designs, plans, drawings, specifications, etc. We had hundreds of meetings both formal and informal. The buyer and builder lived and worked on opposite coasts. This meant plenty of plane rides, daily phone calls, and a handful of faxes each week.

These items—documents, meetings, phone calls, and faxes—meant countless attempts from different groups of people to communicate with one another. This meant countless opportunities for miscommunication. Many of the problems and lessons in this book are about this subject of human communication. If the reader is to learn one lesson from this book, it is that good, hard working, conscientious people frequently misunderstand one another. Such misunderstandings should not surprise or anger anyone. They are normal, and we need to work our way through them.

CONCLUSION

Delphi was one of the most challenging and rewarding projects we have worked on in our careers. We spent three and a half years on it. Several of us had children go from elementary school to high school during this time. Delphi ended by delivering what the users needed. It cost more than people wanted to spend and the wait was longer than people wanted to endure, but the people persevered. In the end, our reward was that we were able to work with people who had the knowledge, skill, and devotion to deliver what many others felt they could not. This is what makes projects worth the years of our lives—the people.

Chapter 2

A Place Where Everyone Knows Your Name: The Project Room

This book contains many examples of bad things that have happened on our project. Many of those bad things trace back to one cause—someone didn't know something that someone else did. Had both people known the same thing, the project would have been smoother and the people would have had less trouble.

This chapter that concentrates on something good to have, something that will help people communicate better—the project room. Establishing a project room is a positive thing the project manager should do on day one. The project room will not ensure that people communicate well, as we know of nothing that will do that. It will, however, help people communicate better.

The project room is a place where team members gather. It has the microwave oven, refrigerator, TV, couch, etc. It also contains information about the project. This includes schedules, descriptions of deliverables, documents, and displays. If someone wants to know something about the project, they should go there.

When people come to the project room, they see outside their own cubicle and know what is happening with everyone on the project. People understand that they are part of something bigger. They acknowledge that each person needs every other person to make this project work. People also see other people in the project room. They can talk about trials and triumphs, ask questions, and share ideas. This is where people learn how and when they can help others.

People on the project begin to know other project members as people. Knowing people as people may be the best effect of the project room. People will talk to other people when they know them. Friends share information

It Sounded Good When We Started. By Dwayne Phillips and Roy O'Bryan
ISBN 0-471-48586-1 © 2004 by the Institute of Electrical and Electronics Engineers.

with friends more than they do with strangers, and friends want to see friends succeed.

In the project room, people can also see the parts of the project that other people are working. The project room gives people an opportunity to help one another. Sometimes, help is a hindrance, but often it is taken in the spirit in which it is given. There are days when people do not have much to do because they are waiting on something from someone. They can spend their time well by assisting someone else. Often, this assistance is not technical or directly related to the project. Picking up someone's children at school, delivering clothes to the dry cleaners, grabbing a prescription before the store closes, etc. can be lifesavers. They are also easy to do when someone is willing and able to help someone else.

DELPHI'S PROJECT ROOM

Delphi had gotten off to a poor start. (The following chapters will relate how that happened.) Although I had been around the "office" for a year or so, I really had not become involved with Delphi nor paid much attention to what was going on. Anyway, I was "chosen" to be the leader for the buyer. Delphi had been under contract for about a year before I came on the scene. Wanting to understand what was supposed to be happening, I called the builder, introduced myself, and arranged a meeting. I told the builder that I was really interested in seeing how everything fit together and would like to see, among other things, the master project schedule. The builder was very accommodating. When I arrived, I found that the builder had a freshly printed master schedule arranged around the walls of the conference room. There were hundreds of events all linked together in a network. The builder had printed out everything on 4 by 8 foot sheets of paper. There must have been 15 or 16 sheets of paper on the walls.

I went through the various views of the project by myself for a day. Engineers working on the project would wander by and look in the door. I would pull them in and ask them about their respective parts of the project. I would point to the task they would be working on and ask if they were on schedule, they would show me the task they were working currently, and we would discuss why we were having problems. The idea was for me to learn from them.

One of the surprising things that happened was that the builder's engineers seemed to learn more than I did. Some had been working on the project for a year or more, but they had never seen the entire plan. I had suspected that the builder's project manager had put up the master schedule just for my benefit and I was right. As we talked, we would wander to a part of the plan on which they were not working.

They would say things like, "I didn't know that was happening now. Who is working on that? I was supposed to help with it, but no one told me they had started."

The problem was that the builder had three full-time "schedulers" who were responsible for "putting the schedule together." The schedulers would go to each of the engineers and ask how many peas (tasks) were on their plate, when they planned to start on each task, and how long it would take. Then they would go back to the schedule room and enter the task's "start dates" and "durations" into the computer. With a little bit of juggling, the schedulers could link the tasks and "get everything to work out."

The schedulers were talking to the engineers, but the engineers were not talking to the schedulers. The information flow was one way—from schedulers the to the engineers.

"To the guy with a hammer in his hand, everything looks like a nail." So it was for the schedulers. The master schedule was the all-encompassing product. Remember that the master schedule had only resided in the computer. It wasn't until I wanted to see it that it was posted where everyone could see it.

We kept these schedules on the walls of this conference room for several months. This was not a great project room as there were no refreshments, microwave, TV, and other things you would like to have in a project a room. It was, however, a big room with several large tables, plenty of chairs, and all those PERT charts.

This room contained information. It was not all high-quality information as Delphi's plans were faulty at this stage. Nevertheless, it was information. When we had questions, we had a place to gather to discuss them. We had plenty of constructive conversations in that room. We would sit in the chairs, put our feet on the tables, look around at the plan, and talk.

Delphi found a better project room about a year later. This room had chairs, walls, huge whiteboards, and a computer with a projector and screen. It was also near the coffeepot and the refrigerator. The builder kept short-term plans on the walls and the long-term plans and documents were on the computer. We solved many problems in that room and changed a troubled project into a successful one.

WARNING SIGNS OF TROUBLE WITH THE PROJECT ROOM

Project rooms help people communicate, but they can have their faults. We have seen project rooms that people avoided. This section describes some of these problems and things that warn us that the problems are coming.

Using a Computer

The purpose of the project room is to share information. We want to bring people together in an environment that engenders discussion and facilitates problem solving.

One of the problems that can occur on a project is that the project room can become a static display. The effective project rooms we have seen were dynamic. People read information with interest and, most importantly, they changed and added to the information.

A warning sign of a project room becoming static is when people use a computer to generate all the project room's information. The most common output of a computer is 8½" × 11" pieces of paper. These printouts are only readable up close by one person at a time. A project room covered with 8½" × 11" pieces of paper in a 12 point font is static. One person reads one item of information. Another person stands at another wall and reads another item of information. There is little or no exchange of information between the two people.

The situation improves if we use a plotter that can print information on large sheets of paper in big print. With this, people can sit in chairs, sip a drink, chat, and read from across the room. While chatting, they discuss the information they are reading. This is more dynamic than the situation described above.

The pretty outputs of plotters can still limit the exchange of information in the project room. People are wary of scribbling a note on the polished output of a plotter. They do not want to "mess up" the display. As a result, they may talk about the information with the person sitting next to them, but they do not add that information to the wall where others can see it.

A further improvement comes when the walls also include sticky notes, whiteboards, big markers, sheets of butcher paper or newsprint, etc. These things invite people to scribble in new information. Fears of "messing up" the room subside when much of the information on the walls is written by hand. Also, people are apt to talk with others and explain what they have written. The project room becomes a dynamic place of information exchange.

Off Limits

A project has a problem if people avoid the project room. They do not gather; they do not share information, and the project does not benefit.

One thing that keeps people out of the project room is when it is located in the project manager's office. Some project managers like to have all the project information in their office. That is convenient, as they don't have to walk anywhere to find information. They think that since all the information needed for the project room is already posted in their office, why waste another room? Why not let their office be the project room? Some project managers do this because they think they are sacrificing their office for the good of the project.

This "sacrifice" by the project manager often dooms a project. People see the project manager's office as a place for people other than themselves. A warning sign of the project manager's office being off limits is when people say things like, "I want to know how the schedule looks, but it's in the boss' office and that is off limits," and "I haven't been invited into the boss' office, so I don't go."

There are several reasons why people feel the project manager's office is off limits. First, it is the boss' office. Even in today's enlightened age, some people wonder about people who spend much time in the boss's office. What are they plotting in there? Second, some people don't go to the boss' office because they don't feel as comfortable there as they do in their regular work area. After all, the boss' office is not common ground. Finally, the project room is for communicating and solving problems. If the project room is in the boss' office, there is a reluctance to disturb the boss. It's like being in the school library or the church.

Posting Harmful Information

The project room is a tool, and like all tools, people can misunderstand and misuse it. Misusing the project room hurts the efforts of the project team.

One warning sign of misusing the project room is when people post information that is harmful to individuals. There is plenty of "bad news" on a project. We can post bad news in a way that shows the project's problems and allows us to work on them. We can also post the bad news in a way that hurts people. That doesn't help anyone or anything.

Some people intentionally post harmful information, whereas others do it unintentionally. It is difficult to guess someone else's motives for posting harmful information. We recommend not trying to guess their motives but, instead, asking these people about their motives. Sample questions include, "Why do you want to post this? How did you learn this? How will this information help the project? How will this information help the other person perform his or her tasks? Have you spoken with the other person about this yet? Did you talk with the other person before you brought the information here?"

These questions help the person understand the intent and utility of the project room. The project room is there to help people work together and succeed. Personal harm doesn't help a group of people.

Not for Public Consumption

Since a project room exists to exchange information, it often exposes problems that lie beneath the surface. One problem is fear of information. Some people are afraid that some information (generally bad news) will become public.

Some things are not for public consumption. These things usually concern individuals. We should not post an individual's salary, health insurance claims, sick days, or home address. We should not post an individual's productivity information such as number of defects generated per week, number of defects corrected per week, or other information that states how well a person is performing on the job.

Information about how the team is performing on the project is appropriate for public posting. Sometimes, however, some people do not want some information posted. They are afraid of that information, and that is a problem the project manager must address.

There are several reasons why people might fear information. One is that it makes them look bad. Suppose they are the lead on the processing software and the information in the project room shows that the processing software is behind schedule. They can take that as a personal affront to them and their team. Suppose their best friend is the lead on the interface team and the project room shows that the interface has overrun its budget. They can take that as a criticism of their best friend.

These fears come from an environment of blame. The project manager needs to remove that environment and replace it with one of problems and solutions. If the processing software is late, it is a problem that affects the whole team, and teamwork is needed to remedy it. If the interface is over budget, that is a problem, and the team will look for budget surpluses in other areas to make up for this problem.

A warning sign of this fear and blame is a statement such as, "This is inappropriate to post publicly."

If a person is afraid to post project news, that tells us something about the person, the news, and the project environment. The person may feel the news reflects badly on them, their team, or a friend. Whatever it means, this is a message, and the project manager needs to pay attention to the message.

CREATING A GOOD SITUATION

We have learned of a few techniques that help us create and maintain good project rooms. We wish we would have learned them sooner and used them more often. Nevertheless, the following discusses some of these techniques.

Devote the Needed Resources

It is important to devote the needed resources to the project room. These include floor space with lots of walls, whiteboards, bulletin boards, supplies, furniture (a few places to sit and a table or two), and appliances (refrigerator and microwave). The furniture and appliances need not be first class. They are often available at garage sales or when upper management is remodeling their offices.

Budget for the project room for the length of the project. This means plan to have the project room from the outset and retain it until the project has been successfully completed and the lights have been turned off. There is nothing that will hurt morale more than seeing management take away the team's gathering place in the middle of a project. This arrangement is a leading indicator that management is cutting cost. People start polishing their resumes in anticipation of layoffs. They spend more time on the phone looking for their next job than working on this one.

Senior management took away a gathering place for Delphi. The builder had an area with coffee and bottled water (the large five gallon bottles that empty into a hot and cold dispenser). I never gave this area much thought, as most offices have a coffee pot and water area. On one visit I noticed the coffee and water were gone. The people told me that the company had removed them. The company had provided these free to the employees for as long as anyone could remember (over ten years), but one day changed its policy. To make matters worse, there was a reason for the bottled water. The water in the fountain tasted bad, and for years there had been an urban legend that the fountain water was unfit to drink (even for animals). The employees were dejected. Why couldn't the company cut its expense in half and ask the employees to pay 10 cents a day? Why couldn't the company do something else to cut expenses? The strangest part was the company would not allow the employees to bring in their own coffee pot and coffee because of safety codes.

Make the Workplace Safe

A prerequisite to having a valuable project room is to make the workplace safe. (Chapter 17 discusses the safe workplace at length.) People are not apt to post information in a public place if they feel someone will use it against them. They will post only good news or will color the news so it looks good.

It is the project manager's job to help people feel safe, and the project manager should lead by example. Examples include visiting the project room regularly, grabbing a marker and posting information on each visit, asking people in the project room questions about the project, and posting requests for help when a task is falling behind. The project manager is not the only one who has the authority to post a request for help. Everyone is responsible for something. Therefore, everyone must feel that they, too, have the authority to post a note requesting help. The project manager must be alert to new postings and determine the best approach for resolving the problem.

Attempting to inspire people by asking them to "just work harder" isn't going to bring a task back on track or engender goodwill among the troops. One element of the safe work environment is for everyone to know that the program manager is not going to shoot the messenger. They must feel confident that the program manager wants to know that they have a problem and cares just as much about their problem as they do. In the big scheme of things, not all problems have the same degree of urgency. Questions like, "Is this a little problem or a big problem?" are often answered in the context of the master schedule. With the master schedule plastered on the walls of the project room, everyone knows which tasks are on the critical path. Hence, everyone has a good sense of priorities. Everyone also knows that each task is related to another task and that there is a kindred nature of everything coming together at the right time.

Engineering and information technology work is often done by one person working alone. When I work alone, it is easy for me to become stuck on a problem and waste days before I find a solution. The right thing to do is ask for help quickly so the project doesn't fall behind. Asking for help is difficult for many people in our field because we think we are supposed to know how to do our jobs. The project manager can set the tone in this area by asking for help publicly by writing requests on the wall of the project room. This act tells everyone that asking for help is acceptable. In our experience, projects in which people ask for help quickly run smoother and have happier and more productive people.

Public Displays

The fundamental reason for a project room is to display information publicly. The basic information to display is the project's plan, its status, and the difference between the two. PERT and Gant charts are the usual way to show the plan. Check marks and notes scribbled on these show the status. The difference between the plan and reality shows where to shift resources to bring the project back on schedule. It also shows people how they can help others to bring their parts back on schedule.

Other public displays should include technical descriptions of the product such as requirements, architecture, and designs. A person should be able to see how their part of the product fits with the others. In addition, all project documents should be in the room. Some of these are best kept in hard copy form. Others can be left on a network server as long as the project room has a computer.

Finally, the project room should have an area where people can post questions. Questions could include, "Where can I find documentation on the debugger? How do I obtain an account on the testing computer? Where is the best fast food place open after midnight? Does anyone know of a baby sitter who works on Sundays? I've got a couple of tickets to. . . ." If anyone wanted to learn anything about living and surviving around the project and the organization, they would come to the project room.

Refreshments

Stock the project room with refreshments. The refreshments do not have to be free, but try to make them inexpensive. We want people to come here instead of the fast food place down the street. The project benefits in many ways when people gather in the project room. The side benefits far outweigh the direct costs of the refreshments.

Free refreshments, pool tables, ping pong tables, foosball, dartboards, giant screen TVs, etc. were scattered about the dot-coms during their heyday of the late 1990s. People in this part of the information technology field came to expect these perks. As with many perks, some people abused them. The refreshments in the project room are not in the category of the playrooms of the dot-com era. The project room is not a perk; it is a tool that helps individual projects succeed.

CONCLUSIONS ABOUT THE PROJECT ROOM

A project is a small community of people that exists for a period of time. Most people like to feel connected to their community; they want to know how their actions affect others and how other people affect themselves. Offices today can become cold, sterile, and lack a feeling of community. A project room allows us to keep project information in a public place that team members visit often.

Try to avoid the following:

- Trying to do everything on a computer
- Making the project room "off limits"
- Harmful information on the walls
- An atmosphere that says "That's not appropriate information to post publicly"

Create a good situation by

- Devoting the needed resources
- Making the workplace safe
- Displaying information publicly
- Keeping refreshments there

Project rooms do not ensure success and happiness. Nothing ensures success on projects, and happiness is something we decide for ourselves. An element of both success and happiness is communication about the project, product, and the people. A project room helps with that.

We built some good relationships in Delphi's project room. One relationship may have saved the life of an engineer named Jessie who helped us from time to time on the buyer's side. He visited the builder alone late in the project and became ill during the visit. One of the builder's employees, Mike, made sure that Jessie made it back to his hotel safely. Later, Mike called Jessie at the hotel to see how he was doing. Jessie wasn't well, so Mike drove to the hotel late at night and took Jessie to a hospital. Jessie stayed in the hospital several days until his condition improved and his wife could come from the East Coast to take him home. All that from a room where we kept schedules, drew plans, displayed status charts, and shared lives.

Part 2

The next three chapters discuss the early phase of a project. Chapter 3 describes the writing and reading of a proposal. This occurs before the project begins, but affects the life of the project. Chapters 4 and 5 discuss things that happen at the start of the project. Chapter 4 is about staffing a project and what happens if we start the project before all the people are on board. Chapter 5 discusses what people do, and neglect to do, at the start of a project.

It Sounded Good When We Started. By Dwayne Phillips and Roy O'Bryan
ISBN 0-471-48586-1 © 2004 by the Institute of Electrical and Electronics Engineers.

Chapter 3

A Charlatan in Expert's Clothing: Writing a Lie—The Proposal

Most contracts between a buyer and a builder begin with a proposal. The proposal states what the builder intends to do on a project should they be awarded the contract. The proposal contains things such as a technical approach to the problem, a project plan, a work breakdown structure (WBS), the hours needed from each of their labor categories, and the rates they pay these labor categories. These items describe the builder's likely cost, schedule, and product quality. The proposal contains few details, as creating those details is too costly for most proposals.

One of the balancing acts a builder must perform while writing a proposal is deciding how much time and money to spend on it. A builder could spend enormous resources creating a detailed proposal. That could be very risky, because if the builder does not win the contract, those resources are wasted. Some builders spend few resources preparing proposals. If they lose the contract, they have not wasted many resources on the proposal.

The proposal is made in response to a request for proposal (RFP). The RFP contains two basic documents. First is what the buyer expects the builder to produce—a specification of the product. This is the "what" or requirements. Second is what the buyer expects the builder to do—a statement of work or specification of the project. This is the "how" or "how much."

The builder takes the RFP, writes a proposal, and sends it to the buyer. The buyer evaluates proposals from several contending builders and selects the best. The buyer and builder enter into negotiations to settle on the details of the contract. If all goes well, the builder follows their proposal and delivers the product the buyer wants on time and within budget.

It Sounded Good When We Started. By Dwayne Phillips and Roy O'Bryan
ISBN 0-471-48586-1 © 2004 by the Institute of Electrical and Electronics Engineers.

As this chapter indicates, the proposal has much to do with how well a project runs. It provides the plan for the project and the promise of a product. In essence, it sets the expectations for everyone.

THE DELPHI PROPOSAL

The proposal on Delphi set our expectations, and we were able to meet only a few of them. This project was a sole-source contract. This means that we as buyers went to only one builder with our RFP. This builder had worked four years on a contract with us to develop two prototype systems. They had worked through thousands of problems to produce a couple of systems that satisfied 90% of our requirements. A sole-source contract was the norm in such situations.

We received the proposal with great anticipation. As with most proposals, this one looked good. Proposals are the best-looking documents most companies produce. Most documents in a technical project are bland—black and white, with only a few figures and almost no photographs. Proposals are the exception. The builder uses their best layout and publications people so that the proposal has color, many figures, and photographs. After all, proposals bring in business, so the company spends the money to make them look good.

Proposals are the epitome of "quap" documents. Quap, pronounced kwap, stands for Quality Uncertain, Appearance Perfect. The proposal for Delphi was an excellent example of quap. It looked good and, as time would show us, its content was dubious.

We brushed aside any concerns we might have had about the proposal. This was a major project, and we were anxious to begin. We amaze ourselves by what mistakes we miss when we want to believe all is well and embark on something. Delphi was one of those cases. The builder's proposal assured us that all was well. We believed them and negotiated quickly without challenging or changing much in the proposal.

Our first mistake with the proposal was that we treated it as if it came from the experts. The builder wrote the proposal, and they knew how to build systems. They knew all the details of each task and had performed market surveys and knew how much materials would cost. We gave them the benefit of any doubts we had. They were ready to start working, and if anyone did not think that was they case, all they had to do was read the proposal.

The builder's first mistake with the proposal was that they did not tell us all they knew. As related in the discussion of planning in Chapter 6, there were a few meetings that occurred before the builder wrote their proposal. Ronald, an enthusiastic person from our side, met with Art, a senior manager from the builder. It is alleged that Ronald told Art what we could afford on the project. If Art's company did not propose to meet those limitations, the contract would not happen. The builder did not tell us that their proposal was written to the constraints given them by Ronald. It was not until all the grumbling started that we subsequently learned of the "alleged" meetings and limitations.

The one thing the builder could have said that would have changed the course of the project was, "Here is the proposal that best meets what Ronald has told us about your resources."

Ronald was the only person on the buyer's side who knew of his conversation with Art. We did not know that the builders were constraining themselves. Our expectations were that they looked at the RFP and told us everything they needed to build the system. We believed that they could do what they said in the proposal. Neither side shared their thoughts as we went through negotiations. We hid our confidence in the builder, and the builder hid their reservations about our constraints.

What the builders had done in their proposal was bid to the alleged budget. Bidding to the budget is not the same as designing to the budget. Designing to the budget means designing an affordable product. When the money is gone, by definition the product is finished. The users use it as is, and when more funds become available, we enhance the product.

Bidding to the budget means making the answer come out right regardless of the truth. The operative words are "regardless of the truth." The builders wrote their proposal, added up the hours they needed, multiplied salaries, and added in the cost of materials. The sum was much greater than what Ronald allegedly told them we could pay. The builder fixed the proposal by multiplying everything by a factor, something like 60%, so their answer would match the budget.

The builder could not perform the project for the amount of hours and money they bid. Well, maybe if they worked really hard and worked extra hours that they did not charge us for they could come close. That was their thinking. They were trying to be positive and they stopped being realistic. Maybe people would not notice the problems for many months. The project would be too far along to cancel, so people would find the funds. Ronald had hinted about that strategy, and the builder had been in the business for years. They had seen this scenario played out before.

In addition to the false assumptions we all had, the proposal itself had several problems. These problems concerned two areas: (1) materials and (2) people. Let us discuss the people first. The proposal contained the names of key senior engineers who were to lead teams working on the project. The assumption was that these people would be available when the project started, but they were not. The senior engineers were busy on other projects. They were good engineers, and companies always have things for good engineers to do. The project was short of staff for over a year. (See Chapter 4 for more on this.)

Junior engineers stepped in and tried to do what the proposal claimed that senior engineers would do. Their lack of experience and knowledge led to many mistakes. These mistakes led to rework that cost the project time and money. The junior engineers gave it their best, and worked long hours and weekends. These long hours cost us more money. We were behind schedule and over budget in the second month of the project. The trials and tribulations of junior engineers are covered more in Chapter 17.

We also had problems with materials. The builder proposed using the same materials at the same cost as they used during the prototype project that preceded Delphi. There were two problems with this. First, the price of the materials had risen since the prototype project. This caused a 10% overrun in the cost of materials. That hurt, but was nothing compared to the other problem.

Many of the parts used in the prototype project were no longer available. In electronics, parts manufacturers build a part for a year or 18 months, then discontinue it. They learn how to make a faster, better, and cheaper part. Our builder learned that many of the parts we needed were obsolete when they tried to order them in the first month of the project. The builder had to buy the newer, better parts, but these better parts did not fit in the existing design. The performance of the better parts was "not exactly" the same. Also, the footprint or physical size of the better parts was also "not exactly" the same. Consequently, the builder had to redesign large amounts of the hardware. That design work was not in the proposal, so the cost kept growing and the schedule kept stretching.

We had a big mess on our hands as the project did not resemble the proposal.

WARNING SIGNS OF TROUBLE WITH PROPOSALS

The story of Delphi's proposal shows how a proposal can set up a project for failure right from the start. There were many things about that proposal that should have warned us of coming trouble. We failed to notice those warning signs. The following discusses those signs and other things about proposals that can warn us of coming trouble.

Proposing to Win

The objective of writing a proposal is to win a contract. That is how business works, and there is nothing wrong with that. The problem is when the builder proposes something that they cannot do. They begin the project, fall behind, and struggle. That wears out their people. On top of that, the buyer becomes angry and sometimes distrustful because the builder is not doing what they told the buyer they would do.

A warning sign of the builder proposing things they cannot do is when they have the attitude, "Let's propose to win, then we'll figure out what is next."

Some builders will propose things they know they cannot do. They simply lie about their ability to meet the buyer's requirements. This is wrong, and in an ideal world liars are caught in their lies and never receive another RFP package from any potential buyer. We do not work in an ideal world. Builders continue to receive RFP packages because for any buyer there is only a small set of builders who have the experience and knowledge to build systems they need.

Some builders make honest mistakes in their proposals. This is because writing a proposal is difficult. The builder is proposing a project in the face of many unknowns and misunderstandings. The builder will make assumptions that may be incorrect. Also, in a competitive environment, it is difficult to obtain clarification from the buyer. The buyer must keep a "level playing field" among the competitive bidders, so the buyer is reluctant to answer questions for one bidder and not for all. The builder, knowing or assuming that the buyer is reluctant to answer questions, will make assumptions about the RFP instead of asking.

We as buyers are uncertain about what we want. We are most uncertain about the difficult parts of a project. Therefore, we may be reluctant to give an answer that will steer builders in the wrong direction. It is no surprise that the builder has difficulty proposing solutions to these uncertain issues.

On top of the technical details, the buyer and builder often struggle to communicate. Human interaction is full of misunderstandings (Chapter 12 concentrates on communication). Most of the interactions that occur before negotiations are via written documents. These introduce many more misunderstandings and may give the appearance of lying.

It is difficult to notice when the builder is proposing to win and cannot do what they propose. The buyer rarely has an opportunity to meet with the proposal writers. If such an opportunity occurs, take it. Ask the proposal writers in plain terms, "Do you feel you can do what is in your proposal? Why do you feel that way?"

The builder on Delphi wrote a proposal to win. This is strange since the situation was for a sole-source contract. They builder still felt that their proposal could lose them the contract. The conversation between Ronald and Art convinced them that they needed the right answer in their proposal. They wrote the right answer and submitted it to us. Months later we learned that several of their proposal writers didn't believe in what they proposed. By then it was almost too late.

Writing Proposals on Weekends

A proposal commits a builder to perform in a specified manner for many months. Therefore, the proposal needs to be correct. Mistakes in a proposal lead the builder to make expensive mistakes during the project.

One major problem in writing a proposal is when a builder takes shortcuts. The trouble with shortcuts is that they usually introduce errors. The best way to write a high-quality proposal is to take time and use best practices.

One common shortcut is cutting from old proposals and pasting into new ones. The basic idea—reuse products and information—is a good one. The problem is that projects are not the same. They have different situations with different assumptions, people, etc. The tasks and solutions proposed for one project probably will not work in another project.

A warning sign of the builder taking shortcuts on their proposal is when they write it on weekends. Builders use some of their smartest people to write proposals, and these people are fully employed on projects during the week. Therefore, they write proposals on weekends.

Writing the proposal on weekends causes people to take shortcuts. This is understandable. We wouldn't want to work on a proposal for four or five weekends in a row. We would take every shortcut available so we could stay home. Most proposal teams do the same.

Our builder on Delphi took one major shortcut while writing the proposal on weekends. They could not call parts suppliers because the parts suppliers were home on weekends. Our builder assumed that parts were available and had not gone up in price. As stated earlier, obsolete parts cost the project dearly. This one shortcut during the proposal writing phase cost the project at least a year and about $10M.

Proposing People

Proposals often contain the names of key people who will work on the project. These people will be the team leaders. This is a normal practice in proposals and is not cause for alarm.

Sometimes, proposal writers will assume that just the right people will arrive on the project at just the right time. These "right people" will complete tasks with few errors and in a short period of time. This assumption can cause big problems on projects.

These "right people" are in the proposal because they are some of the builder's top people. The builder will keep these people busy working on projects. The builder cannot guarantee pulling these people off projects and putting them on your project at just the right time.

What usually happens is the builder has to use substitutes for these "right people." The substitutes are smart, caring people, but they don't have the same qualifications as the people the proposal writers assumed would be available. The substitutes may take longer than proposed to finish their tasks. In addition, the substitutes will make mistakes. That means rework, and that means lots of time and expense not included in the proposal.

A warning sign of this assumption by the proposal writers is when the proposal contains too many names of specific people. As stated earlier, having the names of the team leaders in the proposal is fine, but when names of specialists are in the proposal, beware of upcoming trouble.

On Delphi, the proposal named many key people who would be working on the first day of the project. Most of these people were not available until months into the project. As related above, this caused us many problems. The problems raised the cost, stretched the schedule, and caused enough stress with the builder and us to almost cancel the project.

"They Said They Would Do It"

The greatest potential problem with any proposal is expectations. The proposal sets the expectations for several years to come. When a project does better than expectations, everyone is happy. When a project does worse than expectations, it is a failure.

Delphi experienced this problem of not meeting expectations. The builder proposed $18M for the project. The project delivered excellent systems, but cost $33M. Hence, it was a failure in the eyes of many people. It is easy for people to say, "Give me 50% more money than I propose and I will deliver in my sleep."

As discussed in Chapter 6, after a year into the project, the builder came to us with a new proposal for the project. That proposal called for a 51-month project. They missed that schedule by only 3%. If the builder had proposed that plan originally, most people would have viewed the project as a success. The difference is in expectations.

We work in technical projects with scientists and engineers. Most of these people are logical. They, however, are still people with hopes and expectations. Failing to meet their expectations means a failed project.

The warning signs of expectations are hard to notice. One of the most common is when people expect the history of a project to be like its proposal. Listen for statements like, "The builder said they would deliver in March, so we're planning to use the product in March."

When the builder writes their proposal, they do so at a time when they know the least about the project and the product it should deliver. We urge buyers to manage the expectations of those around them. That includes themselves.

CREATING A GOOD SITUATION

Our experience with Delphi and others taught us a few things about proposals. There are techniques that help create a situation in which we can write and read proposals well.

Determine if this Contract Is Worth Winning

Writing a proposal consumes resources, and buyers seldom pay builders to do this. Therefore, before writing a proposal, the builder should determine if the contract is worth winning. If it is not, the builder should not waste resources on a proposal. This is known as the "bid–no bid" decision and it is common practice with most builders.

A less-common extension of this is "bid–no bid given the circumstances." As discussed earlier, we used a sole source on Delphi. The builder was going to have the contract without competition, so there was no decision involved in preparing the proposal. That is a warning sign—when you can do something without thinking, it is best to stop and think. It would have been wise if the builder had thought about the circumstances for this proposal. They were preparing the proposal knowing that they had to make their answer come out right—make it match the constraints that Ronald and Art had given them. In hindsight, it was unwise of them to prepare the proposal this way.

Our builder won the contract, as they expected. They had terrible problems for a couple of years before they straightened out the project. After that, they had to face the usual problems on any complex technical project. They built good systems, but they suffered through stress that cost them several promising engineers. This project gave the division of the builder a bad reputation (they did after all, overrun the cost and schedule by 50%). The mismatch of expectations and reality (proposal and performance) hurt them, and it may be five years before they change that reputation.

Use the Best

Builders should use their best practices and best people when preparing proposals. Builders often write proposals on weekends and take shortcuts that hurt the quality of the proposal. They use people who have already worked over 40 hours during the regular work week. These are bad business practices. Organizations try to do the best they can using the best practices and people they have. When it comes to writing proposals, however, organizations seem to forget who they are and how they do things.

Best practices include peer reviews, facilitated meetings, and teamwork. We all make mistakes in our work. Peer reviews give us the opportunity to find and correct these mistakes.

Writing documents at work is difficult. Compounding this difficulty is that one person cannot write a proposal. There is not enough time for that, and no one knows all the information that goes into a proposal. This means that the proposal-writing exercise needs structure and organization. One way to provide this is through facilitated meetings. The facilitator, a helper, guides the group through the structure of the proposal and pulls the information from the group. The facilitator's assistants collect the information and put it into the document. This practice reduces the time and cost of the proposal and increases its quality.

Next, and most important, is teamwork. As stated above, no one person can write a proposal. Good teamwork lowers the cost and raises the quality of a proposal. The leader of the proposal team should concentrate on forming and leading a good team. The team leader should let the team write the proposal.

One final practice concerns using a consultant. People do not work on proposals often—usually only every 12 or 18 months. As a result, people do not have enough practice with proposals to become good at creating them. One way to work around this lack of practice is to use a proposal expert. There are consultants available who do this for a living. These consultants and their teams move from company to company helping to write proposals. They have special tools to gather information and create the documents. What is more important is that they have smart people who do nothing but write proposals. These teams know what to do, when to do it, how to do it, and why to do it. The builder provides the information and the consultant provides an excellent proposal.

Pay the Builder to Write the Proposal

Another way to create a good situation with proposals is for the buyer to pay the builder to write their proposal. This is contrary to common practice as builders usually use their own money to write proposals. That is part of the cost of doing business. That, however, is losing sight of the real goal—a successful project and a good product.

Buyers can help builders write proposals by funding study contracts. During the study, the builder examines the upcoming work in detail. They speak with parts vendors about costs, availability, and compatibility of parts. Buyers can do this before issuing an RFP for a competitive contract. They can fund study contracts with three to six companies. Each company would have time to learn about the coming project and create a realistic proposal. The buyer would then evaluate all the proposals and select a winner.

We didn't pay the builder to write the proposal on Delphi. It would have been easy to do so since we were going to use a sole source contract. Our foolish pride kept us from doing what would have been best. Also, we felt we were saving lots of money. Some people in our organization had the attitude that, "The contractor will get plenty rich on this contract. Why should we give them more money?"

It is unfortunate that this attitude prevailed. We could have saved at least $5M on the contract had we paid the builder $100,000 to write the proposal. The builder would have discovered the obsolete parts, learned when senior engineers would be ready to start on the project, and found a host of other little issues that added up to big dollars quickly. There are some things that are right and not popular. Paying the builder to write the proposal is one of them.

Be Realistic

Writing and reading proposals are both full of potential problems. What both the builder and buyer need while doing their respective tasks is realism. Both sides need to understand the difficulties that the other faces and act accordingly.

First, the builder writes the proposal with only a partial understanding of the requirements of the product and the project. It is difficult to predict the future under the best of circumstances. The builder is trying to do this under bad circumstances.

One good technique for the builder is to state their assumptions in the proposal. The builder writes the proposal from their interpretation of the RFP package. There are many times while reading the RFP that they ask themselves questions like, "What does the buyer mean by 'verification testing'?"

The builders decide how they will interpret verification testing and writes their proposal per that decision. In the proposal they should state, "We interpret the term 'verification testing' to mean testing the system to verify every requirement in the product specification."

This helps the buyer understand the types of testing and the man-hours devoted to testing given in the proposal. We have seen too many cases in which the buyer read a proposal only to throw it out because the builder proposed too much or too little effort in an area. The buyer thought the builder did not understand something that was obvious.

Another good technique is for the builder to state all the information they know about the impending contract. Much of that information comes from sources other than the RFP package. The builder should write about conversations they had with the buyer. These include public and private conversations. Had our builder done this on Delphi, we would have understood their proposal much better. We would have seen that they were bidding to a budget they heard about in a private conversation.

Finally, the builder should state what they believe to be most important for the project. Not all sections of an RFP carry the same weight, and not all sections of a proposal carry the same weight. Delphi would have had far fewer surprises if the builder had told us how critical it was to find the parts they needed. We might have been able to help them find parts or allowed them to start buying parts before they became obsolete. No one did any early searching for parts, and we all paid because of this.

The buyer also needs to be realistic when reading a proposal. Given all the uncertainty, a proposal is accurate within 25% at best. In most cases, proposals are only accurate to within 30% or 40%. If a buyer wants more accuracy, they need to pay for it. One way to pay is to fund the builder to write the proposal. Another way to pay is in time. The buyer can spend more time on their own discovering what they really want. The buyer can also spend time with the builder discussing the RFP. Conversations about a document help to reduce the misunderstandings that occur while reading.

The buyer could also spend time talking to the builder after reading the proposal. The buyer should pull information from the builder regarding the proposal. Key questions include, "What are your assumptions? What do you think will be really hard? What do you think are your chances? What could we change that would make this much more likely to succeed? What could we change that would make this much more likely to fail? What else would you like to tell us about this project?"

Some people communicate well in writing, whereas others communicate well in conversation. Writing and reading proposals are important parts of a successful project. Give everyone ample opportunity to communicate well.

CONCLUSIONS ABOUT PROPOSALS

A proposal wins a contract and starts a project. More importantly, a proposal sets the expectations for the project. When people do not meet the expectations of the proposal, others see them as failures.

Given the importance of the proposal, we might expect that builders would write them with great care, but that rarely happens. Builders have many constraints that often cause them to take shortcuts and hurt the quality of their proposal. Buyers don't seem to understand these shortcuts. We see a proposal as a perfect document prepared by experts. We think that since the builder wrote the proposal, they can conform to it without a problem. The difficulties of creating and interpreting proposals lead us to the principle of proposals: A proposal wins a contract, and it can determine if people are successes or failures for the next couple of years.

Watch out for:

- Proposing to win
- Writing a proposal on weekends
- Assuming people will be available
- "They said they would do it."

How to create a good situation with proposals:

- Before writing a proposal, determine if the contract is worth winning.
- Use your best business practices and best people.
- Pay the builder to write the proposal.
- Be realistic when writing and reading a proposal.

Preparing a proposal is difficult. Nevertheless, it is much like creating many of the other products that are part of a system. We can use good principles and practices to prepare the proposal. We can do the same when we interpret the proposal.

A couple of years before becoming involved with Delphi, I was visiting another part of the builder's office park. I was walking through a large area filled with cubicles when I overheard two people talking about proposals. One person said plainly, "I don't lie, I write proposals." I never saw the person or learned his name. There were many days, however, that I wondered if he helped write the proposal for Delphi.

Chapter 4

Leaving the Station before Everyone Is on Board: Staffing-Up

Projects have plans that state who is to do what and when during the project. A common problem on projects is that some people are not available to perform their tasks per the plan. They are somewhere else doing something else. This often occurs at the start of a project when people are finishing work on another project. When people aren't available, the project can fall behind and never recover the schedule.

THE START OF DELPHI

Delphi started before everyone was ready. A number of key people were finishing other projects and were not able to perform their tasks as in the plan. The builder started the project anyway. They told us that they were ready, we believed it, and the project started. Our team did not review the list of people needed to ensure that they were available. This was a big mistake on our part.

Many bad things happened right from the start. The builder had a plan stating that certain people were necessary at the start. Hardworking, knowledgable people created the plan with much thought. Starting the project without the people who were listed in the plan was a way of saying the plan was worthless. It is amazing to consider how the buyer and builder could dismiss the plan so easily. Everyone involved forgot that the plan was there for a good reason.

Delphi began as a follow-on to a project that had built two fieldable prototype systems. The prototype systems met about 90% of our requirements. We began Delphi with the idea of tweaking the designs of the prototype systems

It Sounded Good When We Started. By Dwayne Phillips and Roy O'Bryan
ISBN 0-471-48586-1 © 2004 by the Institute of Electrical and Electronics Engineers.

to meet the final 10% of the requirements. The key people identified to tweak the designs were not available. These senior people were also important to another project we had with the same builder. That project was running just a little behind schedule. The builder's failure to meet the schedule on that other project should have been a huge clue, but at that time we were clueless. We were filled with wild enthusiasm, so we just had to begin.

We started Delphi without these senior people. The builder assured us that the junior engineers could start, the senior engineers would look in on the junior "tweakers," and things would be all right. This didn't work. The junior tweakers were trying hard but were making mistakes, and they weren't making much progress. The senior tweakers were busy trying to get the other project out the door and they didn't have time to look in on the junior tweakers. The clock was running, minutes turned into hours, hours into days, days into weeks, and weeks into months.

As we discovered, tweaking was not the answer. We did not discover that until the junior tweakers had failed to produce the desired results. We were in deep trouble by the time the key people were released from the other program. We had lost months discovering that the builder had underestimated the extent of the modifications required to go from 90% to full performance. If the senior engineers had been on the job from the start, they would have realized the magnitude of the work to be done much earlier. The junior engineers did not have the experience to recognize the extent of the designing that was needed.

Another contributor to our problem was the need for engineers in addition to the senior tweakers. On Delphi, the electrical engineers did the paper design. Once the paper design was completed, mechanical engineers translated the design into layouts. Once the builder discovered that they needed to create more paper designs, they also realized that they needed more mechanical engineers to translate those into layouts. Well, the mechanical engineers weren't available either. Six hundred and seventy-three drawings later, Delphi was delivered.

By starting without the required people, we created a situation in which we were always behind. Being behind usually brings with it many bad behaviors (see Chapter 24 for more on this). The project fell behind on the first day and stayed behind for 18 months. The only thing that pulled us out of the deficit was to admit defeat, throw away the plan, and start again with a new plan.

Another problem was electronic parts and parts that required a long time to buy, i.e., they had long lead times. The system being built had some parts that required months from order to delivery. These long-lead items were critical to the project.

Key people were also needed at the start of the project to identify and order the long-lead items. These people were not available either, and the long-lead items were not ordered as planned. Some of these parts required a year from the date of order to delivery. Because they were not ordered for several months, we still didn't have some of the needed parts one year into the project. Our mistake of starting without these people hit us at a time when we thought we were clear of the big hurdles. Our haste to begin kept hurting us long after we forgot about the slow start.

The problems did not end when the long-lead items arrived. The electronic circuits did not work as the engineers had hoped. The engineers had to change their designs and find replacement parts. The replacement parts were also long-lead items. We rushed purchasing, paid high premiums, and received them in 6 instead of 12 months, but we were still hurting 18 months into the project.

Another problem was that some of the team members felt compelled to help others who were behind, even though the things they needed help with were outside their area of expertise. They were trying to fill in for those people who were absent. Their efforts were admirable, but their results were laden with mistakes. The builder was creating a complex system, and the project needed senior engineers with years of experience to perform the design work. Engineers with little expertise outside their own area, no matter how good their intentions, could not perform the work. They made mistakes, and we did not find those mistakes for many months.

Our next problem was that people hurried when they did arrive on the project. Since they were absent at the start of the project, their tasks were behind by weeks. The people worked quickly—too quickly. They hurried their work in a vain attempt to catch up. The hurry caused design mistakes. The design mistakes meant that the assembly and testing tasks were wasted. The engineers had to redesign, the assemblers had to reassemble, and the testers had to retest.

Delphi was drowning in problems. There is something about having more than one problem at a time. The difficulty of isolating and correcting the problems does not add, it multiplies. We spent most of the second year of the project correcting the mistakes we made during in the first few months.

The cause of these problems was simple—we left the station before everyone was on board.

WARNING SIGNS OF TROUBLE WITH STAFFING

The above horror story shows how Delphi suffered because of lack of needed people. Its main problem was starting the project before people were finished with their other projects. The following describes warning signs of trouble with staffing.

Hurrying to Catch Up

As discussed above, projects fall behind when people are not present when needed per the plan. One common occurrence in this situation is that people hurry. It is not their personal fault that they were absent when needed. They were working on something else. Still, many people feel a sense of responsibility, so when they arrive, they work hard—very hard.

People who work hard often hurry. This means they are trying to do things faster than they are able to. They take a few shortcuts like looking at a product one less time than normal and moving ahead alone instead of waiting until the next day to talk with a colleague.

Hurrying may give the project a few short-term gains as some of the shortcuts taken by hurried people actually work. Most times, however, hurried people make mistakes. Someone may see the mistakes right away and correct them. That costs time now, but not too much. The bad situation arises when people do not see the mistakes now. The mistakes are there, and they will come to the surface eventually. The later they surface, the more they cost to correct.

Warning signs of hurrying usually come in the words people use. One common sign of hurrying is the expression "catch up." An engineer will say, "I didn't finish with the other project when I expected to, but I'm on this project full-time now and I think I can catch up."

A manager will say, "Come on guys, we had some bad luck, but we are going to do better. Let's bear down and catch up."

The manager's words should cause extra red warning lights to flash. The "catch up" phrase is combined with the old "bad luck" phrase. Luck had nothing to do with starting the project before the needed people were available. Managers decided to do that.

We fell into the trap of hurrying on Delphi. The engineers were working on the most difficult part of the project; they were designing complex circuits to achieve the final 10% of the desired performance. This was the most difficult 10%. The engineers were doing as well as anyone could ask, but they were hurrying and making mistakes. These design mistakes caught up with them months later when the parts arrived and the assemblers built the circuits. Few of the circuits worked per the designs. This meant redesign, ordering new parts, waiting, and repeating tasks.

Asking people to hurry and catch up is the same as telling them to make costly mistakes. We did this and paid for it.

'I've Been Helping So-and-So'

Conscientious people go out of their way to help their colleagues. These people step out of their areas of specialization to fill in for those people who are absent. This sounds like a good thing to do at the time. These are smart people, and they feel they can do the work.

People helping others is a good thing as long as it is supervised help. The problem for projects is unplanned help. In unplanned help, people stop doing the work they are scheduled to do. The team accomplishes a task and is making progress. The team, however, is not making progress everywhere as planned.

People give warning signs of unplanned help in their statements. Listen for, "I saw Tom struggling with his design, so I stopped what I was doing and helped him for a couple of days."

Notice two things in this statement. First, the engineer "stopped what he was doing." He had a task to do per the plan. While he was helping Tom, his task slipped. The second item to notice is that he helped "for a couple of days." Helping for 15 minutes or an hour is not a big problem. A couple of days is a big problem.

Unplanned help happened many times in the first 18 months of Delphi. Tasks on the critical path were behind. (When a task is on the critical path, a one-day slip in that task means a one-day slip in the end of the project.) These tasks were behind because the project started without the needed people on board.

To attempt to catch up, some people quit working on their area to help with the tasks on the critical path. That would have been fine if they had only taken a few minutes from their area to help on the critical path. The problem was they took weeks off to help on the critical path. The unattended work fell far enough behind until it *became* the critical path. Since it was already late, the project became even later. The builder repeated this many times and fell behind schedule by a year.

"I've Been Working in Area X"

Similar to helping other people in a project is helping in other areas. Someone is absent (probably still working on another project), so another person jumps into their work. The problem is that they are working on something that is outside their area of expertise. They may be a tester trying to do design or a designer trying to create test plans.

Working outside an area of expertise may be difficult to detect. In intellectual work, like engineering and information technology (IT) projects, people can do many different jobs from their cubicle. Their computer is connected into everything, so they move from design to test to documentation with the click of a mouse. A project manager will not know what they are doing without asking. As a buyer, this is especially difficult to see. We visit the builder once a month and rarely visit people in their cubicles.

The warning sign of working outside an area of expertise is when a person stands and describes their work at a monthly review meeting. They talk about designing a power circuit and it hits you that last month they were writing digital signal processing software. This is learning bad news too late as the damage is already done.

Working outside a person's area of expertise means trouble is coming for a project. The project appears to be moving ahead as people are accomplishing work. When the needed people arrive, and people are confident that they will arrive real soon now, the project will be in good shape. People hope that the schedule deficit will disappear. This substitute working is not so bad, is it?

Substitute work is bad. The substitutes mean well and work hard. They are, however, not the people the project needs. They do not have the training, experience, and skill that the plan requires. They are probably making mistakes, and these mistakes will surface in the coming months. The team will have to correct the work that the substitutes performed. This will hurt the schedule. The project will step back three months, six months, or ten months.

We experienced this on Delphi. The builder was desperate and tried anything and everything to catch up. The result was predictable. The product was riddled with mistakes made by people who meant well but were not qualified to do what the project manager asked of them. This caused much rework and consumed months of schedule time and millions of dollars.

Do Not Confuse Me with the Facts

Many projects are lacking the people the plan requires. It is easy to see when people are missing, but not always easy to admit it. The facts are there, but people don't like them and may choose to deny them.

The facts regarding staffing are simple. To make them visible, the project manager only needs to gather two pieces of information and plot them. The plan contains the number of people needed each month; that is one piece of information. The other piece of information is the number of people actually working on the project each month. It is easy to put these two numbers on a graph. This graph is called a staffing plot. The difference between the plan and actual on the staffing plot is obvious. If there are fewer people present than on the plan, the project has a staffing deficit.

When the staffing plot shows that the project does not have as many people on it as planned, trouble is coming. The project might be on schedule now, but that good fortune is probably short-lived. The project will fall behind schedule, the team will not catch up, and they will probably have made mistakes in the requirements and design.

The builder and buyer both denied these facts on Delphi. About 24 months into the project, I had to do a report on its history. I read through all 24 prior monthly reports that the builder had given to the buyer's team. The builder was short of staff every month for 24 months in a row. Those were the facts, and those facts were right in front of everyone—the builder, buyer, and everyone's upper managers.

Most of the monthly reports, however, contained positive words. The words in the reports admitted some technical problems, but nothing out of the ordinary. The builder even felt they would finish six weeks ahead of schedule (they were 12 months behind in final deliveries). Nothing in the reports indicated trouble with staff or schedule.

This was a complete denial of the facts. The warning sign of denying the facts is when the words and facts do not agree. If the staffing plot shows a deficit of people, the words in the reports should say the same and predict problems in the future.

A mistake we made as buyers was that we didn't compare the facts with the builder's words. We looked at the faces of the builders, heard their confidence, and believed what they said. We wanted to hear good news, so we stopped investigating when we heard good news. It wasn't until that fateful day when I looked through the reports that I noted a difference between the words and the facts. We were in a state of denial. We denied the facts, but the facts did not deny themselves. Trouble came just as the facts predicted it would.

CREATING A GOOD SITUATION

The above sections discussed many of the bad things that happen when projects are short of people. The project suffers, and people on the project work harder only to fall farther behind. This need not be the case. There are things that project managers can do to create a good situation for the people and the project. The following sections relate some of these.

Patience is a Virtue

It seems strange, but when behind schedule because of staff shortages the best way to speed up is to slow down. Most people will take shortcuts and do anything that comes to mind to get back on schedule. Patience is not usually high on anyone's "try anything" list, but it should be at the top. Most errors mentioned previously occurred because people were not patient.

Impatience allows project managers to let people jump foolishly outside their specialty. Patience helps project managers do this wisely. Some people can step out of their specialty, but not everyone. A patient project manager will consider the context and the people. The project manager should allow people extra time to learn, experiment, test, rework, and learn some more. The project manager should also bring in an outside expert for a day or two to review their work.

People do not hurry efficiently, so never hurry someone who is doing complex work. Most projects involve complex work. If they did not, they would be easy. Remember the old saying, "Be quick, but don't hurry."

Patience also means that when people do arrive on the project, the project manager does not rush them. Allow them all the time the original plan allowed. The temptation is to think that since the project is in trouble, a person will work extra hard and make up time. That is wishful thinking that leads to great pain later.

The builder wisely exercised patience at a crucial time during Delphi. They were behind and were not going to catch up. They admitted this to themselves and to us. That was painful and required courage. They stopped all the quick fixes that they had been attempting for a year and created a long, patient plan that they could execute. The builder's managers presented this plan to the managers of the buyers and users. We accepted the plan, and both sides held to this patient plan to the end of the project. The builder met this plan within 3%.

Is Everyone on Board?

Before starting a project, people should ask, "Is everyone on board?"

As the buyer, go to the builder at the official start date. Ask ahead of time to have everyone present. Look at the plan, look at the people on hand, and ensure that they match. Do not let anyone tell you, "Well, a few people are not here today, but they are available."

There is only one answer: "Well, we won't start today."

Be firm in this statement. There are contractual means to keep the builder from starting, so use them.

Standing firm and starting only when ready creates a good situation for a project. There is pain, anguish, and embarrassment at first as people want to meet delivery dates. Realism, however, must guide decisions. Starting prematurely puts people in bad situations in which they quickly fall behind and become failures in the eyes of many.

Strong project managers on both the builder and buyer sides will hold until ready. They will withstand the pressure from people who are not thinking clearly and wait until their team is ready to succeed.

On Delphi, we allowed the builder to start short-staffed and continue working in this manner. They believed they could catch up, and we wanted to believe that too, so we did. All our belief did not change reality.

Use Your Plan

Project managers sometimes find themselves in bad situations like Delphi. The project began before everyone was on board, and it was behind schedule after the first week. The first project manager for Delphi charged ahead blindly. In retrospect, he should have done what we are about to recommend.

The project has a plan, and people made this plan using lots of thought. The project manager should use the plan. It will not, however, work in its present form. That is a given because resources required by the plan are absent. Nevertheless, the plan exists and it provides a place to start.

Post the plan on the wall where everyone can see it and think about it. Now everyone is ready to work on the plan and the project. It is time for a cards-on-the-wall replanning session. Chapter 6 describes the cards-on-the-wall technique.

Work through the plan with the team to first see what work you can accomplish. Next, make a list of the tasks that you cannot perform. The team should generate ideas of how to accomplish those tasks. Some of the people on hand might be able to do some of those tasks. They may need twice the time originally estimated, but they could do the work. The project may be able to hire consultants for short periods to do some of the tasks. It is good to have outside help on tap. No project should start without the builder having identified outside experts who are available to help out at a moment's notice.

Once the team decides on the workarounds, evaluate the schedule again and calculate the new end date of the project. It is important to be honest and open at this point. The project is short of resources; that is a fact. The project will end later than planned; that is a logical conclusion. Neither miracles nor magic will occur; that is only wishful thinking. When doing a cards-on-the-wall session, no one is allowed to put up a card that states, "a miracle occurs here."

The project manager needs to publicize the new estimated end date for the project. This is the most painful step. Upper managers do not want to hear bad news, and most people do not like to tell managers that they cannot do what was expected. The project manager must understand that he and his team have not failed. They are working without resources that were promised to them. The situation has changed and the estimated end date for the project will change accordingly.

Following the above steps will help create a better situation for a troubled project. The project manager is working with a public plan. This lends stability to the project. The team is working from a foundation that they created and own. This is familiar territory, and familiarity often lends comfort.

The plan and reworking of the plan also gives a degree of confidence to the team. The project manager is facing big problems, but is not panicking. He is working through the problems in public using a logical progression of steps. The lack of resources is a change, and change is normal on projects. No one is ignoring the change or acting like it will go away on its own. Everyone is being honest and open about the situation and its implications.

Most of the project managers on Delphi handled their bad situation well. Even in the darkest days, the plan was posted on the wall. The team members had a place to look for guidance on their next task. They knew what they were trying to do today and what they would do next.

The project turned around when the builder discarded most of the original plan and created a new one. A detailed cards-on-the-wall session helped the team create the new plan, and they used it from that day to the end of the project. As related in Chapter 6 on planning, the public plan allowed them to replan when necessary and create detailed plans for short, yet important phases of the project.

CONCLUSIONS

We learned the hard way about leaving the station before everyone was on board. There were many pressures to start the project regardless of the staffing situation. We could not resist the pressures and we suffered because of that.

It is sometimes necessary, however, to suffer some pain at the start than to suffer greater pain later. Mistakes that hurried or inexperienced people make early are expensive to fix later.

This leads us to the principle of staffing: Have the people you need on hand when you need them, especially at the start of the project.

Watch out for:

- "I'll catch up."
- "I've been helping so and so."
- "I've been out working in area X."
- "Don't confuse me with the facts."

How to create a good situation:

- Have patience.
- Ask, "is everyone on board?"
- Use your plan.

People perform the work on projects. If the people are absent, the work does not get done. Those statements seem so simple, but we often miss such simple things in the heat of a project. Look around a project area, even if the area is virtual. If people are not present, do not expect work to get done.

Late in Delphi, we embarked on a side project to enhance some of the software in the system. The builder's software lead, Jim, planned how they would complete the enhancements in the time we desired. Having experienced so many problems with staffing at the start of Delphi, we knew enough to ask the question, "Do you have the people to do this work as planned?"

Jim, having also lived through the problems of leaving the station without everyone on board, answered yes. He showed us who would be doing what and when. He had real names of real people in his plan, and how many hours each person was to work each week. Some, including himself, were scheduled to work more than 40 hours each week. Jim had already received commitments from these people to work these hours and from the company to pay the salaries. We were a bit skeptical, but approved of the plan. The enhancements effort began, proceeded per the plan, and finished on time, on budget, and with a good product. That was most satisfying.

Chapter 5

After The Party Is Over: Letting Everyone Do Their Own Thing

Builders win a project by having a buyer select their proposal from several competing proposals. After the buyer notifies them of their winning, the first thing the builder does is have a party to celebrate their success. What the builder does immediately after the party often determines the path of the project.

At the start of a project, people are anxious to build the product. They have considered the situation—the customer, the market, and the product—and have ideas. They can see the product in their mind, and like a kid in a video game store, they cannot wait to do something.

The energy and desire to start are apparent. All that is needed is for the project manager to focus and direct this energy. Oftentimes that focusing and directing does not happen, and the desire to build the product leads to impatience. Engineers, programmers, and others start doing what they know best. They design, code, and do whatever is the core job of their profession. In other words, they do their own thing. This "do your own thing" phenomenon often leads to skipping steps like planning and creates problems.

It has been said, "If you have no place in particular to go, any road will do." It follows that, if any road will do, you do not need a roadmap. Project plans are like roadmaps that focus on time instead of roads. For example, "We need to be in Kansas City on Tuesday." How are we going to travel—fly or drive? Driving requires more time. This question of time occurs on projects as some things take longer than others, and we need to start those things sooner. Without a plan, however, we do not understand which tasks take longer and need to be started first. Without a plan, any road will do.

Although we have used schedule and planning almost interchangeably, there are many other plans that are used in the life of a project. One is the project management plan. The project management plan encompasses the program technical requirements and the project management requirements. One side turns the requirements into specifications. The management side contains the configuration management plan, the test and evaluation plan, the manufacturing plan, and the quality management plan. Then there is the system engineering management plan. This is where technical requirements and the project management requirements come together.

At this point, many readers are rolling their eyes and thinking, "Wow! If you had to do all that, when would you have time to do any real work?"

We are guessing that response because we have heard it and seen it in action. The following story is about attempting "real work" without having a foundation—without having a plan.

GAMMA

I was once involved in a project, I will refer to it as Gamma, where the best of intentions gave way to everyone doing their own thing. This was a $50M project. The buyer organization decided to build a system using a different strategy from the usual one as used on Delphi. In most buyer and builder projects, the buyer has a contract with a single builder. The builder may choose to have subcontracts with other builders. The subcontractors deliver subsystems to the prime builder, who integrates them with other parts to produce a system for the buyer.

In Gamma, the buyer organization decided to have some of its own engineers play the role of the prime builder. The buyer would contract with several builders who would deliver a subsystem to the buyer's facility. The buyer would then integrate the subsystems with a few other things to create a system.

There are advantages and disadvantages to this strategy. There are some cost savings in that contracts with several builders usually cost less than going through one primary builder. There is some cost increase in that the buyer must supply more of its own people. Sometimes, the buyer has less money for contracts and more people available. In such cases, the strategy used in Gamma has more advantages than disadvantages.

Gamma began when a project manager in the buyer's organization proposed this strategy to the buyer's and user's upper managers. The managers agreed that given the context, the strategy was appropriate. A series of meetings led to the decision, and Gamma began. The key people in the buyer's organization were Dave, the project manager, and John, the system engineer. Dave would perform the usual project manager tasks of planning, organizing, staffing, leading, and controlling. John would take care of the technical matters.

The Gamma team held a party to celebrate management's decision to let them play the role of the prime builder. They had convinced the managers to let them run this project their way. They would do "most of the engineering" work, while the many builders would supply subsystems. This would be great. The team was confident that they could fill the role usually performed by a builder, and they would show the managers that they could do it much cheaper than a builder.

After the party, Gamma fell into what happens with many projects. People forgot what they were supposed to be doing and started doing their own thing. Dave, the project manager, became an absentee manager. He already had a full-time job and spent his time doing it instead of managing Gamma. John, the system engineer, would take over. John, however, had neither the knowledge nor the desire to be a project manager. He had the title of "system engineer" and was going to prove to himself and the world that he was a system engineer.

John interpreted system engineering as handling the technical details, and the best way to handle the details was to hold them in his hands. John concentrated on touching every piece of hardware that went into the system; he became infatuated with gadgets. One famous gadget was the rack fans—those little fans that pull air through a rack of equipment. John discussed the subject of rack fans for weeks. He spent hours on the Internet researching the many different types of rack fans available, the amount of air they moved, the different ways to mount them in a rack, and the different options of airflow. Whenever someone was talking about the system in the rack, John's mind focused on the airflow through the rack. He would start at zero and go through the entire rack fan discussion with the people in the room.

John's enthusiasm for technical matters overshadowed his need to do other things. A project needs organization, planning, and leadership from its project manager. The team had created a high-level plan and used it to convince their managers to let them run Gamma. They now needed a detailed plan to guide their daily activities. The old expression, "the devil is in the details," had real meaning on Gamma. This plan did not exist, and John did not ensure that the team create it. He kept the rough plan in his head and convinced himself that the team was abiding by it. The team members, however, were not sure where they were headed and what they were supposed to be doing. They looked to John for guidance, and he did not provide it.

A project also needs other items to use as a foundation. One example is configuration management. Gamma was complex and filled with important details. Proper configuration management helps the team identify, label, and manage those details. Before the team can perform the configuration management tasks, they need a configuration management plan. The Gamma team had promised management that they would create and abide by a configuration management plan, but John was caught up in the excitement of hands-on engineering. He neglected to write the configuration management plan.

The same holds true for other items like quality assurance and integration and testing. The team needed to complete plans and documents for these items. They were to use these things to manage the project's details. John, however, had them doing "real engineering" before creating the necessary foundations.

Gamma proceeded along well enough for several months. Every month, John would spend an hour telling the managers of the great progress that the team was making. The managers neglected to ask about things that projects need to do to support the engineering. They didn't have much time to probe the team and, besides, John was capable and so were the members of his team. The managers had selected John for this job, so he must have been good. They rarely, if ever, made mistakes about job assignments.

After about six months, Gamma collapsed. John and his team suffocated under a pile of details. The project infrastructure did not exist to help manage the details. The engineers followed John's lead and plunged into doing their own thing—engineering. They neglected to build the foundation as Dave and John had promised.

The managers decided to change the direction of Gamma. They brought in a devoted project manager to do the things that had not been done. Their intervention occurred time to save the project from cancellation, but not from wasting six months' worth of resources.

WARNING SIGNS OF EVERYONE DOING THEIR OWN THING

Gamma is one of many projects that faltered because people did what they liked instead of what they should have done. The people on the project were smart, worked long, hard hours, and had good intentions. Nevertheless, the results were poor. In retrospect, there were signs that people could have seen to warn them about what was happening.

Does Anyone Really Know What Time It Is?

Projects comprise countless little details. Attempting to manage each detail one at a time is a nightmare. Projects need foundation pieces that help group the little details into manageable chunks. A problem in projects is attempting to proceed without first building this foundation. One key foundation piece is a plan.

A warning sign of this "project without a foundation" is when the foundation pieces are not visible. As the buyer, we should be warned if we find ourselves asking, "Where is the plan?"

We should see the plan posted in a public place where everyone can see and use it. If we do not see the plan, this means one of two things. Either (1) people are not using the plan or (2) the plan does not exist. Both of these explanations are bad for the project.

The plan is the most visible foundation item, but not the only one. If the plan is not present, odds are that the other necessary items are not present.

These include the configuration management plan, the quality assurance plan, and the integration and test plan. These items should be sitting on the table. If they are not, they probably do not exist.

The absence of the plan and the other items means that no one has built the foundation of the project. People appear to be working, but it is not evident that their activity is leading to anything meaningful.

The project will probably have trouble in the future. People are doing tasks, but they are doing them out of order. Creating designs is good, but if the configuration management system is not in place, there will be problems. Engineers will change their designs, and without a change control system, they will confuse themselves and one another. They may also have ideas about testing the system. An integration and test person needs to be analyzing the designs, learning the type and quantity of test equipment needed for those designs, and canvassing the market to learn how and when they can obtain that equipment. Otherwise, test time will arrive, test equipment will not be present, and people will not be able to test the system.

Gamma went through these problems. The shame was that the warning sign was apparent to anyone who would look. I looked for the plan when I first arrived, but could not find it. Plenty of people working on the project also asked for the plan, but John, the system engineer, worked around our requests. John's managers mistakenly assumed the plan was complete and the team was using it.

The one simple question from the managers, "May we see the plan?" would have triggered further investigation and maybe saved the project months of time and millions of dollars. The managers never asked that question and the plan never appeared. The "do your own thing" continued its course. With nothing to support the details, they piled up high enough to suffocate the team.

The Dog Ate My Plan

The previous section discussed how the absence of a plan warns of coming problems on a project. Another part of this situation is the builder's response to the question, "Where is the plan?"

Sometimes the builder will not simply say, "We haven't finished the plan."

Instead they say things like, "We tried to print it yesterday, but after four hours it was still printing. The plotter broke. We tried to make it on the printer, but that makes too many little pages. When we plot it on a single C-size sheet, the print is too small to read. This project has too many tasks to print."

I have found myself waiting to hear the builder say, "The dog ate my plan."

The builder is offering excuses for doing their own thing. In a sense, the builder is embarrassed. They know they should be building a foundation by finishing a plan, a configuration management plan, a quality assurance plan, etc. They stated that they would do them when they wrote their proposal.

They feel like children. An adult has asked them a question, and they are giving a childish answer.

Making excuses is a warning sign of trouble to come. It points to the real problem—that using excuses to cover skipped tasks is acceptable. In the future, if there is something people do not want to do, they will skip it and create excuses. The thought goes that something may seem important in theory, but this is a real project. These are real engineers working here and they are doing real engineering. They do not have time for clerical work.

It does not matter if an engineer considers a configuration management plan to be clerical work. Projects have many tasks that are not the core of the engineering profession. These tasks are, however, important because they enable designing, building, programming, etc.

Gamma had a high-level plan. The project manager and system engineer used it to sell the project to their managers. The plan was on a viewgraph, actually two different viewgraphs that held two different plans. After the managers approved the project, the project manager and system engineer never replaced these viewgraph plans with a real plan.

People on the project kept saying, "We need a plan, we need a plan."

Some people were so frustrated that they took a plan from another project and tried to change enough of the task names so it would appear that Gamma had a plan. This attempt was futile. People were in the middle of flurries of unplanned activities. Since there was no plan, people were confused as to what they should be doing. Since they were confused, they were too busy to make the plan. This cycle repeated itself endlessly.

Doing Something Else

There are many reasons for lack of progress on a project. One reason is that the builder's engineers are not doing what they should be doing.

This is similar to what we discussed in Chapter 1. There, the project was short of people, so some people worked outside their areas of expertise. The case in this chapter has everyone on board. The problem is people are not doing their jobs because no one is ensuring that they do. Instead, they are doing their own thing.

The buyer is warned of this by comparing what should be with what people say. The buyer looks at the statement of work (SOW) and the builder's proposal (see Chapter 3 on proposals). The proposal states what people should be doing and the products that should be ready. The buyer asks, "Where is such and such? Is it ready or almost ready like the SOW and proposal stated?"

The warning sign is when the builder responds, "We didn't finish it because so-and-so was helping someone do something else."

The proposal and the plan listed items that were due on certain dates. Those items and dates are there for good reasons and ignoring them means ignoring the reasoning. Doing something else means two things. First, it puts the project behind schedule. Second, it sends a clear message—just do your own thing.

Gamma suffered through this situation. No one ensured that people were doing what they were supposed to do. Dave, the official project manager, disappeared and was not replaced. John, the system engineer, became the unofficial project manager. This didn't work as John turned a bad situation into a disaster.

John had a great imagination. He would walk the halls with ideas bouncing around in his mind. As he entered his office, the idea that happened to be in the front of his mind became the most important thing to do that minute. He immediately tackled that task and delegated parts of it to team members. The team members wanted to help, so they jumped in and did what John asked.

The problem was that John's big idea of the day rarely connected with his idea of yesterday or tomorrow. Brilliant people were working diligently on random tasks. It's a shame, but random tasks do not make a project. Months passed and the team was no closer to providing the user with a system than when they started.

CREATING A GOOD SITUATION

The temptation to do what comes naturally is a strong one. We have seen it ruin projects and have discussed the particulars of Gamma. There are things a builder's project manager and a buyer can do to help people do what they should. The following sections discuss some of these actions.

Today is the First Day of the Project

The first thing to do to avoid everyone doing their own thing is to have day one of the project start at day one, not day 21. This requires two attributes: patience and discipline. Patience allows a project manager to keep people from diving into the product. There are tasks to perform first, and a project manager should have the team do these first.

Discipline gives the project manager the strength to say no to requests to "skip that other stuff and get on with the project." Many project managers are amazed at how passionately engineers can argue for jumping into the engineering. The reasons seem good and the engineer's arguments are earnest. Saying no is not easy, but it is possible.

The buyer also plays a part in holding people to day one on day one. Distance is the ally of the buyer in this case. Distance helps the buyer see that doing the foundation work, no matter how mundane it may seem, is important.

A one-size foundation does not fit all. It is important that the buyer determine how much foundation work is needed prior to launching the project. There is foundation work that the buyer needs for visibility and monitoring progress and there is foundation work that the builder needs. This may not be easy. Some may see you as holding back progress, but you are staying with what people decided was best to do. There will be time available to change, so keep an open mind. Nevertheless, keep to the plan.

Staying with the plan and working on day one's tasks on day one sets a precedent. The builder's project manager and the buyer are stating that the project will stay the course. They are not blindly following a doomed plan. They can change the plan, but in a disciplined manner.

I do not have a story related to staying on the plan for Gamma because we never did that. On Delphi, however, we learned our lesson in time to save the project. We finally created a good plan for Delphi (see Chapter 6 on planning). We used that plan from its inception to the end of the project. There were plenty of troubles, and we did plenty of replanning. That is part of using the plan in a patient, disciplined, and thoughtful manner.

If Today is Tuesday, We Must be Having Hamburgers for Lunch

The prior section suggested beginning a project at the beginning. This section's suggestion is to stay with the plan every day of the project. The buyer should ask for each day's product on that day. If the detailed plan is due 30 days into the project, the buyer should ask for it on the 30th day of the project. This is using the plan in a disciplined manner. We trust the builder, but we have paid money for intermediate products. We want the products in our hands when they are due.

Asking for items when they are due sets and communicates expectations. The builder will realize that we want items per the schedule. They will look at the schedule and have the products ready, if for no other reason than making products is often easier than making excuses. This expectation also encourages the builder to look ahead. One benefit of looking ahead that is the builder will note problems earlier. It is good to know bad news as soon as possible because this allows time to work on problems. It is better to use time to work on problems than to let problems work on you.

Gamma began with a general plan. The plan had a few milestones or key dates on it. The upper managers considered this plan and approved the project. These managers, however, never met with John, the system engineer, on these key dates. The milestones came and went and the promised products did not appear. The team, especially John, received the message that the managers were not interested in the plan and its intermediate products.

On Delphi, we used a simple calendar on the wall. We penciled the dates of coming events and products on the calendar. Every visit to the builder included a review of the products that were due that month. The builder did not always have the products in hand. Most of the time they did, and the rest of the time they had an explanation and a new date when the product would be ready.

Red Means Stop

There are times when the buyer should stop all work on the project. This is a harsh action, but it may be necessary. The situation where stopping work is justified is when products are not done on time and people are working on other things. One example is when the plan is not finished but people are creating designs. When and how will these designs be turned into a product if there is no plan? Another example is when the configuration management system is not in place but people are programming. How will the programmers control and coordinate changes without a configuration management system?

Stopping work on a project is difficult. One reason is that the project is behind schedule, people are working, and it seems that the best course of action is to keep the work going. The problem is that the builder's team is doing tasks out of order. Their misdirected efforts have put them behind schedule now and will really put them behind schedule in the future. Continuing work will only make the situation worse.

Stopping the work creates a better situation for the project. The builder's team is working on tasks out of order, but they probably do not see this. If they did, they would have changed direction on their own. Stopping work causes a temporary setback, but it also forces the builder to create a foundation for the project. The foundation will help the team recover from the temporary setback.

Given the above advice, we have rarely been able to stop work on a project completely. On several projects, we were able bring work almost to a halt. Careful thought allowed us to keep some work in progress. Nevertheless, the main effort went into finishing the project's plan and other foundation documents. The goal was to create the items that permitted people to do the "real work."

Discipline and Respect

This chapter deals with a subject that resembles the question of maturity. Projects have problems when people do what they want instead of what they should. Several suggestions here come close to sounding like an adult keeping a child in line. This is a danger. It is important to apply discipline to projects and, at the same time, respect the people working on it.

The first principle is discipline. We have decided to do something, and it requires discipline to implement the decision. The project manager should tell people what to do, but without squashing them. This is where we respect people. We work with adults on projects, and all conversations should be adult-to-adult, not adult-to-child.

Adult-to-child direction sounds like, "I am the boss and you are not, so just do what I say."

Adult-to-adult interaction means that we all try to do what is right, not just what I say. We have best practices based on experience. The project manager should discuss these practices with the team. This is more difficult than adult-to-child direction, but it works much better in the long term.

There are two usual situations when the project manager must step in with discipline and respect. The first is when a project is just starting and some people want to jump ahead into doing their own thing. As in the earlier section, the project manager needs to say, "This is day one. This is what we will do today. We will do this first because it will enable us to do other work later."

That is the discipline statement. The respect statement is, "I will listen to all ideas. If we think that changing course will work better, we will."

The second situation is when the project is doing poorly and needs to change direction. It is easiest if the current project manager is on hand at the start of the project.

This project manager can say, "I made mistakes at the start of this project. I allowed people to jump ahead in the work. I need you to help change this project. We will start now by doing what we should have done at the start."

It is more difficult if a new project manager comes into a troubled project and must work with the team that was present at the beginning. The best way we know to change this is to state, "This is the first day of a new project."

The concepts of discipline and respect apply to the buyer, too. The buyer must use caution in the middle of a troubled project. The temptation is to shout, "You messed up this project and now you will do it right!" That has plenty of discipline, but no respect.

We suggest inclusive language such as, "We have had problems with priorities. We will do things differently now. First, we need to do some background work. This will take time and will take each of you away from what you know best. Stay with this for a while. We believe it will work. We believe this will create a better situation for all of us."

This is adult-to-adult talk. We discuss problems and solutions, and not people.

I came into Delphi when it was already in trouble. Other chapters discuss the difficulties we had with guessing budgets, telling people what they wanted to hear instead of the truth, and other dysfunctional behavior. Turning Delphi around was difficult, but we did it. One key to the change was the attitudes and actions of the builder's project manager (see Chapter 11) and the buyer's team.

We used candid talk, patience, and understanding of the other person's situation. We used inclusive language and tried to remove fear and blame. The

ideas are simple, but acting on these ideas is often contrary to our first responses.

For example, it often feels right to blurt out, "Damn it! Can't you guys do
anything right?" It is more difficult, yet more effective to state, "This is disappointing to me, and I can see by your expression and posture that it is disappointing to you as well. What do you think we should do?"

CONCLUSIONS ABOUT EVERYONE DOING THEIR OWN THING

Engineers design and build things, and programmers write programs. These
actions are the core of their respective professions. People enter their professions because they love these tasks. Projects comprise many tasks, and a large
portion of them are not from the core of engineering and IT. The products of
these tasks, however, form the foundation of projects. They enable the core
engineering and IT tasks to occur in a meaningful environment. They may not
be exciting, but they are necessary.

There exists this tension among tasks. The technical people want to do
what they know and love, but the project first needs people to do other
things.

This brings us to our principle of letting everyone do their own thing in
projects: Ensure that people work to the plan instead of doing their own
thing, especially at the start of the project.

Watch out for:

- Having to ask "Where is the plan?"
- Hearing excuses.
- Hearing, "So-and-so is doing something else."

How to Create a good situation:

- Start day one at day one.
- Ask to see items when they are due in the plan.
- Stop all work if items are not done on time.
- Have discipline with respect.

The temptation to do what we like is strong. The result, however, is often
chaos. We need to guide people patiently through the less-exciting tasks in a
project. Then we can cut them loose to do what they love.

Before I started working on Delphi, I was assisting a buyer team that was
working with another builder on another project. It was to be a challenging
project involving modifying a large amount of complex software. One of the
things the builder needed to do right after their celebration party was create
detailed work packages for their programmers. These packages would allow

the builder and buyer to track the progress closely and understand the status of the project.

Month after month, we visited the builder and asked, "Can we see the work packages now?" The answer was always, "We didn't create them yet. We were really busy doing such and such this past month."

The builder never finished the work packages and they never finished the product, either. In a year, the project collapsed because no one knew what they were to do or how much work they had completed. We cancelled the project after wasting a year and $5M. Doing your own thing can be fun for a while, but it usually catches up with you.

Part 3

The next five chapters discuss project management basics. Chapter 6 is about planning and what happens when we fail to plan. It also describes a practical and effective technique for planning. Chapter 7 discusses requirements and the critical role they play in a project. The topic of design is discussed in Chapter 8. That chapter emphasizes the relationship between requirements and design and what can happen if we incorrectly reverse their order. Chapter 9 is about schedule tracking and the mishaps that occur when we fail to read the calendar. Chapter 10 discusses what happens when facts disagree with theories and how we can avoid many of these problems via risk management.

It Sounded Good When We Started. By Dwayne Phillips and Roy O'Bryan
ISBN 0-471-48586-1 © 2004 by the Institute of Electrical and Electronics Engineers.

Chapter 6

Months Have 30 Days in Them, Except Those That Do Not: Planning

A plan is a calendar with events and tasks written on it. We want those events to occur on the day they are written on the calendar. Calendars have not changed much in the past few hundred years. Each week has seven days, months have 28, 30, or 31 days, and a year has 365 days (every four years we receive a bonus day).

Everyone knows these calendar facts but, on projects, we often act like we have our own unique calendar. We put events that should be 30 days apart in the same week and we schedule events that should be 90 days apart in the same month. We attempt tasks that must come in a sequence (obtain a driver's license before driving across country) in parallel. Those seven-day weeks confuse us because we are accustomed to base-ten math instead of base-seven. Then someone walks in and reminds us that we only work five days in a week instead of seven.

All but the simplest projects cannot succeed without a plan. That statement has eluded many of the projects we have seen. This chapter discusses some of those misadventures, as well as a few basic things that help us plan.

PLANNING DELPHI

We had several plans during Delphi. The first few plans did not work. Our later plans worked well, as we were able to hit our targets within 5%.

We had several problems with our planning. The first was that our builder used a dictated plan or a "right answer plan." This sounds like a Three Stooges routine, but Art told Dale the "right answer plan," Dale told Harry the "right answer plan," and Harry told Ronald the "right answer plan." We are getting ahead of ourselves.

We had a number of problems with "our" plan. The first problem was that we used the "right answer plan." It was a "flow-down" plan. That is, Art told Dale and Dale told Harry and Harry told Ronald. Art "dictated" the plan to Dale who dictated it to Harry. Harry said, "yes sir, but." Irrespective of the "but," Harry signed up for delivering on an impossible schedule. Harry really knew he could not deliver, but he said he could. He bought into the "lie."

The question is where did Art obtain the "right answer plan?" Rumor has it, and this is all rumor, that Ronald gave it to him. Before the project began, Ronald, the working-level lead of the buyer's team, met with Art, a senior manager with the builder. Ronald told Art how much money the user's organization had budgeted for the project and when they expected to receive the product. Ronald strongly hinted that the builder's proposed plan should agree with what Ronald's management expected. If the builder needed more money and more time, Ronald felt in his heart that his upper managers would cancel the project before it started.

Ronald felt this way because he had briefed his managers on the "right answer plan" long before he spoke with Art. Ronald's managers liked the "right answer plan" and told him to proceed. Now all the builder had to do was come through with the "right answer plan."

Ronald opined to himself that once the project started and was going well, his managers would find the money needed to complete it. This type of planning—"start now and we'll scrape up the money later"—happens. The builder came in with the "right" plan, and the project began.

Trouble hit the project quickly. The builder was not ready to start, had staff shortages, and fell behind schedule. They also had technical problems that increased the amount of design far beyond the plan. The accompanying cost increase was beyond what people expected.

Both sides, the buyer and the builder, made major personnel changes about one year into the project. The builder changed their project manager, and the buyer brought me in as our project lead. I was told that things were going to smooth out and the project would move through to the end without major problems. These personnel changes brought in new perspectives. My initial investigation showed that the plan was not going to work, not then, not ever. We needed a new plan that would take the project to a successful end.

The buyer visited us monthly. Their project manager, Fred, and his manager, Leo, brought adjusted plans with them on each visit. One plan showed a one-month delay in deliveries, and the next plan showed a three-month delay. The further we went, the further behind we fell. We had no faith in these plans.

After we saw several anemic plans, we decided to start at zero and planned the remainder of the project in detail. Our upper managers convinced (demanded) Leo and others at the builder to work with us on this. We held a two-day cards-on-the-wall planning session with the builder in the project room. (The next section describes this technique.)

We created a pretty good plan, but the most important outcome of the cards-on-the-wall session was that we could see the size and complexity of the project. We had been fooling ourselves into thinking the project would last about 28 months—the "right answer plan." The real answer was 48 months.

We experienced several "Aha!"s during the planning session. Bruce, an engineering manager, quietly documented the structure of the product. He showed everyone what a few people knew—how the components built upon one another to form the system. The structure helped the engineers set priorities on their work each day. It made no sense to build three copies of one component when we needed one support component and two other components that sat on top of it.

Someone else discovered the essential steps in building our product. The system was complex, and building the hardware required about 10,000 individual steps. We were able to find four basic tasks that we needed to perform to build a component. We then laid out these four tasks for the several hundred components in a system. This fell into a matrix that we shaded as we completed steps. This large matrix helped us gather status and keep track of progress for the project.

People from different organizations met and learned what others did in their respective parts of the company. One key conversation was between a lead designer, Ray, and an assembly manager, Jim. These people had worked for the same company for years, but did not know exactly what happened across the hall. They casually talked through what happened when an engineer obtained a component from the assembly area and tested it. The test usually showed that a change was needed. The engineering department would route the component through a bureaucratic maze back to the assembly area. The assemblers would spend an hour doing the work and route the component back through the company to the engineer. There was three days of routing for one hour of work. Ray and Jim worked out a way for the assembly rework to be performed and documented properly and have the component back in the engineer's hands in half a day. What they learned allowed us to cut a year from the schedule.

The most important outcome of the planning was that we became a team. There were several people in this session that were new to the project (me included). We learned each other's area of expertise and style of working.

It would be great to say that the plan we produced carried us through to a successful completion, but that was not the case. The builder's managers, Leo and his manager, Bill, decided that they could not bring the 48-month plan to our managers. They felt that we would cancel the project if confronted with this. We fell back into dictated plans. The difference this time was we knew what the plan should be.

The builder presented a shorter and less-expensive plan to us. I did not believe this optimistic plan—the new "right answer plan"—and told my managers my opinion. My managers understood my skepticism, but decided to give the builder a chance. At the same time, they started looking for money and support from the users for a long and expensive project.

We tracked this optimistic schedule for six months. As predicted, it did not work. At the end of six months, we were already four months behind. It seemed as though the project would never end.

Our upper managers had a series of serious telephone conversations with the builder's managers. Our side wanted a final, no-nonsense plan that the builder could meet. Our managers would go up our management chain and ask for the money. They did not want to do this without a 95% chance of success.

The builder held a private cards-on-the-wall session. Leo and Bill visited us and presented their plan. This was a real plan instead of yet another "right answer plan." This one showed a 50% overrun in cost and schedule. The $20M project would cost $30M and take 48 months. It was not good news, but it was news we could believe.

My managers went through a series of meetings with the users and the sponsors of our program. They convinced people, many people, that the product was necessary for our user and that we had no other source for it. This was painful, but less painful than canceling the project. Everyone agreed to proceed.

Sure enough, Ronald was right. His managers did somehow find the money needed to complete Delphi. Down in my heart, I feel that Delphi would have gotten the "go-ahead" with a real plan in place and there would have been much less grief if the proper planning had occurred up front.

This realistic plan stayed with the project for a couple of years until project completion. In the end, the project plan called for 51 months or 220 weeks. The builder delivered six weeks late. That was within 3% of the plan, and that was pretty good.

THE SELF-FULFILLING PLAN

A common situation in planning is that people do not want to spend the time and effort to plan. They are paid to build systems and write software, not plan. These people do not like to plan and they do not plan well. This combination means, that they often delay planning until the last possible moment or beyond.

I represented the buyer on the software portion of a project in the mid-1990s. Tom, the lead software engineer for the builder, did not like to plan. In fact, he did not like to do much of anything but write programs. Requirements analysis, design, planning—they all fell into the pile of things Tom did not like. Tom was good at programming and good at leading a team of programmers. He was a solid, honest, and down-to-earth person whom people liked and trusted.

The story begins with Tom about to embark on a three-week part of our project. We wanted Tom to sketch out a plan for us. Tom said, "I know how to do this; it's all in my head. Trust me and let me start now."

We did trust Tom, but we did not have faith in Tom's ability to hold this phase of the project in his head. We also did not want to risk money without a plan.

Tom continued with, "It'll take me longer to plan this than to do the work."

We urged Tom to plan this on a single piece of paper. All we wanted was to see that he had thought through the steps with his team. Tom did not say it, but he was upset because he felt we did not trust him. Tom had always come through before—well, almost always—and he thought that we just did not understand software projects like this. The planning would take longer than the project. Well, maybe it would not take three weeks to plan the project, but it would seem that long. It was only a three-week phase of the project. What was the big deal? Tom "agreed" to create the plan, and we were satisfied.

Tom proved his prediction. He complained, stalled, and found other things to do besides plan. In three weeks, the plan was not ready, and he was right—the planning took longer than the three-week project.

The three-week project? Well, it was not done either. All that "planning" kept Tom from "working." The phase of the project failed because Tom did not want to make a plan, and we did not realize that Tom would rather see his prediction come true than the project succeed.

WARNING SIGNS OF TROUBLE WITH PLANNING

We have learned a few lessons about problems with planning. This section gives a few warning signs of coming problems. We have often seen and rarely heeded these warning signs. Our advice is that if you see one of these things, stop and think.

"I Was Not Involved"

A common problem in planning projects is that people use a dictated plan. Someone, usually a manager, dictates when the team will deliver the desired product. Any planning that ensues is merely a charade to arrange tasks that finish on the dictated date. The project begins, the dictated date passes with no product, and everyone lives and works in agony until they finish the product.

Dictated plans do not work. People, however, tend to accept them and try to make them work. There are various reasons for this doomed behavior. One is that people use dictated schedules so often they think this faulty process is normal. The boss says what to do, and everyone tries to do it.

Another reason people use dictated plans is that they are being passive aggressive. They do not believe the plan, but it is not theirs and they have no stake in it. They will work quietly every day and watch it fail. Afterwards, they will blame the manager who dictated the plan. That will show everyone whose fault it is; everyone who is not laid off because of yet another failed project.

The buyer usually does not know that the builder is using a dictated plan. We did not know that the builder on Delphi was using a dictated plan. The builder created their schedule while writing their proposal. To us, it looked like a polished product with much thought behind it.

A warning sign that the builder is using a dictated plan is when some of the builder's people mumble things in the hall like, "I was not involved in planning this," and "I told them this plan would not work."

We heard these murmurs in the hall on Delphi, but did not recognize them. As told earlier, our builder used dictated plans several times. They kept telling us what they thought we wanted to hear. They felt that reality in planning would cause project cancellation. It took us many painful months to convince them that we wanted a product (nine systems) and we needed a realistic plan.

"I Think We Can Beat that Date"

Related to the dictated plan is planning to produce the right answer. Instead of dictating a plan, a manager hints at it. In dictated plans, the manager says, "You will deliver on 1 May."

In planning to produce the right answer, the manager says, "I want you guys to plan the project. I think you can deliver on 1 May. Come back to me with the results of your planning session."

A planning session ensues; it may be a good cards-on-the-wall planning session. The final answer, however, must agree with the hint. The project must end on 1 May, and the product must meet all requirements. The planners adjust task durations to ensure they sum to the right date. If the project appears to be 20% too long, the planners cut the duration of each task by 20%. Whatever it takes, the planners produce the right answer.

Things fall apart once the project starts as tasks take longer than planned. Given the numbers above, the team usually falls further than 20% behind. This is because they take shortcuts, and shortcuts only make the situation worse. Shortcuts introduce errors that require time to correct. Teams in these situations often fall 50% behind the "right answer" plan and 30% behind the realistic plan.

Planning to produce the right answer happened on Delphi. We participated in a cards-on-the-wall planning session at the builder's facility. The session went well, and we were developing a realistic delivery date. During a break, we talked with Leo, one of the builder's senior managers. We told him about the date that we thought the planning would produce.

Leo grimaced, turned his head, grinned, and told us, "You know, I think we can beat that date."

That was a warning sign. "I think we can beat that date" revealed that planning to produce the right answer would occur five minutes after we left the builder's facility. We, however, did not notice the sign. After we left, Leo hinted to his team that they could beat the date given by their plan by a few months. A week later, Leo visited our office and told us they would deliver a few months earlier than the cards-on-the-wall session indicated. His team succumbed to the pressure, shortened their tasks to produce the right answer, and failed miserably in their attempt to meet the date.

Delusion is one of the worst forms of a "lie" as it is a self-inflicted "lie." Leo knew that they had not been able to finish anything as scheduled. In Leo's new "I think we can beat that date" plan, they were to assemble the components even faster than on the old "right answer plan." Leo was deluding himself, deluding the team, and deluding the company.

"Planning Is A Waste of Time"

Some people do not like to plan tasks in a project. One way to understand this is with the Myers–Briggs Type Indicator. That is the groups of four letters that indicate how people prefer to obtain energy, gather information, make decisions, and take action. The last of the four letters is either a J for judging or P for perceiving. The Js prefer to decide now, make a plan, and move on with the work. The Ps prefer to postpone decisions and planning in case additional information becomes available. Hence, people who are Ps prefer not to plan. People who are Ps can make plans, but they prefer not to make plans today, tomorrow, or this week.

A project has a problem when people do not want to plan. Sometimes people will do anything else but plan. These people are probably strong Ps, i.e., they really hate to decide now.

A warning sign that a project is having trouble with planners not planning is when people make excuses. Some of the excuses we have heard include, "Planning is a waste of time. I can do the task faster than I can plan it. There is no reason to plan because the marketplace will change and we will have to plan again." The people making these statements may be strong Ps. They are not inferior people, but they are probably in the wrong job. In projects, the user is paying for us to work and deserves to have an idea of how much time and effort is required to build the product they want. That is what a plan provides.

There is only one reason for a person not making a plan. That is if they can pay the cost to make a product from their own wallet. If they can, they can cover the risk incurred from launching into tasks without a plan. If a person is sure they can succeed without a plan, let them put up the money to cover the effort in case it fails.

Avoiding planning was Tom's problem in the self-fulfilling planning story. Tom felt that all time spent on tasks other than programming was a waste. He told us, "The plan would not change the outcome of the project. Just let me work and I'll call you when I'm done." These excuses were warning signs that we had a person in charge of planning who preferred not to plan. We did not notice this warning and have someone else plan for Tom. We all suffered because of that.

Picnic Planning

Projects need good plans. As stated in the previous section, a plan provides an idea of how much time and effort is required to build a product the user wants. If a project does not have a good plan, it is risking the user's money every day.

A problem on projects is when people mistake "a plan" for "the plan." I can sketch "a plan" for a multiyear $50M project in half an hour on a sheet of paper. I would not advise anyone to back that plan with money. Such a project needs people to spend a week in a good planning session. That session would produce "the plan" for the project.

A warning sign that people are trying to use "a plan" is when they engage in "picnic planning." This is where people are sitting around as a group and someone asks another person, "How long do you think it would take to do this project?" It's like asking, "When do you think we should have our annual picnic?"

An unsuspecting person might venture a guess in this public forum. It's just a guess at "a plan" that no one would use, or so the person assumes. Sometimes, the person asking the question will record that answer and circulate it as "the plan."

Never fall into the picnic-planning trap. Answer, "That is an important project. You deserve a good estimate as an answer, and I cannot give you one at this time."

This illustrates one attribute of planning. People often consider an estimate and a plan as 100% accurate. They will neither ask how you created the plan nor for your estimate of its accuracy. When starting work on a project, always ask the source of the project's plan. If it was a picnic plan, stop work and create a real plan.

Relating to the Plan

Optimistic people can be wonderful. They say things like, "We think we can build the product because we've gathered the necessary people and technology and have planned the work."

Unjustified optimism, however, can be a terrible problem on projects. This is especially true in the area of planning, as many projects have failed because the planners were optimistic without justification. They felt things would work, they could solve problems quickly, and outsiders would deliver everything as promised.

A warning sign of unjustified optimism is when people make statements about the plan that have no relation to the plan. For example, "We will deliver the software per the plan because the sky is blue."

We had more than our share of unjustified optimism on Delphi. As mentioned earlier in this chapter, Leo was a senior manager on Delphi. He worked hard, was a smart person, and was optimistic to a fault. When we asked about his team performing per the plan, his favorite response was, "We have a good team, and the guys are working really hard."

It was positive that Leo felt good about his team and their efforts. That feeling, however, had no relation to the plan. We needed to know if the resources were available so the team could accomplish the tasks in the plan. It seemed that Leo believed the project would succeed if he said, "the guys are working really hard" enough times. The guys were working really hard, but they never had the things they needed in their hands. The hardware components were not available, someone else was using the test equipment, and the corporation was rebuilding the test lab. Those barriers were slowing the engineers because no one had planned. No one ensured that the things were ready at the same time the people were ready for them.

Leo's answer was a warning sign that although the people on the team were doing their best, the things we needed for the plan to work were missing.

CREATING A GOOD SITUATION

There are many problems related to planning. We have also learned of a few techniques that help create a situation in which planning works well. None of these are easy, but we feel they are worth the effort.

The Cards-on-the-Wall Planning Session

An excellent planning technique is the cards-on-the-wall planning session. This is where a project team gathers and plans a project. The name cards-on-the-wall comes from how people write tasks on cards and stick them to the walls. You connect the task cards with string to show task precedence. In the end, the walls are covered with a network of tasks or a project plan. A cards-on-the-wall session may lasts two or three days for a multiyear project, one or two days for a one-year project, or a couple hours for a multimonth project.

Cards-on-the-wall planning sessions usually produce good plans. There are several reasons for this, with the first being that the people who know the work best—the project team—create the plan. They know what they need to do a job and about how long it will take them to do it.

A second quality of cards-on-the-wall sessions is that the team owns the plan that comes out of the session. Ownership means the team will work hard to see the plan succeed. This is the opposite of what usually happens when a team receives a dictated plan. Teams do not own dictated plans. If the dictated plan fails, that is another sign of poor management and does not reflect on the team. Teams that own their plans want to see them succeed.

There are several elements that help lead to a successful cards-on-the-wall session. First, use a facilitator and other helpers. The facilitator asks a steady stream of questions to pull information from the project team. The facilitator concentrates on logistics, participation, and process. This allows the team to concentrate on the plan.

Next, plan to plan. This is something the facilitator can do for the project team. The facilitator arranges a good planning room (with lots of walls); gathers materials (stacks of cards, rolls of string or yarn, scissors, markers), and provides refreshments. Planning to plan helps ensure the right people attend from start to finish.

Another key element is participation from all attendees. Again, the facilitator works on this. A good facilitator will not try to have everyone participate in the same manner. Different people have different styles of working, thinking, and contributing. The facilitator will observe everyone and allow them to participate in their own way.

There are several cautions to heed in a cards-on-the-wall session. Sometimes people compete with one another to see who can save the project the most money. These subtle competitions lead people to underestimate the duration of tasks, as they want their department to look better than all others. A variation on this is simple optimism. We all want to see the project proceed quickly, and the excitement of a planning session can lead people to shorten their estimates.

Another caution is relying on automated tools. A good use of automated tools is recording and changing the plan during and after the session. The facilitator should bring a helper who records the growing plan on the wall with an automated tool. The plan will change often and drastically during the session. This is the reason for having a tool—for entering and modifying. Note that the tool records the plan. People do not use the tool to create the plan. There is only one keyboard and one small display. People use cards, string, and big walls to create the plan. That allows many people to create and see at the same time.

The second mistaken use of the automated tool is believing that it will manage the project. Tools do not manage projects; project managers manage projects. Chapter 11 discusses the things the managers should do.

A number of good things happen during a cards-on-the-wall session. There are several "Aha!" events that occur. The story of the Delphi cards-on-the-wall session relayed several of these. The first was when Ray and Jim learned how their departments could work together to save time. The next was when Bruce documented the structure of the product. This allowed everyone to see and understand the product. The understanding helped people set smart priorities on their work. The last "Aha" was when we learned the four basic steps to building every component. That allowed us to monitor our progress and adjust our efforts.

Most important, the project team members learn that the other people in the cards-on-the-wall session are people. They talk about hobbies, families, and aspirations. These relationships pay great dividends during the project itself. People will take time to stop by and talk to the friends they made during the cards-on-the-wall session. These friendly conversations often lead to discussions that benefit the project.

Cards-on-the-wall sessions are appropriate in many circumstances. An obvious one is when creating a plan before a project starts. Another use of the technique is when a project is about to enter a critical phase. The team can use the technique to plan the phase in great detail. There are times when projects are in trouble and there is a need to plan the rest of the project from scratch. Cards-on-the-wall works well there, too.

Scale Your Plans

As with most practices that have worth, people can abuse planning. A three-day planning session is not necessary for a three-week project. People should scale planning to the project at hand. Use large plans when necessary and use small plans when they are sufficient.

Delphi went through its major plans and replans as described earlier. During the final couple years of Delphi, the builder held a dozen smaller cards-on-the-wall sessions. These planning sessions provided detailed schedules for short but critical phases of the project. The builder usually drew these short schedules on a whiteboard in the project room. Bruce, a meticulous mechanical engineer with a background in drafting, drew them neatly by hand. Everyone could see the tasks, the dates, and the results.

Keep Plans Public

One way to help plans work is to keep them in public. We have found the best way to do this is to post them in the project room (see Chapter 2). There are several things about public plans that help a project. First, this shows that the project manager feels the people on the project are adults. The project manager is not holding the plan in a secret place and showing a little bit of it at a time the way adults sometimes share candy with children. It is out there for everyone to see and use.

A public plan is open to criticism and improvement. Plans are rarely correct, and a project manager should not try to act like the plan on his project is an exception. People can look at a public plan and suggest changes. A wise project manager will listen to those suggestions.

A public plan also shows that the project manager is open with his work. The plan is the responsibility of the project manager. Putting it on display shows humility and a willingness to improve work products. People should welcome peer review of their products, and the public plan shows that the project manager welcomes peer review of his.

The builder on Delphi posted their plans during the final two years of the project. The short planning sessions created those plans that Bruce drew on the whiteboard of the project room. Everyone saw them everyday. Everyone saw the progress and lack of progress of the project against the plan. People helped others when they fell behind, and sometimes the entire team threw up their hands and admitted that they could not meet the schedule. Nevertheless, everyone was honest and open with the plan and their progress. This meant much to our users. The builder told us the truth, we told the users the truth, and we all worked together.

Plan for Real Life

A good technique in planning is to plan for real people living real lives. As much as we may wish we had ideal people working on projects, we do not. Real people take vacations, become ill, have babies, retire, resign, make mistakes, need training, and all sorts of other things.

When starting a cards-on-the-wall session, ask people to write their planned absences on a large sheet of paper on one wall. People usually know months in advance when they will take their vacations, have babies, and retire. Do not try to talk anyone out of their planned absences, as denying real life will not make it go away. Use the real information in the plan. The planned absences do not waste time on projects. Ignoring them wastes time on projects.

The big waste on projects is the time spent scrambling to catch up. When someone is sick, others have to shift around to do their tasks. They stop work on their own task, try to figure out where the other person was on their task, try to learn that task, and then do it. Most of the wasted time is spent discussing how in the world the other person could let us down by becoming sick. It's funny how we talk about things like that as if the other person were enjoying the flu. People do not plan sicknesses, so we do not know when they will occur. People do become sick, so we can plan in extra time. Allow every person at least one sick week per year on a project. Add that week to their tasks. If they have an exceptionally healthy year, the project may complete ahead of schedule.

Another thing that consumes time is correcting mistakes. There are many techniques that help prevent mistakes and catch them early when they are easier to correct. None of these techniques catch 100% of the mistakes. We always have to stop and correct mistakes as they are another part of real life. Since mistakes always occur, we can plan for them. Add five to ten percent to the project schedule to correct mistakes.

A final thing that takes time is training. People who know what they are doing perform faster and make fewer mistakes. No one is born knowing what they need to know to work on a project. That is another part of real life. We can wish for people who have all the abilities we need, but wishing will not make it so. Plan time for people to learn through formal training or just through hard knocks, but plan for it.

During the early phases of Delphi, the builder did not plan for real life. One key engineer named Lee allowed himself to fall victim to this mistake. The plan had no room for people taking a day off, so Lee worked every Saturday and half days on most Sundays for a year. He grudgingly took a day off on the Fourth of July to take his kids to the beach. That was the only day he took off for a year. Lee quit the project and quit the company. He took a lower-paying job at another company because he wanted to spend Sundays and holidays with his family. A lack of real life in the plan drove away a key engineer.

Know the Context of Planning

A good technique to avoid problems and wasted time with planning is to understand the context of a plan. People often ask for plans and estimates. The reason for asking varies and drives the effort and accuracy of planning.

The first thing in finding the context of a plan is to know who wants the plan. This does two things. The first is that you know who to ask the rest of the context questions given below. The second is that the person who wants the plan brings context with them. Some people like to know how long it would take to implement every idea that pops into their head. If this person asks you for a plan for a different idea every week, do not spend much time creating them. Some people are in a position to make things happen. If a manager several layers above you asks for a plan, spend some time and energy on it.

The next thing in finding the context of a plan is to ask the person what they will do with the plan. Sometimes people want a plan because they are curious. A simple plan will suffice here. At other times, people are trying to create the budget for next year. They need a higher-quality plan and they probably need a conservative estimate so they can budget enough resources. There are even times when someone needs a plan to decide whether or not to start a project. A high-quality plan is in order here, so spend the resources to create one.

A key to planning is to know how the desired accuracy of the plan. Sometimes, people want a ROM (rough order of magnitude). They only want to know if the plan is one, six, or ten months long and needs $100K, $500K, or $1M. Sometimes, people want a 50% plan. This is one in which there is a 50/50 chance of the project succeeding with the plan. Sometimes people want a 95% plan—one with a 95% chance of the project succeeding with the plan.

Once you know the context and have made a plan, provide the context with the plan. Tell people the assumptions used while making the plan. Tell them the accuracy of the plan, the resources consumed while planning, and what you would and would not do with the plan. State openly, "This is a ROM plan. I spent four hours creating it. Do not bet the company on it."

On Delphi, Leo visited our managers monthly. He always brought a new plan with him. We had difficulty interpreting the word "plan" as he used it. No one was sure how Leo made the plans. We did not know his assumptions, his resources, or his accuracy. Leo brought plans because he felt that was the best way to keep us from canceling the project. It gave him a form of legitimacy and justified his visits. We did not buy any of that, and the builder's senior managers removed Leo from the project six months later.

CONCLUSIONS ABOUT PLANNING

Planning a project is difficult, as we have to make predictions about things in the future. This is hard enough, but we often make these predictions with incomplete and incorrect information.

One thing harder than planning a project is attempting a project without a plan. No one knows where they are or what they are doing. Maybe planning is the lesser of two evils.

This leads us to our principle of planning: Plan the project, and plan in as much detail as necessary.

Watch out for:

- "I was not involved."
- "I think we can beat that date."
- "Planning is a waste of time."
- Picnic planning.
- Not relating to the plan.

How to create a good situation:

- Hold a cards-on-the-wall session.
- Scale your plans.

- Keep plans public.
- Plan for real life.
- Know the context.

Planning may be difficult, but it is not impossible. We saw people predict a 220-week project within six weeks even though they needed several painful tries to create this plan. The hardest part was convincing them that we wanted to hear the truth as they knew it. This leads us to our best advice about planning: plan projects as best you can and honestly tell people about your results.

Back in the early 1990s, three gentlemen and I spent a day and a half in a cards-on-the-wall exercise. We planned a project that would run six months and cost a couple million dollars. The next week, we presented this plan to our managers. They considered the project a few days and decided not to do the project.

One colleague smuggly remarked, "I told you that all that planning stuff was stupid. You guys wasted two days with those silly cards and string."

Our division chief stepped forward and said, "I disagree. Forty-eight manhours of planning gave us the information we needed to prevent wasting six months and $2M."

That was the best planning for a nonproject I ever did and it taught me a big lesson about planning. Planning gives us information. How we use that information is up to us.

Chapter 7

Be Careful What You Ask For, You Just Might Get It: The Requirements

Requirements describe the problems we are trying to solve. In effect, they express the work that we want to improve [2]. All activities of a project stem from how we gather, state, and interpret the requirements.

We often have problems with requirements. The major cause of these problems is failure to communicate among people. (We address these communication problems in Chapter 12.) We misunderstand one another, and our misunderstandings do not become evident until after we have consumed large amounts of resources. Another reason for problems with requirements is that we can misunderstand what they are and the role they play in projects.

THE PORTABLE CONTROLLER

This story relates a classic example of a little requirement "creep" that resulted in significant unforeseen consequences. The system we built on Delphi was to be operated with a portable controller. The obvious portable controller was a laptop computer. We, however, ended up with a second portable controller—a palmtop computer. This palmtop computer caused problems for almost ten years.

This all started back in the early 1990s on the contract that preceded Delphi. Laptop computers at that time ran the basic DOS operating system with simple text displays. They were big and heavy compared to what we have today, but they were sufficient.

It Sounded Good When We Started. By Dwayne Phillips and Roy O'Bryan
ISBN 0-471-48586-1 © 2004 by the Institute of Electrical and Electronics Engineers.

Early in the project, a few members of our team visited COMDEX in Las Vegas. They ran across a palmtop computer. This was not like the Palm Pilots and other personal communication devices that we have today. It had a small QWERTY keyboard, a text display of 25 lines, and fit in your hand. It was a real novelty for the early 1990s.

The lead for the buyer team at the time was an energetic and creative engineer named Ronald (the same Ronald discussed in chapter 6). Ronald was sure that the palmtop computer would be great for the users. It was smaller and lighter than the regular laptop computer. Ronald figured a way that he could hold the computer in his palm and tap the function keys (F1 through F10) with his thumb. He envisioned how the builder could program these function keys ("quick keys") as shortcuts to common operations. Ronald championed this idea with great zeal.

Years later, it would be hard to find any user who thought that the palmtops had any merit. Back then, however, there were some people who thought the palmtop was "pretty neat." Some eagerly participated in a user working group to define the functionality of the quick keys.

Ronald had deftly inserted the new little computer into the project. The users wittingly or unwittingly became coconspirators when they eagerly participated in defining the functionality of the quick keys. Once "in," none of the users ever expressed any interest in pulling the palmtop "out." After all, it was a novelty, and it might have some use under some circumstances. No one anywhere down the line ever said, "This is a dumb idea."

With time and lack of interest to reassess the need for it, the "pretty neat" thing became a necessity—a backdoor requirement. After a while, no one was sure how the palmtop was introduced into the project, but at one point somebody felt it would be a good thing.

The builder worked to fit the control software into this palmtop computer. To accomplish this, the builder chose a user interface toolkit that worked in DOS. They optimized the code for size (not much memory was available) and speed (not much of a CPU was available). The optimized code eventually worked well.

Time marched on and the Windows movement made DOS obsolete. The user interface toolkit, however, worked only in DOS. We stayed with DOS on the laptop computer just to keep the palmtop computer working. After all, it was a requirement, was not it? Or was it just something good to have? We were all a little confused at this point, but we did not have the resources to change everything. We stuck with the palmtop controller and its DOS software.

Delphi itself started in the fall of 1997. Laptop computers became smaller, lighter, faster, and did everything better. Ronald was no longer on the project. His replacement, Don, was the leader of the buyer's team. The builder was ensuring that all software changes worked on the palmtop. Don saw that retaining the palmtop computer was costing the project a lot of money.

Don went to the user with this predicament. None of the users at that time could remember when Ronald had found and promoted the palmtop computer. They now had no interest in it. The palmtop computer, however, was written into the requirements, and Don had to struggle to take it out. He spent days talking with users and managers of users. The users finally agreed to remove the palmtop from the project. They signed memos stating their position and backed Don in configuration control meetings. The palmtop computer was gone, but its software, bound to DOS, was still with us.

Don left the project in the fall of 1998, and I became the leader of the buyer's team in January 1999. We were going to use one of the new laptop computers available. The trouble was they were not made to run DOS. There were DOS windows available and even some DOS simulators, but those were not exactly DOS. They were not what we needed to keep the software, a legacy of the palmtop computer, running.

The builder discovered that they could not go to the store and buy a laptop computer that would run the control software. They could search the world of laptops, make many phone calls, ask many obscure questions (and be answered with "You want to do what?"), and buy something close to what they needed. Our builder could throw in old device drivers, old copies of this and that, and make the laptop work.

By the year 2000, we finally had to confront our problem. We could not depend on using old pieces of software from companies that no longer existed. We decided to move the control software to the latest Windows environment. That would cost about one million dollars. This was a reasonable cost given the complex nature of the software.

All this effort and expense was needed because someone thought it would be a good thing to use a smaller controller. That good thing became a requirement, and that requirement drove the project for almost ten years. Although migrating the software to the Windows environment would cost around a million dollars, we really do not know how much it cost us to stick with the palmtop for all those years before we were forced to do something.

This is the nature of requirements. They drive a project for better or worse. Eliminating requirements helps drive the project for the better.

A FEW WORDS ABOUT REQUIREMENTS

A large problem when working with requirements is the vocabulary used. We easily slip from black and white requirements to emotional arguments. We go from, "The system shall transport 100 tons of steel," to "How dare you question my dedication to this project!" The following may help understand such problems and help to avoid them.

There are five words to discuss in the area of requirements [1]. These are

1. Requirement
2. Attribute
3. Constraint

4. Design
5. Derived requirements

We discuss them below.

Requirements

If we care about something, it is a requirement. The level of detail does not matter. Some requirements are at a high level at which we care about large things. For example, "The system shall transport ten tons of gravel." Other requirements are at low levels at which we care about small things. For example, "The system shall use 36" tires with 3/8" tread."

If something is important to us—if it is a requirement—we must state it and have the builder do it.

The requirements form "shall" statements. Each requirement begins with "the system shall." For example, "The system shall carry 1,000 gallons of water." "The system shall calculate square roots." "The system shall store names of one million people."

All requirements are not equal. People often act as if requirements are equal, but they really are not. For example, making the user happy is great, but keeping us out of jail is more important. Storing names of one million people is fine, but finding the one person we need in a few seconds is important.

Attributes

An attribute describes something and lends properties to that something. The requirements state what the system shall do, whereas the attributes describe the system.

The attribute forms a "shall be" statement. "The system shall be small." "The system shall be easy to use." "The system shall be blue."

We should attach attributes to requirements. Suppose a requirement is, "The system shall hold the names of one million people." Now suppose there are the following attributes:

a. The system shall be easy to use.
b. The system shall be blue.
c. The system shall be small.
d. The system shall be fast.

Which of the attributes can we attach to "The system shall hold the names of one million people"?

We can attach (a), (c), and (d). Now we have, "The system shall hold the names of one million people. The system shall be easy to use. The system shall be small. The system shall be fast."

Now I know that it shall be easy for me to store the names of a million people, I can store them in a small system, and I can do it quickly. We are now describing the system, and someone can build it.

Constraints

The constraint forms an "it shall fit inside or play with" statement. Constraints limit the system. We might want a fast system, but are we able to have a system that needs liquid nitrogen to cool it? Probably not, so a constraint would be, "The system shall fit inside my shirt pocket."

Constraints bring us back to earth. They remind us that there are many things we know, but we need to say them. If we do not constrain the system, the builder can do almost anything. Sometimes, we want the builder to think freely without any limits, but sometimes we cannot afford that.

Design

Design is how we build the system we want. We leave the design up to the builder.

Design is a "do not care" statement. We do have an interest in how the builder builds something, but as long as they deliver the system we want, we do not care about the details. If we care about some details, the details that we care about must be expressed as requirements.

Sometimes, it is hard to accept that there are things that do not reach the "we care" level. Caring is a sign of a good person, and we are good people, so we should care. Sometimes, however, we let our caring take over our better judgment. We want to tell the builder how to do something. We are certainly smart enough to tell them exactly what to do. We want to design and build it so badly that we interfere.

This is the common problem of putting design and implementation into requirements. Our egos and exuberance can overcome our judgment. We tell people the details that we want. These details may be our desires, but they may not be necessary. Do we need the builder to use material X? Do we need the builder to use manufacturing process X? Do we need the builder to use packing and shipping process X? If we do need X, then X is a requirement. Otherwise it is a want, a desire, and a do not care.

There are times when we can help the builder. We know something about the application because it's for us. Because we know how we will use it, we can make suggestions about some implementation details. These suggestions may help the builder when they are stuck with a problem. We should treat these suggestions as suggestions, not as requirements.

Derived Requirements

Halfway between requirements and design are derived requirements. In order for the system to do X, the subsystems shall do A, B, and C. We, the buyer, do not state what the subsystems shall do. The builder derives the requirements for the subsystems from the requirements of the system. Hence, the term "derived requirements." Suppose we want a system that weighs less than ten pounds, and the system has three subsystems. Their weights must sum to less than ten pounds. The builder can derive the weights of the subsystems to be two, three, and four pounds. We do not care about the weights of the subsystems.

There are two ways to treat derived requirements. The first way is to treat them like requirements—we care statements. In such a situation, we know the high-level requirements, but do not know the requirements for the subsystems. We will pay the builder to derive these. Once the builder states the derived requirements, we accept them. We will now treat them as we care statements. The builder cannot trade around the derived requirements. Continuing the example, the builder cannot build the three subsystems to weigh three pounds each because that causes the first subsystem to exceed its weight requirement (two pounds).

The second way to treat derived requirements is to leave them as we do not care statements. We state the big requirements, and the builder goes on from there. The builder derives requirements for the subsystems, but owns these. The builder is free to trade requirements among the subsystems as long as they meet the system requirements. Continuing the example, the builder can build the three subsystems to weigh three pounds each.

The key to working with the different methods of derived requirements is to state it clearly in writing. We wanted to keep control of the derived requirements on Delphi. We wanted the subsystems to be interchangeable, so if subsystem A of system number one failed, we wanted to be able to swap it with subsystem A of any other system.

Our problem was that we did not state clearly our desire. We assumed that everyone knew what we wanted. Many of the builder's engineers also assumed that and worked in that direction for months. Finally, someone read the contract. The contract did not say the subsystems were to be interchangeable. The builder stopped working in that direction. We lost the ability we wanted, but we saved ourselves money.

Another thing about derived requirements is that requirements can be decomposed differently. The buyer and builder may not agree on a logical decomposition. This is where we have to be careful as to what is important to us. Do not leave anything to chance; if it is important, do not leave it for others to divine. State it as a requirement.

WARNING SIGNS OF TROUBLE WITH REQUIREMENTS

We have learned a few warning signs of impending trouble when working with requirements. This section discusses a few of those warning signs.

"I Think They Mean X"

A big problem on projects is when people misunderstand the requirements. The builder will build the wrong product if they misunderstand the requirements. It is as simple as that.

Miscommunication is a big part of misunderstanding. There are at least two parties involved in communicating requirements. The sender of the message is one. If the sender gives a confusing message, the receiver will misunderstand it.

"Confusing" messages come in all forms. For example, "The system shall store the last message it receives." Which message is "the last message?" Is it the final message received before midnight? Is it the final message received before someone reboots the system? Is it the final message received before someone makes a backup copy of all system data? Is it the most recently received message?

A warning sign of miscommunication is when someone says, "I think they mean X instead of Y."

This shows that people are not certain about the requirements. If the user and builder do not work out the uncertainty, the builder will build the wrong product.

Confusion or confused requirements are warning signs that should not be ignored. The following paragraphs provide examples.

The buyer should know whether or not his requirements have stabilized. If they have not stabilized, he is not ready to enter into a contractual agreement. The builder should not proceed further until resolving the requirements and communicating them clearly.

Builders be wary when the buyer's requirements are vague rather than explicit. It is probable that the buyer's needs have not coalesced yet. Do not bet that the buyer will know what he wants when he sees it. Vaguely stated requirements do not constitute a license to steal. Your company's reputation is on the line, so help the buyer articulate and document what he wants.

There is a good chance that before the product has been delivered, the people who "know" what was wanted will move on to bigger and better things. With vaguely stated requirements, the "new kid on the block" will interpret the requirements in a new manner, and there is a good chance that the product will take a left turn at the kitchen table and end up in Wichita.

If the buyer really wants the things he cares about, and the builder did not think they were important, there will be an impact on cost and schedule. The cost will go up, and it will take longer to get the product. There is also the paperwork needed to make the change. Requests for Change (RFCs) and Engineering Change Proposals (ECPs) take time to coordinate and process.

In the story of the portable controller, the builder could have asked us questions like, "Is the palmtop controller the most important thing to the user?" A wonderful statement would have been, "I thought portable software was more important than a little controller."

These would have pointed to possible misunderstandings on our part. We might have reconsidered the situation and spoken with our users about it. Did the users really want the little controller? Did we misunderstand how important it was to them? We were going to spend millions of dollars to accommodate this. Was it worth this expense?

"They Know What I Mean"

A part of miscommunication in requirements is when the buyer implies a requirement, hoping that the builder will infer it. Sometimes, if the buyer and builder have a long and good working relationship, they think enough alike and this works. Such long and good relationships, however, are rare.

Take, for example, "The system shall work when covered with 12" of snow." The buyer is implying that the system will also work when wet because snow is wet. The builder might infer this other requirement, but might not. If these requirements are important, if the buyer cares about them, the buyer should state them explicitly.

A warning sign of implying and inferring is when someone says, "They know what I mean," or "I know what they mean."

An infamous case of implying and inferring was with the space shuttle Challenger in the mid-1980s. The requirement was that the shuttle function at a low temperature of 40°F and above. The shuttle would be launched from Florida, and the temperature does falls below 40°F in Florida. Was NASA implying that the shuttle should function at all temperatures known to occur in Florida? As we learned, the builder did not infer that. They built the shuttle to work at 40°F. NASA tried to operate the shuttle on January 28th 1986 in rare but cold Florida weather.

It is possible for a buyer to conduct a project with implying and inferring. They must, however, state that clearly. Start with, "We are not sure about the details here. We will tell you what we are thinking about, and we will pay you to work with us to discover the details."

In the above example, the buyer could write, "We know the system will be covered with snow. We do not really know much about the conditions that accompany snow. We will pay you to study that and help us write the requirements correctly."

A Requirement is a Requirement

An earlier section discussed requirements and derived requirements. These two are different, but treating them the same is another major requirements problem that can occur on projects.

A case in point was with the palmtop controller. We required the palmtop controller. The only way that controller would work at the time was using DOS, so the builder derived DOS as a requirement. We went along with that, and DOS became a derived requirement.

The builder squeezed software into that tiny DOS memory space. They did a great job of optimizing the code. The cost kept climbing; the computer world went away from DOS, and we should have, too. We did not because DOS was a requirement. At some point, we forgot that it was a derived requirement, treated it as something essential, and paid dearly for this mistake.

The warning sign was that we did not keep separate lists for requirements and derived requirements. Everything went into one list and became of equal importance. If we had a traceable list of derived requirements, we would have noted that DOS was not a requirement. It was derived from the palmtop controller. As soon as we dropped the palmtop controller as a requirement, we would have dropped DOS, too. That would have freed us from years of expense.

Requirements Creep

Many projects suffer from "requirements creep," which comes in all shapes and colors. Warning signs of requirements creep come in the form of requirements clarification. People say, "Well, obviously, you really did not understand what we meant by that."

The buyer's people can cause havoc with requirements at project reviews. At these reviews, the builder's people usually hang on every word spoken by the buyer's management. Warning signs include the statements, "You mean that it doesn't do X? What happens if Y? I did not know that!"

These indicate that someone really does not understand something. Fault can lie with the stated requirement, the derived requirements, or limitations and constraints imposed by the manner in which the requirements are being implemented. The fault can also lie with managers from the buyer's side who are not up to date on the project. They simply do not understand what is happening.

Managers like to make decisions, as that makes them feel important. Not to disappoint the buyer, the builder, who has been hanging on every word, will try to accommodate the buyer's manager by throwing him a bone. Sure enough, the buyer's manager will bite. Bones come in all shapes and sizes in statements like, "Well if you would like X, we can do that."

Sure enough, the manager makes a "constructive change." Constructive changes are like credit cards, in that you get it now but you still have to pay for it. Misconduct occurred, but who is going to tell the boss that he goofed?

Many times, the users cause requirements creep. When things begin to come together and people have a better understanding of what they are getting, they try to help out. They provide suggestions such as, "Wouldn't it be nice if. . . ."

Of course, that statement may not be asked at the formal review where the builder's program manager can assess the cost and schedule impact. It may be asked informally of the guy who is doing the work at his desk or workbench.

The implementer thinks about it for a few milliseconds, says, "Yes I can make it do that," and before you know it, it is done. Sometimes, it takes a little longer, and before you know it, it has a life of its own.

Requirements creep can be initiated by builder personnel. Designers like to design and engineers like to pull every bit of performance they can out of the design. They do not want to let go. They say things like, "I can get you X amount more performance if. . . . I can make it go faster if. . . . It will jump over tall buildings, if. . . ."

If the system meets the requirements, be satisfied and move on. Pry it loose from the engineer's hands, and start him on something else. Do not buy into these can-do, "if" statements.

Putting Technology Into Requirements

Another problem in the requirements area is when we mix design and implementation with requirements. The requirements are a statement of the problem, whereas the design and implementation are statements of solutions.

When we mix the solution with the problem, we make the particular solution a requirement. In a contractual relation, the builder must use the solution the buyer has stated. That is a legal issue. In internal projects, this is not a legal issue, but the builder still must use the solution. Mixing the solution in with the problem causes trouble because it limits the builder from doing their job of finding the best solution.

This is what happened to us in the palmtop controller story. The palmtop computer became a requirement. To remain legal, the builder had to use the one specific little computer that we wanted. They had no option of looking at other small computers and recommending one that would work without the restrictions contained in the one we found. We were so smart in the short-term, but this cost us in the long-term.

A warning sign of mixing the solution with problem is the use of technology in requirements statements. For example, "The system shall use disk drives with at least 100,000 hours MTBF (mean time between failure)." This requirement contains a technology (disk drives). It does not allow the builder to find some other means of data storage that has the same MTBF.

Another example is, "The laptop computers shall have at least 10 GByte of disk space." This requirement forces the builder to use a certain type of disk drive on a laptop computer. A better solution might be to have a laptop with a wireless connection to a large server. The server could store all the data better than the laptop. The requirement also forces the builder to use a laptop computer. It rules out the possibility of letting the user speak into a cell phone that is connected to a server containing voice recognition software.

An allowable form of mixing design into requirements is when stating constraints (discussed earlier). For example, "The system shall use disk drives made by ACME Disk Drive, Inc."

That is a valid constraint if we already have a maintenance contract with ACME and we want all new systems to fit into that contract.

"If They Can't Understand This"

Specifying requirements is difficult. We are surprised to find that many people are surprised when difficulties arise while trying to understand written requirements. It can be a major problem when people expect the requirements process to be easy.

A warning sign of the problem is when someone says, "If they can't understand this, they shouldn't be in the business."

We usually hear this from a buyer. They have written a requirements document, and the builder keeps asking them questions about it. The builder only wants to understand the problem so they can build the right system.

The "if they can't understand" statement is a cry of frustration. We have seen some buyers accuse the builder of using the questions to stall for time. The builder must have something else happening in the background that is occupying their best engineers. They ask questions only to delay the project and blame the delay on the buyer.

Sometimes this cry of frustration is wishful thinking. The buyer states the requirements poorly and hopes the builder will understand the intentions instead of the words. This wish rarely comes true.

People are anxious to start "the real work" instead of haggling over requirements. We must remember, however, that to write is to be misunderstood. We are working with complicated high-technology systems. There will always be confusion with requirements, and it is best to seek clarification on everything.

TECHNIQUES THAT HELP WITH REQUIREMENTS

We have learned of a few techniques that help us when working with requirements. We wish we would have learned them sooner and used them more often. Nevertheless, the following discuss some of these techniques.

The Straight Story

We have found it helpful to try to communicate requirements in a straightforward manner. This involves ways to express the requirements and to pull information from the builder about the requirements. Writing requirements is not like writing a mystery novel in which the author drops hints along a twisted path leading to the final scene.

Communicating begins with the builder understanding the user. We need to quiz the user. Ask repeatedly, "Do you mean X?" When the user says, "Store one million names," ask, "Do you mean first, middle, and last names of one million people? Do you mean first and last names only? Do you mean Mr. or Ms. and last name only?"

We should think of at least three interpretations of what the user wants and ask about each interpretation. Be specific, no matter how far-fetched an interpretation seems. Stating specific things aloud often brings hidden desires and misunderstandings to the surface.

Next comes the communication with the builder. Try to state things in a simple and straightforward manner. Use small words and short sentences with only one requirement per sentence. The "shall," "shall be," and "shall work within" statements given earlier work well.

The time to make sure that there is no confusion about what the builder must build is long before anything is ever built. If I think I clearly understand what I want, and I think that I have clearly and concisely articulated my requirements, I should run them by the prospective builders. Ask them, "Are these requirements clear enough for you build it for me? What do not you understand? Where are the cost drivers? Now that you know as much as I do, tell me in your own words what I want."

Phrases such as "verification test" and "prototype unit" mean different things to different people. Ask the builder to state their interpretation of terms.

Be wary when people answer questions with the same words you used. For example, "Well, in a verification test we verify that the system meets the requirements." That answer does not tell me anything.

Finally, allow the builder time to study the requirements document and then ask them questions. "What would you do with this problem? What are some rough solutions that come to your mind?"

Another question to ask the builder is, "What three requirements changes would change the design dramatically?" This question looks for things that might change the entire project. It causes all parties—the builder, user, and buyer—to consider things that may not have crossed their minds.

We wish we had asked this question when we pushed the palmtop controller requirement on our builder. Maybe the builder would have launched into a discussion of operating systems and personal computers. We might have foreseen a day when DOS would not be prevalent. This would have shown us some of the downside of tying a system with a ten-year lifetime to something that might disappear in two years.

Review Early and Often

Visiting the builder early and often to see their design and implementation shows us what the requirements mean to them. The design and implementation of a system express the builder's understanding of the requirements. If the builder shows us gallons of green paint in storage, we can see that they are not going to paint the system red. We will never see these cans of green paint from the opposite coast of the country. We will only see them if we visit the builder early and often.

Looking at the builder's work will also show us things we forgot to include in the requirements. The steps on a fire truck should not be tall because fire fighters carry heavy gear and cannot climb tall steps. Did we forget that? The surface of these steps should have nonslip coatings on them. Did we forget that also?

The builder's work can also trigger a new requirement that we want to include. The danger here is that we think of ten new requirements every week when we visit the builder. Requirements creep can overload and kill a project just like forgotten requirements. There are ways to save new requirements for the next iteration of a system.

Manage the Requirements

A technique to prevent problems is to manage the requirements. Requirements management is simple in principle but difficult in practice. The Software Engineering Institute's (SEI) Capability Maturity Model (CMM) spells out requirements management in basic terms. Requirements management means to:

1. Establish a common understanding of the requirements with the user.
2. Document that understanding.
3. Make changes in an organized manner.

How could anything be simpler? One, two, three, and we are done.

As with most things, the problems with requirements management come with people. Technical people run projects. We move up through the ranks of engineers until we are the head engineer on a project. The next step up the ladder is the project manager. Most technical people like to work on technical problems. It does not matter that an engineer is sitting in the program manager's chair. The engineer is still an engineer. Requirements analysis is a technical problem. Technical people gather information, draw diagrams (use-case, data-flow, etc.), and analyze them to prepare for design. Requirements analysts use all their technical skills and apply themselves wholeheartedly.

Requirements management is a management problem. People solve management problems by working with people, not things. Requirements management involves holding meetings, reaching agreements face-to-face, and keeping detailed records. Many technical people see requirements management as a clerical job, and most of us hate it. Meetings never seem to end and they produce no conclusions.

Communication skills and practices seem to be a waste of time to most technical people. They are, however, helpful in understanding the requirements and controlling changes to them. Without managing the requirements, they run out of control, grow, creep, scramble, and choke us. Well, maybe they do not do it on their own. Maybe we help them do all these distracting things.

Senior managers should provide help to the project manager. Real help can take several forms, with the simplest being providing a full-time requirements manager. This is a person who understands technical issues, but likes and is good at managing things. The requirements manager conducts all the face-to-face meetings and keeps all the detailed records. This person has the personality and temperament to keep the user happy and the technical people out of trouble.

Project management is about the management of change. Requirements are going to change throughout the life of a project. Everyone associated with a project should stay focused on what we want the builder to build. Requirements help us focus. We focused on what we needed when we wrote the requirements and we must focus on the requirements as we progress through the development cycle. If things change, manage the change.

Basically, the buyer has to weigh the impact of a change before the change is made. The Delphi story in this chapter demonstrates the unforeseen consequences of a single change in one small system. If Delphi was one of a number of systems that were to be incorporated into a larger system, i.e., the Space Station, such a small change in the requirements could have impacted the performance of many of the other systems. Fortunately, the palmtop only affected Delphi.

Draw Boundaries

Another technique that helps create a good situation with requirements is to determine carefully how much work we will attempt. A basic technique is to draw the boundaries of the system.

I once worked on a project in which we built a software system that would schedule resources. There were many things we wanted the system to do. We had the opportunity to draw a boundary around these desires, allocate some of them to the software, and leave the rest to the user. For example, we could have a person interpret our policies for resource allocation. Instead, we allocated this task to the software.

First, the builder struggled to write the software. Interpreting policies means wading into many areas of gray instead of the nice black and white that computers do well. Second, once finished, the software was hard to use. The users hated it, so the system rotted on the shelf.

A better idea would have been to write simple software that did not do much. We could have drawn the system boundaries so that the people interpreted the gray policy areas. This would have given the users a simple system that they would have used. Once people use a system, they see the value of it. This builds support for the system and helps provide resources to upgrade the system later. People upgrade useful systems and throw away systems that are hard to use.

A similar thing happened with the dot-com businesses in the late 1990s. The companies krew their requirements well. Their mistake came when they drew the boundaries around what the system would do and what the consumers would do. Prior to going on-line, the company's employees would enter the consumer's orders. The employee was serving the consumer and compensated for the system's faults. Once the system went on-line, the consumer had to enter his or her own order. Consumers are not tolerant of faulty order-entry systems. The consumers revolted against companies with poor Web sites. Those companies failed in part because they moved their consumers inside the boundaries of the system.

The Stranger

A final technique that helps create a good situation with requirements is to bring in someone who knows nothing about the particular set of requirements. This person has no preconceptions.

Let this person read the requirements and talk about them. Ask the person about what they read and what they would build. Look for things that confuse this person. Do not dismiss confusing areas with, "Well, there is a certain amount of background that our builders know, so they will understand the document." Revise areas that confuse the outsider. This is a good way to judge the quality and clarity of your requirements.

CONCLUSIONS ABOUT REQUIREMENTS

Requirements describe our situation, so we list what we care about in our requirements. We state what we need, discuss it until we all understand it, and go on to build the system. This all seems so simple, but reality is not so simple.

Our principle of requirements is: What the builder understands to be your requirements will drive everything in the project.

Watch out for

- "I think they mean X."
- "They know what I mean."

- "A requirement is a requirement."
- Requirements creep.
- Putting technology into requirements.
- "If they can't understand this, they shouldn't be in the business."

To create a good situation,

- Communicate in a straightforward manner.
- Review early and often.
- Manage the requirements.
- Decide how much work to attempt.
- Bring in someone who knows nothing about the requirements.

People rarely "just understand" what we want. We have to talk with people, draw and write what we hear, and ask plenty of questions. Skipping ahead and hoping the builder will do it right rarely works. The best advice we have is to be patient, forgiving, and persistent.

The biggest requirements exercise we had on Delphi came right after the builder came forward with their final plan (see Chapter 6). The builder told us their plan and also told us that it was based on "clearing up a few misunderstandings" with the system requirements. We needed a month of meetings to "clear up these misunderstandings."

We were so mad at the builder. We had just given them 50% more money and 50% more time to deliver systems, and they were not grateful. Instead, they were demanding that we ease many of the requirements. They were mad at us, too. They were cleaning up our messy and mistake-laden requirements document, and we were not grateful.

Tempers flared often during this exercise, and I still wonder how everyone stayed calm enough to keep the project going. The builder just wanted to understand what we wanted, and we just wanted them to understand what we wanted. In the midst of all these good intentions, we felt like strangling one another. That is the nature of requirements and people.

REFERENCES

1. *Exploring Requirements: Quality Before Design,* Donald C. Gause and Gerald M. Weinberg, Dorset House Publishing, 1989.
2. *Mastering the Requirements Process,* Suzanne Robertson and James Robertson, Addison-Wesley, 1999.

Chapter 8

If I Could Just Find a Question for this Answer: Designing Before the Fact

People who work in technical fields love to have answers. We work our way through problems and produce an answer that astounds others. Sometimes in the business world, we have an answer before we have the question. We "know" the project should build something using computer X and software Y. The early answer steers our thinking, but it also limits it.

There are occasions when we do know an answer before others are sure of the question. Those occasions, however, are usually in simple or frequently occurring situations. Most situations in the business world are complex and rare. An early answer keeps people from thinking through the entire situation.

This chapter discusses situations in which people suggest designs before first understanding the requirements. They have an answer and are in search of a question. Those situations can wreak havoc on projects and with people. Patience, discipline, and maturity are required.

THE PROBLEM SOLVERS

I worked four years in a computer processing lab during the early 1990s. We had a local area network with over 200 Unix workstations, three dozen mini-computers, and four supercomputers. I was in the support area and managed the people who maintained the computing resources.

Computer hardware advanced at an alarming rate during this time (it still does). Every six months there was a new wave of hardware available. Our users wanted to keep up with the new hardware, so, twice a year, after the

It Sounded Good When We Started. By Dwayne Phillips and Roy O'Bryan
ISBN 0-471-48586-1 © 2004 by the Institute of Electrical and Electronics Engineers.

computer hardware salesmen visited the users, they drew up their list of needs. The users "required" 20 or 30 new computers. Note that the users did not want new computers, they required them.

Another technology that changed rapidly was the data flow through computer networks. The basic Ethernet moved data at one rate. A new technology came along that moved data at a higher rate, and a year later, yet another technology came along that moved data even faster. About once a year, the users came in with a new data rate requirement.

The message the users gave us regularly was, "Technology X exists, we require it."

We always asked back, "What is the requirement? What has changed in the work that makes you need added capability? What is your new function?"

There were no new requirements. The work was the same, the processing load was the same, the functions were the same, but the user's desires changed with each visit of a salesperson. We were chasing the technology imperative. If a technology existed, our users required it. We bought it, installed it, maintained it, and we had fun doing it. Like most technical people, we loved to have the newest tools and technology.

Somehow, our users convinced the lab managers to buy the new computers they wanted. We had the budget available, and the managers did not see the need to spend time thinking before spending the money. Therefore, we bought new computers every six months and new network hardware every year. We could process and move data faster than anyone.

In spite of all the new, more powerful equipment, the lab did not process more data. We were busy doing other things. First, we spent time acquiring, installing, and becoming familiar with the new equipment. Next, since people expected new equipment twice a year, they needed to be ready with the specifications for the next purchase. Therefore, they spent time reading catalogs and meeting with computer salespeople. Finally, the users quickly tired of the new equipment. They anxiously awaited the next round of new equipment. This meant they discussed what was coming and how they would use it to process more data.

All these activities left little time for processing data. The users changed their jobs from processing data to buying new equipment so they could process data one day in the future.

Our users did not understand the difference between requirements and design. They did not think the statement, "Buy me a 200 MIP workstation" was a design. They thought it was a requirement. They did not see it as an answer; they thought it was a question.

WARNING SIGNS OF TROUBLE

We had big problems in the processing lab. The managers were spending money, and the users did not produce anything to justify these expenditures.

The combination of money spent, effort spent, and no results frustrated everyone. Working in that lab consumed four of the worst years of my professional life. This was because we were working on answers before we knew the questions. In retrospect, there were signs that should have warned me of this backward approach. The following two sections discuss different ways that people express an answer before they have a question.

The Block Diagram

A block diagram is a simple sketch of a design. It shows how various elements connect together to form a system. This is a good way to explain a complex system on one piece of paper. We need to remember that a block diagram is an expression of an answer, not a question. It is a design, not a requirement. A mistake in systems analysis and design is treating a block diagram as a requirement instead of a design. If someone thinks the block diagram is a requirement, the ensuing project and its aftermath will have problems.

A warning sign of the incorrect use of a block diagram is when someone presents a block diagram as the first artifact on a project. They are presenting the answer before anything else.

This happened often in the lab. The users would come in with a block diagram of how the network would look when new computers were installed. They told us that they required the hardware to look like the block diagram. Too often, we grabbed their block diagram, sped out of the room, and proceeded to build to "their requirements."

These were difficult and costly projects because a block diagram does not contain many details. It is easy to draw a line on paper that connects two squares labeled "processing system 1" and "processing system 2." It is often difficult to implement these drawings as each processing system has specific hardware and software interfaces. We usually had to modify interfaces so they would connect with incompatible interfaces on other systems. The effort required to do this was more expensive than the new equipment the users bought.

This brought much frustration to the users. They felt that we were dragging our feet and raising the cost of projects without reason. This ill will only solidified their belief that they needed to give us designs before requirements. They believed that the cost of projects would be prohibitive if they ever let us analyze a situation and document the requirements before finding a design.

We Will Use Technology X on the Project

We in the technical fields often enjoy the technology. We may have a favorite programming language, database tool, or brand of computer. Technologies are solutions, and the mistake is thinking of them as problems. A warning sign of the mistaken view is when someone mentions technology on the first day of a project. They confidently proclaim, "We will use object-oriented programming, agile methods, Java, XML, parallel processors, and wireless."

These technologies may be good for the project, but how can anyone know that on the first day? No one has had time to think about the problem.

Selecting a technology before understanding the requirements overconstrains a product. In theory, a new problem has an infinite number of possible solutions. The more possible solutions available, the better the chance of finding and using an excellent one. Selecting a technology early eliminates many possible solutions.

There can be legitimate constraints on projects. If an organization uses XYZ computers and has a maintenance contract with the XYZ company, a constraint is that all new projects use XYZ computers. Software can also be a constraint. If an organization stores all its data in an ABC database, it is wise to constrain future projects to use the ABC database.

We were not dealing with constraints in our processing lab. The users often "required" that we change everything. In one case, we switched from an OS/2 system to a DEC/Unix system to a Sun system in only two years. Each change required new hardware, operating systems, and porting application software.

I have experienced problems when people specified a technology too early in a project. I worked on a project in the mid-1980s in which we built a large communications system controlled by a central computer. The operators controlled the system via text menus on black and white terminals (this was back in the days before the GUI). Standard terminals existed from previous projects, and our organization had already written a software menu system for those terminals. Someone specified that we would use those standard terminals and existing software on the project. That reuse made sense on day one.

Two years later, that reuse did not make any sense. Analysis of the system led the team to select a computer that had a good real-time operating system. The best way to work with the operating system was to write programs in the C language. The existing terminals used the FORTRAN language for the menu system. The programmers spent most of their efforts interfacing the control code written in C with the menu code written in FORTRAN. A careful analysis would have shown this problem before programming began. No one did this analysis because someone had specified the FORTRAN code on the first day of the project.

HOW TO CREATE A GOOD SITUATION

The desire to produce an answer quickly is a strong one. We rewarded people with quick answers when we were children, and we still equate being the first with being the best. As discussed earlier, quick answers are not often good ones, especially when they precede the question.

We have seen techniques that help with the problem of answers coming before questions. The following sections describe some of these techniques. I wish I had this collection and the ability to employ them when I worked in the processing lab.

This is Business

We do things at work for an employer. Doing things for an employer carries the constraints of business. These constraints of business suggest that we build products for business reasons. At home, I write books and computer programs. Those things are hobbies, and I do them because I enjoy doing them. I enjoy the practices I do at home, but those practices do not all fit in the constraints of business, so I cannot use them all at work.

In a business situation, there are two main reasons to implement solutions. These are (1) return on investment and (2) meeting requirements. If spending $100,000 on new computers allows a business to process more data and earn $150,000, that brings a return on investment of plus $50,000. That is good for the business, and that is a good reason to buy those new computers.

If a business has a new requirement to process more data, and buying $100,000 worth of new computers is a necessary step in processing that data, we buy those computers. They enable the business to meet its requirements.

In the processing lab, we did many things that did not make business sense. If our users said, "I need a 200 MIPS workstation," we bought it for them, installed it, and maintained it. We gave little thought to a return on investment or meeting a new requirement. We operated the business of the lab as if it were a hobby at home. If something looked liked fun and seeemed interesting, we did it. The cost of all this fun caught up with the processing lab. Senior managers removed many of the lab's managers, brought in new people, and merged the lab with other organizations.

Managing a business by the book may chase away good technical people. Therefore, it is good to manage a business so that there is some room for technical play. We suggest scheduling a part of each person's week for technical enrichment. This includes self-study, experimentation using the facilities of the business, and training.

Allowing for technical play is not business suicide. It helps technical people to be happier at work. It also helps to instill loyalty in the person to the business. This results in lower turnover, and that, too, is good for business.

First Things First

Now that we have established that we do things at work for an employer, let us move to another fundamental area. The project manager should challenge the project team to find solutions to the employer's problems.

First, take charge of the problems. Use skilled people to study the situation and form problem statements. This is not easy, as it is difficult to find people who can do this. Second, put the problems in front of the project team. Communicate what is happening, where the employer wants to go, and what the project manager sees as roadblocks. Distribute the problem statements so the maximum number of smart people can see and think about them.

We are stating the obvious in this section. Sometimes we need to do this, as we can forget the obvious. Establishing the problem and allowing people to think of solutions is a fundamental. This method is not always the best way to do things. Some people have made discoveries accidentally, and others have made breakthroughs during moments of crisis. Still, this is a business, and using a fundamental approach usually provides a good return on investment.

Patience with Projects

Project managers should exercise patience with projects. Start a project with one or two analysts to study the situation and formulate a problem statement. We have seen that it is a good idea to keep this work quiet.

Bring in problem solvers only when you have completed the problem statement. If the problem solvers arrive too soon, they jump on things. They start suggesting solutions before the problem statement is ready. In that case, the project manager is back where he started. He has a group of people anxious to implement their solutions. Those solutions may be good ones, but they may not be appropriate for the current problem.

It is not easy to exercise this type of patience with a project. There are so many people telling the project manager to stop wasting time with questions and let them run with their answers. The project manager becomes the bad guy, the person who is standing in the way of progress. The project manager often gives in for no other reason than fatigue. It seems that he is the only one bringing what he thinks is right to a project. The principle is no longer worth the headaches, and the project manager lets people do as they wish.

Patience from the project manager does help create good projects. We are trying to solve problems, and there are techniques that work well most of the time. Knowing the question before searching for the answer is one of those techniques. It does not work best in every situation, but it does work well in most situations.

Some organizations do allow other approaches for some projects. Skipping steps, taking risks, trying "wild" ideas are things that have their place in a balanced organization. It is good to use them when appropriate and when senior managers understand the probable costs and low probability of success.

We did one project in the processing lab that way. The senior managers took a risk by letting the research and development people manage a development project. The head of R&D "knew" the answer before the project started. The senior managers believed him and wrote a big $6M check. We used some techniques that were not the usual for our organization, and it worked in this one high-profile instance. Unfortunately, this success was not the norm. We had many large failures using this same approach.

With the help of some new managers, I eventually succeeded at establishing a patient process for projects in the lab. We analyzed requirements, found solutions to the real problems, planned projects, and implemented them. It was not spectacular, but it worked. These processes were good for the lab, as soon thereafter our budget was cut in half. We were able to survive with less money because we were now being patient in our projects.

Switch Between Requirements and Design on Purpose

A project manager should keep an open mind about the order of design and requirements. Sometimes, designs precede requirements. Requirements can sit quietly in the background where we do not notice them. A new answer popping in without a question can be a flashlight that illuminates our requirement.

Allowing people to talk about solutions while discussing problems can help set the stage for good projects. There are several reasons for this. First, is the iterative nature of learning—a few questions, a few answers, a few more questions, and so on. The key is to move back and forth among questions and answers on purpose. The project manager should set up decision points and criteria and use them in a disciplined manner. Try not to bounce back and forth by accident, on a whim, or out of frustration.

Another reason to alternate among questions and answers is that it is an admission that we do not have all the right answers and approaches. Running projects is a complex endeavor. There are many wrong ways to conduct a project, and there are many right ways to do so. Maybe knowing all about the question first is not the right way to do this project.

Finally, switching back and forth between requirements and design shows that a disciplined approach to thinking can work. Changing views from requirements to design and back means we are trying new things, but we are doing this in a disciplined manner. We are thinking about the content of our discussion and our transitions.

It is also good to be open and honest about the transitions. The project manager should stand up and state, "Now let's stop requirements analysis for a while and look at design. I do not think we are through with the requirements yet, but we seem to be stuck. Some solution ideas may help us get unstuck. Then we can go back to the requirements. We won't throw away any design ideas we discover, but we won't make any binding decisions."

I have seen this approach work many times. Once, we were trying to find a tool for an employment recruiter to use while visiting college campuses. The obvious answer we all had was to buy a laptop computer. This was in the late 1980s when laptop computers were not as common as they are in the early

2000s. The laptop seemed to solve all our unstated problems and, besides, we really wanted to buy a few because they looked like so much fun.

We began by discussing the recruiter's requirements. It was futile to keep people from talking about the laptop computer, so I stopped trying. I announced that we would bounce back and forth among requirements and designs. We did this and it helped us learn about the recruiter's needs.

A typical exchange began with an engineer stating, "A laptop computer has a word processor on it." The recruiter would reply, "That sounds good. I have to type reports about my interviews. I do this at night in the hotel room while doing my expense calculations."

A second engineer would add, "Expense calculations? I just read that the laptops can run the popular spreadsheet applications. We need to research those to find a good one for you." The recruiter would reply, "Oh that would be nice if I could do all these chores with the same machine. Then maybe I could mail in everything the next morning."

Another engineer would light up, "You send in your information during your trip instead of at the end of it? We could buy a modem to go with the laptop so you could send them in electronically."

These conversations about solutions helped the recruiter remember requirements; the new requirements helped the engineers think of solutions, and the cycle repeated itself many times.

The Answers Shelf

There are times when great answers walk in the door in the absence of a question. This usually means that resources to implement those answers are also absent. The standard advice from this chapter would be to discard the answer until someone has stated the question. Here is where we break away from the standard advice. The project manager should act in a constructive manner in such situations.

We advise saving the answers. They are the product of inspiration and enthusiasm and they are probably good. I try to have a convenient place, I call it an "answers shelf," where I hold good ideas. This can be a special disk directory on the network, a group of folders in a file cabinet, or a pile of 3" × 5" cards.

There are several reasons for saving answers. First, this saves good ideas, and we can always use good ideas. Maybe we cannot use this good idea on this day, but there may come a day when we can use it.

The second reason for putting ideas on the answers shelf is that this tells people you value them and their ideas. It is a good thing for an organization to try to keep people with good ideas. Those people are more likely to stay if they feel the organization appreciates them.

It is easy to squash people's enthusiasm. A person rushes in with a answer; they are willing to work hard and long to implement it and their enthusiasm will make it work. Telling them to back up, think a few months, and first find a good statement of the question lets all the air out of their balloon. The project manager should guide people carefully in these areas.

The act of saving the idea physically helps keep it in my mind. Use a little fanfare when saving an idea. Take a few minutes of everyone's time to explain the idea and where you are storing it. More people will know about it, and this increases the chance that someone will remember it when the right question arrives.

The project manager should visit the answers shelf periodically (monthly, quarterly, etc.) and publicly. A good reason to keep ideas in a box of folders is that it is easy to bring that box to regular staff meetings. Flip through the ideas with the staff and try to find a question that has surfaced that fits any of the ideas. This shows the group that you value their ideas and you are trying to use them.

CONCLUSIONS ABOUT ANSWERS AND QUESTIONS

In an ideal world, questions always precede answers. We do not, however, work in an ideal world and we have yet to work with ideal people. Thought processes often produce answers before we know the questions. This is not surprising, as most technical people are problem solvers. They see solutions first, and they want to implement them.

As a manager or a buyer, work on this issue. If you do not, your problem solvers will run wild with their answers. In the processing lab, the managers let the problem solvers do this for years, and these answers eventually hurt us.

This leads to our general principle for finding questions for answers: Design answers only after understanding the question.

Watch out for warning signs such as,

- Drawing the system block diagram on the first day of a project.
- "We'll use technology X on this project."

Try to create good situations by remembering

- This is business.
- First things first.
- Switch among requirements and design only on purpose.
- Be patient with the project.
- Use the answers shelf.

Creative people can work well with those of us who are a little boring. We, the boring ones, can channel the creative, problem-solving abilities of others in disciplined ways.

To paraphrase Lewis Carroll, "If you do not know the question, any answer will do."

We often had a problem with design before requirements on Delphi. This was because although we had requirements for the system, we did not have requirements for the major components of the system. When the builder had a system problem, they would come forward with a design change for a component.

The builder told us, "Here is the design for component X that will solve our current system problem."

We would ask, "What is the performance requirement for component X that this design will meet?"

The builder would reply, "We do not have one."

Our next question was, "Then how do we know this will answer the question?"

The builder's answer was, "We do not know."

We had this discussion on many occasions and never came to a logical conclusion. Somehow, we applied enough brute force and ignorance to build a good system. Maybe if we used a more refined application of engineering and logic, Delphi would not have been so difficult.

Chapter 9

A Miracle Occurs Here: Schedule Tracking

There are a number of ways to depict the project's schedule, and different levels of management require a different level of schedule detail. There are Gantt charts, PERT, CPM, etc. All of them have one thing in common—a project start date and a projected end date. The Gantt or bar chart can depict early start and early finish and late start and late finish times for each activity or any subset of activities in the project. The Gantt chart can further indicate progress and highlight the critical path, i.e., the longest pole in the tent. Except for a few software management tools, the Gantt chart does not normally indicate interdependencies between events and activities. Networks, on the other hand, are comprised of events and activities together with their interdependencies, and reveal the string of events requiring the most amount of time to complete, hence, the critical path. In theory, the analysis of these networks can preclude the need for crisis management. This is the technical and tool side of schedule tracking.

On the human side, I remember an old cartoon about some scientists. One scientist is pointing to a blackboard while explaining its contents to several colleagues. Equations lead in sequence to a fuzzy area on the board just before the answer. The scientist explains, "A miracle happens here."

The schedules of many projects remind us of that cartoon. People are not completing tasks and building products on time. The facts indicate that the project is in trouble, and the only way the project can deliver a good product on time is for a miracle to happen.

This need not be the case, as most people we know can track a schedule. It is matter of reading words on a calendar and asking people if they are finished with a task as the schedule indicates. People are either behind schedule,

It Sounded Good When We Started. By Dwayne Phillips and Roy O'Bryan
ISBN 0-471-48586-1 © 2004 by the Institute of Electrical and Electronics Engineers.

on schedule, or ahead of schedule. Nothing could be simpler, but schedule tracking also involves working with people, and that is rarely simple. The following describes many bad things that can happen in schedule tracking or trying to follow a schedule. It also suggests things we can do to make schedule tracking a little easier.

NOT BEING ABLE TO HIT THE BROAD SIDE OF A WALL WITH A PENCIL

We hit a wall during the second year of Delphi. We essentially accomplished only two months worth of work during the entire year. We discuss this year again in Chapter 21. We had several problems that year. One, related in this chapter, was producing parts and tracking schedules. Another, discussed in Chapter 21, was obtaining parts from outsourced vendors.

As a reminder, the project was to build nine systems that involved hardware and software. The technology employed was multichip modules (MCMs), sometimes referred to as "chip and wire." Basically, MCMs are considered the new generation of hybrid circuits that provide at least an order of magnitude higher electrical performance and orders of magnitude reductions in weight and volume. Each system comprised nine (hardware) modules. The nine hardware modules housed 127 circuit card assemblies. The 127 circuit card assemblies (CCAs) accommodated some 8,700 parts or components. Now multiply that by nine (1,143) and you have the totality of the scheduling issue. There was also the chassis, removable dividers, covers, etc., not to mention the drawings that had to be completed in a specific sequence before parts could be ordered and assembly could start—687 of them.

The builder had four major steps in the production and assembly of the circuit card; four major steps in integration, assembly, and testing of each module; and four major steps in integration, assembly, and testing of each system. The project plan showed how many circuit cards were to move through each step each week.

The builder chose to track progress by looking at the production numbers. At the end of each week, we and the builder compared the planned production numbers (number of sections, modules, and units through steps 1, 2, 3, and 4) with the actual ones. For example, at the end of a week the plan was to have 127 CCAs through step 2, 10 CCAs through step 3, and 2 circuit cards through step 4. The actual numbers could have been 45 CCAs through step 2, 5 CCAs through step 3, and 0 CCAs through step 4. That showed the builder was behind schedule.

We did not like this method of tracking progress. We would rather have tracked progress using the schedule in the form of a network of tasks. The builder, however, convinced us that using the production numbers was the way they always managed projects. This company had built many systems that contained thousands of parts for decades. They always used the production numbers to track progress.

We used this method to track progress for six months. The numbers showed were about six weeks behind. For example, after week 26 the production numbers showed that we should have been at week 20.

One day, we looked hard at the schedule and discovered that the builder was six months behind. That had to be wrong. Further investigation showed that it was right. The builder was six months into the plan and six months behind.

We went to the network of tasks and began tracing through it. We checked off the tasks that were done, and we found what we were seeking and hoping not to find. There was a chain of tasks that was six months behind. Because of problems with parts vendors, the builder had not accomplished anything on several threads of tasks.

The production numbers had fooled us. They showed that the builder was only six weeks behind.

There was a fundamental problem with tracking progress with the production numbers. The builder was ahead on some things and behind on others. All items produced in the project were not of equal value. We, however, were treating them as if they were. Those things that the builder was ahead on inflated the numbers and hid the critical items that were behind schedule. Using production numbers to monitor progress was a good step, but it was not sufficient.

I wanted to punch my head through the wall. We had a schedule; a good, complete schedule for this project. We, however, had stopped tracking to it.

Further study of the plan revealed some mistakes in how we had linked tasks. The mistakes in the plan meant we were another six months behind. This made us a total of a year behind schedule! At this point, we lost all confidence in everything we were doing. We stopped most of the work and went back to the drawing board.

We had accomplished things during the six months. The hardware team had built hundreds of circuit cards, dozens of modules, and a few units. Nevertheless, a complete system was not in sight.

Remember that, in theory, network analysis should reveal interdependencies and problem areas that are neither obvious nor well defined by other planning methods. The key words are in theory, analysis, and should reveal. We were dazzled by the numbers but failed to properly assess progress in terms of the critical path for each system and once again found ourselves in the crisis management mode.

WARNING SIGNS OF SCHEDULE AVOIDANCE

The episode in Delphi described above was a disaster. The builder lost a year of schedule and we failed to realize it as it was happening. That story, however, is not the only one we could tell. In hindsight, each schedule disaster we experienced had signs along the way hinting at coming trouble. The following sections discuss some of these.

Schedule? What Schedule?

One of the bad things that can happen on a project is that people are not us-ing the schedule. They are either not seeing the schedule or not seeking the schedule.

Some projects suffer from a lack of visibility. The project manager does not post the project schedule and other important items in the project room (see Chapter 2). The schedule is usually on a disk drive somewhere, but a person would need to know where it is and also how to use the project management software. Many people do not have enough interest in the schedule to seek it.

It is fairly easy to learn if people are using the schedule or ignoring it. We ask people basic questions during routine visits. The conversation is, "How does the progress on your task relate to the project schedule? Are you ahead, behind, on track?" The person may hem and haw and shuffle their feet, or say something without meaning like, "Oh, I guess I'm doin' OK." Further probing sounds like, "Well, are you three days ahead of the schedule or two days be-hind the schedule?" If the person still seems uninterested in the conversation, we suggest, "Let's go look at the schedule. Where is it?" The moment of truth is fast approaching, and we eventually hear the warning sign, "I've never seen the schedule."

In some ways, people working on a project do not need to know the sched-ule. They need to know what they are building and how to build it and they need to be able to do their work within the time limitations they are given. It is not essential that they know what everyone else is doing and when they are doing it.

At the same time, it is important that everyone sees the schedule. This gives people an idea of how they fit into the project. When people have not seen the schedule, we know they are not using it. If they are not using the schedule, what are they using? If the project is not using the schedule, it is probably be-hind schedule.

This is what happened to us in the Delphi story above. We learned after the fact that the builder's engineers never looked at the schedule. It was posted on the wall, but none of them were interested in it. The project manager was con-vinced that using the production numbers would tell him where were they were. The builder was wrong, and we were wrong for letting them ignore the schedule.

A Vote of No Confidence

A schedule is a tool for the project manager and his team. It provides a bench-mark to let them know where they should be, what they should be doing, and if they need to make changes in their activities. If a person loses confidence in a tool, they stop using it.

The buyer can learn of this by using a conversation similar to the one given above. In this case, however, the continued prodding about schedule leads to the dreaded punch line, "The schedule is never right."

I ran into this situation early in Delphi. I visited the builder by myself and spent a day tracing through the schedule (see Chapter 6 for more details). During the day, people walked by and I asked them questions about the schedule. I pointed to their part of the schedule and at the task they should have been working on and asked about the status. Most of the engineers moved my pointer from today's task to one that should have occurred weeks in the past or should occur weeks in the future.

I asked why they were working on tasks that were so far away from today. Most gave me the "schedule is never right" reply. They were doing what they felt was most important. It probably did not fit in the schedule, but that did not matter because "the schedule was never right."

This is what happens when people lose confidence in the schedule. They stop using it and instead spend their day doing what they think is most important on that day. This "most important" item often changes from day to day or even in the middle of a day. Good people spend time wandering aimlessly from task to task. When someone awakens from this stupor, they learn that the project is far behind schedule.

No One's Job

The previous two problems related to a schedule that was neither visible nor dependable. Few people will use a tool with those properties. The underlying problem is that no one has the full-time job of maintaining the schedule.

Projects, especially large projects, have intricate schedules. There is much work involved in gathering information and updating those schedules. In most projects, the project manager saddles himself with schedule maintenance. The warning sign of trouble is when the project manager says, "Maintaining the schedule is so important that I will do it myself." That sounds good, but the execution is often weak.

A project manager has many things do to in a day. Knowing where people are in the schedule is one of them. The project manager should talk to everyone every day to learn their status (see later). The project manager should not spend time updating the schedule with that information. That task is like bookkeeping. It is not the most difficult task in the world, but it does take attention to detail and time.

When the project manager tries to maintain the schedule, he usually fails. When faced with limited time and seemingly limitless duties, the project manager must decide what is done and what is left undone. The bookkeeping tasks of schedule maintenance often go undone. If we were forced to choose between facilitating two groups of engineers in solving a key technical problem and updating the schedule, we would choose the technical problem. So do most project managers.

One of Delphi's project managers fell into this schedule maintenance trap. Fred (see Chapter 11) decided to maintain the schedule. When he entered the information into the schedule software, he saw the information at the level of detail he wanted. That desire to know the situation was admirable. There were, however, other ways for him to know that information that did not consume his time and prevent him from doing more important tasks. Fred tried—oh, how he tried—to do everything, but he couldn't. No one could, so Fred suffered personally, and the project fell behind.

"No One Talks to Me Anymore"

Some people on projects feel that schedules are important. Note, we did not write that everyone feels schedules are important. Someone is paying the bills for the project and eventually paying the salaries of the people working on the project. These people care that they receive a product on a date that meets their desires.

Many projects suffer because people working on projects do not care about schedules. At times in Delphi, we had a schedule, it was mostly correct, and someone owned the task of maintaining it. This person, however, often told us that she was having trouble. Her warning sign to us was when she said, "No one ever tells me where they are. I have to drag it out of them."

I heard these words while spending a day studying the schedule at the builder's facility (see discussion above). I asked the schedule maintainer about some items that did not make sense to me. She told me about her troubles in gathering status. The engineers were supposed to come to her every Friday morning and tell her what they had accomplished. She would then enter the information in the schedule and send out a new copy to the project manager. The engineers, however, were not reporting their status to her.

When people do not report status as they should, this indicates that they put a low priority on the schedule. Their technical work is more important than this "schedule stuff." This is a common situation, as people do technical work because that is what they like to do. They spent years of their lives training for it and they did not spend years of their lives training how to report progress to a bookkeeper. That should be someone else's job, shouldn't it?

This would be nice if it were true. The reality of the work world is that reporting status is important. Without it, project managers cannot manage projects. Projects fail, companies lose business, and engineers lose their jobs.

Engineers want to keep their jobs and will do what they should if they understand why. They do not like to report status because they do not make the connection between status and successful projects. The project manager has the job of helping them make this connection.

Someone is Mistaken

As the story at the start of this chapter related, once we worked through all the above warning signs and related problems, we found mistakes in the schedule. These were not mistakes in judgment or in estimates. They were mistakes in linking tasks in the schedule.

Schedules have links between tasks. A task has inputs—the engineer needs a document, materials, or assistance from others before starting a task. Other tasks must come first to produce those inputs. Creating a schedule requires looking at each task and ensuring that all the prerequisites are in place. Linkage mistakes occur often in large and complex projects, as the precedences and linkages are not always obvious.

A builder usually finds these mistakes when starting a task somewhere in the middle of the project. They are ready to do something, but missing one key ingredient. This case is a false positive. The schedule mistakes show a situation that is better than reality. Here, the builder stops working, thinks a while, and starts a series of tasks to create the needed item. While creating that item, people stop working. They often drift to other projects, never to return.

Another case is a false negative. The schedule mistakes lead the builder to believe they are in a worse state than they really are. They have the needed ingredients, but do not realize it. A little thought will show the builder that they are in good shape and can continue as planned. The trouble with such situations is that people usually do not apply a little thought. Instead, they charge into action. Someone hurries off and produces something that they already have in hand.

A linkage mistake cost Delphi six months. We all thought we were in pretty good shape until one morning an engineer discovered that products he needed to do his job were not available. Several people studied the schedule and found the missing link. The thing that broke our hearts is that the resources to do these tasks were available when we needed them. The people were sitting idly by because they did not know they were supposed to be doing something.

A mistake in a schedule is difficult to find. We analyzed Delphi's schedule over and over again, but our analysis did not find the mistakes it contained. The one thing we learned was that if a schedule has one mistake, it probably has several others. We found mistakes in Delphi's schedule early in the project. Our mistake was that once we corrected these, we stopped looking for others.

The Computer is Down

Large projects have large and complicated schedules. We have seen schedules with over ten thousand tasks, and it is easy to become lost in such a morass. One answer we have today is using a good project management or schedule tool. Microsoft's Project and Scitor's Project Scheduler are two good tools. Like all tools, however, we can have problems with our tools and these problems point to other problems.

When visiting a builder, we often ask to see the latest printout of the schedule. An answer that sends chills down our spines is, "We're having trouble with the project management software."

This is a warning sign of problems for the project. The project manager is depending on the software to show him how the project is doing. If the builder is having trouble with the software, they do not know the state of the project. The tool may be too complicated for the builder or it may be too complicated for this project.

This happened on a project similar to Delphi. We visited the builder in the first month of the project. They could not show us their schedule because they were having trouble with their schedule software. They were lost, but we did not recognize the warning sign. One problem led to another and, two years later, we had to throw out half the requirements from the product. The builder had been lost from the first month and had wasted their resources. They had consumed all the project's resources, but had no product in hand. We added money and time to the project so we could pass along something to our customer.

Fear of the Calendar

A schedule is a funny looking calendar with tasks written on it. The schedule has no expectations, desires, or feelings. It is just a bunch of facts. Who would avoid looking at the facts? A warning sign that we have heard from some builders is, "We do not use the schedule to track progress."

Sometimes there are ways to track progress on a project without using the schedule. This happens in "3 by 3" projects. These have three people working for three months. The project and team are small enough so that each person can hold the project in their head. This is also true when projects use many short iterations. Each iteration is short enough for everyone to know what to do without a formal schedule.

In larger projects, however, the schedule seems to be the tool that leads to the most consistent success. When people avoid the schedule, they are avoiding the facts. A well-maintained schedule shows that a troubled project is in trouble since people often do not like to hear that their project is in trouble. If they have a feeling that things are not going well, they avoid studying the schedule as it may confirm their feelings.

As related earlier, this is what happened to us on Delphi. The builder did not want to look at the schedule. Instead, they tried to track the project via production numbers. Those numbers fooled us into thinking that we were not in bad shape. An all too late analysis of the schedule showed that the project was a disaster.

THINGS THAT HELP US TRACK SCHEDULES

The above shows that many projects have troubles because the project manager does not track their schedules. We have found that if the environment is good, people are more apt to track their schedule. The following sections discuss things we have seen that help create a good environment. They do not guarantee project success, but they increase the odds in our favor.

Talk to Everyone Every Day

Several times in this book, we have recommended that the project manager talk to everyone every day. Here we go again. This time it relates to creating a situation in which people will use the schedule.

There are several sets of questions the project manager should ask. The first set is, "What are you doing? What are you supposed to be doing?" If the answers to these two differ, the next question is, "Why do not these two match?" The answers to these questions tell the project manager if people know the schedule and are is using it.

Another set of questions begins with, "Are you being interrupted?" If the answer is yes, the next questions include, "Who is interrupting you? What is interrupting you?"

One of the major reasons people do not stay with the schedule is that other people stop them and ask them to do other things. The project manager should find out who is interrupting the person. This is not so that the project manager can reprimand the other person, but so he can understand what is causing the other person to seek help and provide that help.

Another question is, "How can I help you stay on task?" People drift off task for a reason. Sometimes it is personal, in that the person does not find the work interesting. Address that by finding them interesting work or changing the work so that it is more interesting. Other times, it is because they are helping other people. It is good to be helpful, but sometimes people need to stick to their own tasks.

If a coworker needs a little help, it is fine to provide it. If a coworker needs much help, it is best to tell the project manager so he can find the needed resources. Telling the project manager is not placing blame. It is giving information to the person who is best able to provide help while still moving the project forward.

A Visible Schedule

People tend to use what they see. Therefore, we suggest placing the schedule in the project room (see Chapter 2). Items in public are visible. People see them, talk about them, and think about them. The schedule goes from the realm of someone else's idea to something real that people use every day.

Posting the schedule in the project room also shows its importance. The project manager is telling everyone that this is what will guide the project. If it were not important, we would roll it up and stick it in the corner of someone's office.

In addition to posting it publicly, the project manager should use it publicly. When someone completes a task, the project manager should go to the schedule and place a check mark on that task. The schedule on the wall should show a progression of checked-off tasks. The marks on the wall indicate that the team is inching toward success. A good sign is when people go to the schedule and check off the tasks themselves. Going to the wall is a sign of accomplishment.

In the earlier Delphi story, Fred posted the project's schedule on the wall in the project room. Fred, however, did not use the schedule, and it became part of the wallpaper. Later in the project, Peter (see Chapter 11) kept the project schedule on the wall of the project room and used it. Moreover, he used the whiteboards in the project room to update the schedule frequently with the assistance of the team. That was one of Peter's actions that kept the project moving forward.

Use the Numbers

People have emotions. Yes, even engineers have emotions. They are an important part of working with people on projects. Feelings about a project change daily if not hourly. We do not recommend being heartless, as emotions and dealing effectively with emotions play a major role in projects. Emotions, however, can lead a project manager astray.

There are numbers that indicate the health of a project relative to its schedule (see the next section). We encourage project managers to look at and use numbers. Suppose ten tasks were to be finished by the first of May, and only five were finished by that date. Those cold, cruel, and heartless numbers indicate that the project is in trouble.

This is not a condemnation of the people working on the project. Success requires many factors, and many of the factors are out of the control of the team members. We need to appreciate the people, but find the numbers that predict the time and cost of the finished project.

Countless times during the troubled parts of Delphi, a builder's senior manager told us that the spirits were high on his team, the people were working hard, and that things would change for the better real soon. We wanted to believe him, but he could never show us any numbers that indicated a turnaround was looming. We explained our desire to believe and the role that hard numbers would play in our actions. He, however, could not find the numbers. The reason was that they did not exist. The project never had that wonderful turnaround that he predicted.

An Earned Value Tutorial

One set of numbers that helps predict project completion is the earned value system. This is a number-based management system created in factories in the late 1800s. The earned value system was adopted and promoted by the U.S. Department of Defense (DoD) during and since the 1960s. The earned value system has good application in most projects. For more information, see Reference [1].

One unfortunate aspect of the earned value system is its name. The word "value" has many meanings and tends to confuse more than it helps. In the earned value system, value denotes an amount of work. If we plan to do ten hours of work at $40 an hour, the planned "value" is $400. If we accomplish this ten-hour task, we have "earned" $400 of value for the project.

The earned value system is best explained by an example. Suppose a project has 20 tasks, and every task is 40 hours long. Also suppose that every task is performed by someone paid $50 an hour. This is a $40,000 project, so there is $40,000 of value in it.

The first element of the earned value system is the planned value or budgeted cost for work scheduled (BCWS). Suppose in the first week we are to do three 40-hour tasks. The planned value for that week is 120 hours × $50/hour = $6,000.

The second element of the earned value system is the earned value or budgeted cost of worked performed (BCWP). Suppose in the first week we complete two of the 40-hour tasks. The earned value for that week is 80 hours × $50/hour = $4,000.

The third and final element of the earned value system is the actual cost or actual cost of work performed (ACWP). Suppose in the first week the first 40-hour task only took 35 hours, the second 40-hour task took 55 hours, and we did not complete the third 40-hour task. We paid people for 90 hours of work or 90 × $50/hour = $4,500. The actual cost for the first week is $4,500.

Now let us discuss the third task for the first week. We worked 35 hours on it, but did not finish it. We do not give ourselves credit for this partially completed task. We only give ourselves credit when the task is completed. This is known as one-zero earned value and is the most commonly used form of earned value.

Now let us take stock of this project after one week. We are a little behind schedule because we did not finish the third task. Let us look closer at the numbers. To do this, we calculate two ratios. These are (1) the cost performance index (CPI) = earned value/actual cost and (2) the schedule performance index (SPI) = earned value/planned value.

In this example, the cost performance index (CPI) = earned value/actual cost = $4,000/$4,500 = 0.88. We want the CPI to be 1.0 or greater, so in this example we are overrunning the planned cost of the project. Continuing the example, the schedule performance index (SPI) = earned value/planned value = $4,000/$6,000 = 0.8. We also want the SPI to be 1.0 or greater, so again in this example we are behind schedule. We are spending more than planned and accomplishing less than planned. No one can argue with these numbers.

The earned value system is worthwhile because of its predictive power. The Department of Defense has used earned value on thousands of projects. One important observation was that the CPI does not change much after one-fifth of a project. If a project is 10% over budget a fifth of the way through, it will most likely be over budget by at least 10% at completion.

There are several prerequisites to using the earned value system. The first is to scope the work. This means to define it and put a boundary on it. The next prerequisite to using earned value is a work breakdown structure (WBS). A WBS looks like an organization chart for a project but is used to define and assign work.

Suppose a project is to build a CD player. At the first level, a CD player comprises hardware and software. The first level of the WBS is 1.0 Hardware and 2.0 Software. Under hardware and software we have design, implementation, test, and manufacture. Therefore, the next level of the WBS under 1.0 Hardware is 1.1 Design, 1.2 Implementation, 1.3 Test, and 1.4 Manufacture. The next level of the WBS under 2.0 Software is 2.1 Design, 2.2 Implementation, and 2.3 Test. The breakdown of work will continue in detail to individual tasks or detailed work packages. In the above example, we had 20 tasks or detailed work packages. They were 40 hours each at $50/hour. This all fell out of the WBS. Now we can monitor the tasks and report on them with numbers.

The final prerequisite for using the earned value system is honesty. If someone works 50 hours to do a 40-hour task and we only pay the person for 40 hours of work, we have lied about the difficulty of the task. The person worked at 80% of what we estimated. This means trouble is coming, and we need to do something. If we only pay for 40 hours of work, we are hiding the trouble. We are assuming that everything else will be fine.

The earned value system is valuable, but not sufficient for tracking a project's schedule. We must also track the critical path of the project (see later). The earned value system, however, will provide us with the valuable SPI and CPI numbers. If SPI and CPI show trouble, it is time to look hard at everything. We cannot afford to let enthusiasm erase the numbers.

Before leaving the subject of earned value, look again at the prerequisites. We have a complete plan, are monitoring the tasks for their cost and schedule, are watching and managing closely, and everyone is being honest about their hours and challenges. If we have all this, we will be in good shape regardless of what else we might be doing.

The earned value system is one of those techniques in which using the technique is not always the point. The point is doing everything so the system is valid. So use the earned value system. All the preparation will help put the project in good shape.

The Critical Path

An important part of tracking a schedule is to watch the critical path. This is a string of tasks through the schedule that does not have any slack. If a task on the critical path slips one day, the end date of the project slips one day. This is why it is called "critical."

The project manager should combine watching the critical path with using the earned value system. The earned value system gives values to tasks that we can interpret. The critical path looks at only the most important tasks. Neither technique is sufficient by itself. Together, however, they provide the project manager with information to manage a project.

Consider two examples in which one factor is good while the other is bad. First is the situation where the earned value numbers appear good and we are behind on the critical path. This means we are working well on all tasks not on the critical path. The project, however, is falling behind schedule.

The opposite situation is where we are on or ahead of the critical path, but we have poor earned value numbers. This means we are putting extra people on the critical path tasks and ignoring many other tasks.

Both of these examples are bad for the project. The project will fall behind schedule and overrun costs. If either factor is poor, the project manager should stop and examine the schedule to find the reasons. Try to ignore feelings of optimism and enthusiasm and find the reason why the numbers are bad.

SOME CONCLUSIONS ABOUT TRACKING THE SCHEDULE

We work with engineering and IT projects, not the weather. Things that seem like miracles do not pop up with a change in the wind. To deliver a product on a certain date means that people complete prior tasks on certain dates. All these tasks and products link together in a schedule.

If we are not following the schedule day by day and person by person, we do not know where we are in the project. We do not know if we will deliver a product on a certain day and we do not know if we will keep our commitments.

This brings us to the principle of tracking schedules in projects: Track the schedule and always compare it to reality.

Watch our for:

- "I've never seen the schedule."
- "The schedule is never right."

- "I'll maintain the schedule myself."
- "No one ever tells me where they are."
- Mistakes in the schedule.
- "We're having trouble with the project management software."
- "We do not use the schedule to track progress"

Try to create a good situation for schedule tracking by:

- Talking to everyone every day.
- Putting the schedule on the wall in the project room.
- Using the numbers.
- Using earned value.
- Watching the critical path.

We had an odd schedule-tracking situation on the Gamma project discussed in Chapter 5. The project manager needed to schedule a major design review at a builder's facility in Florida. The project manager looked at "a" calendar and selected a couple days during a particular week. The problem is that he did not look at "the" calendar and did not track the design review on "the" schedule. The week he selected was also the week that all the counties in Northern Virginia (population over one million) let out school for spring break. Thousands of people had already made their reservations to go to Disneyworld and other attractions in Florida. The Gamma project was trying to send over 20 people to the same place on short notice. These people scrambled to find any flights that would take them anywhere within driving distance of the builder's facility. These were educated, experienced, and accomplished people and all they had to do was read a calendar. Such are the perils of tracking a schedule.

REFERENCE

1. *Earned Value Project Management,* Quentin W. Fleming and Joel M. Hoppelman, Project Management Institute, 1996.

Chapter 10

Getting Mugged by the Facts: Risk Mitigation Strategies

Nothing hurts a good theory as much as being mugged by the facts. Projects start with theories; plans one class of theories. We think tasks will start and stop on time and projects will move forward. The facts come along, and we hope they will agree with the theory.

When the facts mug the theory, we are often surprised. The mugging often has bad consequences for our projects because we did not identify this possibility, watch for its approach, and plan for its occurrence.

THE STORY OF DON THE BUYER

Let us relate a story of a young man named Don who was the project manager for a buyer. He was managing a contract with a builder to provide a product for his user. Don met with the builder once a month to learn the status of the project. At one of these monthly meetings, the builder told Don about a problem they were having. Don's user was not represented at the monthly meeting. Don was the only person in the buying organization to know about the problem.

The problem was not a big one, and the builder was confident that they could work through it before the next monthly meeting. Don went along with the builder's assessment. He was not concerned because the builder often reported problems that they cleared up in a few days.

Don chose not to tell anyone in his organization. Don did not like to bring problems back with him from the builder. The few times he did that, he had to explain the problems in detail at meetings. Everyone wanted to know everything about the problem. They wanted to know how much it would cost

It Sounded Good When We Started. By Dwayne Phillips and Roy O'Bryan
ISBN 0-471-48586-1 © 2004 by the Institute of Electrical and Electronics Engineers.

and how much time it would take to fix. Don and no one else knew accurate answers to any of those questions. The people did not seem to understand that problems were a natural part of projects. They made such a big deal out of these things.

Don hated those probing questions. He felt so small and defenseless while being questioned. The other people in his organization who worked with builders did not have any problems to report. Don hated being the only one with problems.

At the next month's review meeting, the builder reported that the problem was still present. They had unsuccessfully tried a few things to correct it. Don realized that the problem was growing. It had not affected the critical path of the project yet, but if they could not correct it in two weeks it would be on the critical path. That would mean that each day spent on the problem would delay the end of the project a day.

Once again, Don was the only person in the buyer's organization at the meeting. What was he to do now? The little problem had grown to a medium-size problem. If he told people about it, they would have him go to twice as many meetings and answer twice as many questions as normal. Don could feel the tension in his body.

The problem was growing, but the builder was paying more attention to it. They were bringing in extra people to work on it. With this help, Don hoped, they would surely solve it in a week or so. Don decided not to tell anyone about the problem. He would wait one more month.

The next monthly meeting began with a discussion of the problem. The builder still did not have a solution. The problem was now a major one as it was on the critical path and delaying the completion of the project. Don had no choice; he had to tell people in his organization. The meetings, questions, grilling, and blaming were coming. Don thought about resigning instead of facing these.

We know of many people who have gone through this situation. They had a problem on a project. Fear, among other things, kept them from telling people about the problem. They feared the questions, they feared looking bad, they feared admitting problems. If the problem would just go away, they would not have to tell anyone and they would avoid the situation they feared. They often chose to hide the problem. In most cases, the problem usually did not go away. Eventually, the problem was too large to hide any longer.

In this story and in many others, Don was mugged by the facts. He thought things would be fine, and the builder thought they could solve the problem soon. No one faced the problem, and the problem clobbered them.

WARNING: FACTS APPROACHING

Don had trouble when the facts collided with his theories and wishes. The rest of us failed to help Don with his predicament. There were things we could have noticed to indicate coming trouble. We saw these things, but did not realize what they meant. The following sections discuss signs of coming trouble.

"That Can't Be Right"

We love our theories. When time shows one of out theories to be true, we are elated. We feel so smart and gratified. There are times when we desire this gratification so much that we ignore and deny facts for a while. Denying facts is a big problem on projects.

A warning sign of this denial is when people say, "That can't be right. Let's go on anyway." The speaker has dismissed things quickly. Dismissing facts is a problem, but not as bad as the conclusion. Deciding to go on invites disaster.

As usual, there are two sides to any story. It is not wise to quickly accept news that dooms a project. Stopping and changing the direction of a project is expensive. A good project manager will not do that because of one piece of data. The person bringing the data could have been mistaken so it is wise to check on it more than once.

At the same time, it is not wise to dismiss news quickly. News that changes the complexion of a project is serious. Project managers should investigate it with an open mind. The project manager can have some people on the project go forward, but he should also have others stop their work and investigate.

Ignoring facts is foolish and can doom a project. The obvious way this hurts is that people are continuing on a project as if things were going well. They build parts of a product that depend on other parts that other people are building. The trouble is that these other parts will not be present when needed. They are failing, we know they are failing, but we are ignoring those facts. A project manager can ignore facts for a time, but they will catch up and mug him later.

Another way in which ignoring facts hurts a project is that the project manager is throwing away resources. Facts are resources. They are available to use for the good of the project.

Don the buyer denied facts. He had an unfounded hope that everything would be fine. That is what the theory said. The facts indicating otherwise were presented to him, but he ignored them and went on as if they did not exist. They caught up with him and the project in a couple of months.

"That's Just His Personality"

There are people in most organizations who see the downside of every situation. When nine people think the project is going well, one person will say that things are bad. A project manager who wants to believe theories will often ignore the bearer of bad news at the peril of the project.

This warning sign usually sounds like, "Don't worry about that. Joe reported it, and he always brings bad news. That's just his personality."

It is not easy to work with people like Joe. There are days when the project manager wants to hear good news and see people who have a positive outlook. The pessimist walks by and the project manager ignores him. He does not want to talk with someone with a frown on his face and predictions of doom. Sometimes the pessimist is right. They may see something in the project that others are missing. It is worth the effort to listen and investigate what they report.

Ignoring the bearer of bad new brings several problems. The first problem is the immediate effect. The project has troubles and the project manager is denying them. He should take action, move resources, and address the trouble. Instead, he is moving on obliviously.

The second problem is that the project manager is dismissing people. They are telling him important information and he is ignoring them. Why should they expend their energy in the future to bring him news he needs? His actions are saying that he disregards them. Their morale drops, and low morale is contagious.

Don ignored news because of its source. The builder had brought him bad news before and much of that was not so bad. The builder worked around it without major affect on the project. He thought that they might be crying wolf once again. This time Don was wrong and he and the project suffered.

"Don't Bring Me Problems Without Solutions"

Projects have problems, and the project manager is responsible for the project. Sometimes, project managers will add these two statements together and surmise that the project manager owns all the problems. That is an unhealthy attitude. No one person can own all the problems in a project, as the weight would crush them.

A warning sign of this unhealthy attitude is when a project manager proclaims in desperation, "Don't bring me problems without solutions."

The project manager cannot stand the weight of yet another problem. He wants a solution so the problem will disappear.

We who work in technical fields are problem solvers. That may not be written in our job description, but that is what we do. Some people feel that when we have a problem, we should find a solution. If we discover a problem without a solution, we have only done half of our job.

This view has some merit, as we want people to work through as much as they can. Sometimes, however, a person has a problem and does not have a solution. They are tired and encountering a problem depletes their energy.

They cannot find a solution today, so they tell the project manager what they know—the problem.

We believe that this idea of no problems without solutions is wrong. Suppose someone has a heart attack in the office. I do not know what to do; I have no solutions. Should I tell someone or keep quiet until I have a solution? Of course I should tell people. Someone in the office may know exactly what to do, and if I keep quiet, the person with the heart attack will die.

Don the buyer lived with this idea of problems and solutions. He had a problem and did not have a solution, so he kept quiet. Someone else in his organization may have had a solution. This does not mean that they were smarter or superior to Don, but maybe that problem hit them last month and they learned a solution. Don felt that no one could help him. He kept quiet hoping that someone would find a solution and report the two at the same time. That wish did not come true.

ON RISK MANAGEMENT

At this time, let us look at the subject of risk management. We have found that if we understand risk management and use it effectively, we can avoid the sad story of Don the buyer.

A discussion of risk management begins with a definition. A risk is a potential problem. If support for our system depends on a part built by an outside vendor, that is a potential problem. The outside vendor may not deliver the part on time or may not deliver the part with the quality we need. The outside vendor is a risk to our project. We can manage this and other potential problems. The classic steps in risk management are (1) identify, (2) analyze, (3) plan, (4) monitor, and (5) act.

The first step is identifying potential problems. This begins by asking the question, "What could possibly go wrong?" There is a probability (between 0.0 and 1.0) that a potential problem will become a real problem. We state the potential problem and the probability that it will occur. Next, we state how much time, money, and other resources the problem would cost the project. The next step is to analyze the risks identified. After writing the risks, we classify them by their type. Usual classifications include outside vendors, personnel, technical, political, and cost.

The next step of analysis is to rank the risks. One way to rank the risks is by their probability of occurrence. Another is to rank them by their cost to the project if they occur. A good method is to multiply the probability of occurrence by the cost in dollars to the project. This gives a dollar value to the risk.

The next step in risk management is to plan to deal with a risk should it occur. We should plan both preventive and reactive measures. First, what can we do to prevent the potential problem from occurring? This usually means gathering and employing some extra resources. This can be expensive, but is often worthwhile. We use judgment in this step, as spending a million dollars to prevent a thousand-dollar problem is foolish. Second, how will we react if the problem occurs? We should know who we will call to lend expertise to work the problem and what they will need as resources. The problem has not yet occurred, but we should make calls ahead of time to ensure that the resources will be available.

A key element in planning for reactive measures is to set triggers. At some point in time, the risk will almost be a problem. We need to know when that will happen. We do not want to call in resources too soon, but we do not want to wait too long like Don the buyer in our story. The trigger is the right point in time. If task A is not done by date B, we will do C. If it is still not done three days later, we will do D, and so on.

The next step in risk management is to monitor the project. We have identified potential problems, analyzed them, and planned to deal with them. Now we watch for the triggers we set. A project manager has many things to watch, but the risk management triggers are some of the most important.

Finally, we need to act. We have the background information at hand as well as the information from the project. We should make decisions and communicate those to the people on the project. If we have done all the risk management steps, this should be easier (not easy). We can tell people what is happening, what has happened, and why we are changing directions (implementing our risk management plan) on the project.

It is much easier to act in the heat of a project if we have performed the risk management steps. We thought through the potential problems and planned our way out of them when the situation and our emotions were calm. The actual problem is probably not the way we thought it would be. We are, however, far ahead of where we would have been had we not thought about this. The mugging the facts are giving us is not as bad.

In classical risk management, we write a risk management plan that records the results of (1) identifying, (2) analyzing, and (3) planning for risks. This can be done before the project begins. If such formality does not fit a project, it is good to do these things informally on a whiteboard or on a set of 3″ × 5″ cards pinned to a wall. This provides a living risk management plan. As risks come and pass, we take them off the wall. If a risk becomes a problem, we record the details of what happened, how we reacted, and what resources we consumed. This information can help in future projects.

Risk management is a critical part of project management, but it has one major problem—the word "risk." Risk is fun. At least our culture sees it that way. The 1980s Tom Cruise movie "Risky Business" is one example. Cruise's character took a risk, came close to catastrophe, but got away with it and had a thrilling and fun time.

Our culture's perspective on risk is a bad influence on project managers. New project managers think of fun when they hear about risk management. These popular but misguided thoughts contribute to poorly managed projects.

Risk in a project means "potential problem" not "potential exhilaration and potential fun." A project with risk is a project that has potential problems (do not they all?). We can use the five steps of risk management on those potential problems.

To separate pop culture from proper project management, we suggest the PM-RMUT (project manager's risk management understanding test). Every time someone says the word risk, apply the PM-RMUT by substituting the words "potential problem." If the result does not make sense, we have a person using the fun version of risk and we may have a big problem. Try this with common cultural phrases such as "we take risks here" and "risks have big payoffs."

There are things we can do about this risk business. First, maybe we should change the name. Instead of presenting risk management information, discuss managing potential problems for a project.

For example, "A $10M project has several potential problems. There is a 50/50 chance these problems will occur and this will be a $13M project."

That communicates more than saying, "The project is risky."

A second strategy is to plan projects with the potential problems in mind. The simplest way is to set aside a management reserve to handle problems. Some organizations do not allow a management reserve. In those cases, structure the project to absorb extra costs. Set problem triggers as early as possible. If a potential problem becomes a real one, drop features from the project and use those resources to handle the problem.

Finally, talk with people about managing potential problems (risk management). Use informal and simple instruction from an understanding person. Also, listen to people and the way they discuss risk.

ADDRESSING THE FACTS

There are times when it is difficult to accept the facts on a project. The facts are mugging our treasured theories and crushing our egos. As discussed earlier, ignoring the facts only hurts projects more. We have seen practices that make it a little easier to receive news that contradicts to our theories. The following sections describe some of these.

Admit the Facts

Projects have problems. If there are no problems, there was no real project but only an exercise in confirming something that was already accomplished. Admitting the existence of problems is a first step in dealing with them. The second step is admitting that problems exist first as potential problems or risks. Hence, all projects have risk. Admitting the existence of risk is a big step in creating an environment in which facts do not surprise us and mug our theories.

Once we admit that risks exist, we can work with them. Someone once said that risk management is project management for adults. We agree with that concept. Adults can discuss that they make mistakes. Their theories can be wrong, their project can have potential problems, and they can record these and plan how to deal with them.

Being able to manage risks helps projects succeed. When the project manager practices risk management, he is not (as) surprised by problems. He knows they may come, he has set aside extra resources to apply to them, and he has acknowledged them to his managers.

Don did not want to admit that risks and problems existed. He felt the pain of admission was greater than the pain of a failing project. Hence, he ignored the signs of growing risk and approaching problems. This was Don's failure, and also a failure of his managers. They created a situation in which discussing risk frightened Don.

Measure Twice

Part of risk management is monitoring the status of the project. Information comes to the project manager daily, and some of the information indicates trouble for the project. The facts may be mugging the theory. When this happens, the project manager should measure twice and think before acting. Measuring twice is not an act of unbelief or of ignoring possible problems. If the data are correct and there is a problem, the project manager will soon commit resources to address it. Extra resources are scarce, so the project manager should be sure about the problem before committing them.

The project manager should measure twice publicly. People should know why the project manager is asking them to check their data twice. We trust our people, and they should know that we trust them. People, however, make mistakes, and it is possible that someone made a mistake with the data.

The project manager should always think about the data before acting. We advise bringing in a few people and going through the information. The project manager is under pressure to act quickly and correctly. He can relieve some of this pressure by asking for a little help.

As discussed earlier in the book, I arrived on Delphi and started noticing things that did not make sense. I looked at the information several times with the builder and the other members of my team. We confirmed that things looked bad for the project so we took this news to my managers and requested action.

The action came, but it came several months later. There were many meetings, discussions, information-gathering trips, and analyses of the situation. Our managers decided to commit the resources needed to complete Delphi. At times it seemed that the deliberations would never end. I thought our managers were dim-witted to take so long. They, however, were looking at the information twice, just as I had done. They were also thinking, just as I had done. These steps took time, but it was wise to take them.

Put Out the Welcome Mat

While monitoring the project and its risks, people bring the project manager information often. As discussed earlier, some people always seem to bring bad news. Regardless of the source and type of the news, the project manager should welcome it. Information allows us to act for the good of the project and its people.

The worst thing the project manager can do is to blame the messenger. Lashing out at people who bring bad news means they will not bring news next time. We will be like the users that Don the buyer was trying to serve. They knew nothing about the problems Don was seeing so they could not help.

Not blaming the messenger is simple in theory, but sometimes difficult to practice. When someone brings in bad news, the natural tendency is to be disappointed. We must always ensure that everyone knows we are disappointed with the news and not the messenger. I cannot let the messenger deliver the news and run off while I am thrashing about on the floor. Tell them the reason for the reaction immediately, and thank them for bringing the news.

In the story above, Don did not want to bring news of problems home to his organization. He felt they would shoot him. In our experience, most people in organizations like Don's do not think they are shooting the messenger. They feel they are trying to learn about the situation. A common way of learning about a situation is asking for briefings. People in organizations want all the information in a presentation and they want to ask questions. They see this as the most efficient way to learn. Don saw it as punishment for bringing bad news.

It is easy to interpret a desire to learn as a desire to shoot the messenger. We should all take great care of our messengers.

Public Data

The volume of data associated with a project can be overwhelming. Something that helps with all this information is posting it publicly in the project room. Posting the data in public helps the project in several ways. This is one way of welcoming the messenger. Posting all data avoids singling out any one messenger for special treatment (punishment) as everyone's data are in the open.

While posting data publicly, be sure to post all the risks for the project. This lets everyone know that there are potential problems. If one person knows that his potential problem is not the only one on the project, he will not feel as threatened.

We need to be careful with the names of people when posting data. There are many practices we do (see Chapter 16 on internal design reviews) where we look closely at products made by individuals. Key to those practices is that we do not pin numbers on those individuals. It is good for everyone to see that we are having schedule problems with the mailing database. It is not good for everyone to see that Mary is having schedule problems with Mary's product. If we single out Mary, she will never tell us anything again.

One big advantage of public data is it decreases the pressures on the project manager. Don was attending monthly reviews with the builder by himself. He was the only person in his organization who saw the data. He alone carried the burden of the information that could spell problems for everyone and he alone had to decide what to do. That should never happen. Organizations exist to group people together to accomplish things. An organization that allows one person to do it alone is doomed.

What? Me Worry?

One last way to create a good environment for accepting facts and acting on them is to practice whiteboard risk management. The earlier discussion of risk management practices may seem daunting. There are textbooks on the subject that go into far greater detail and some of those are scary. Your organization may not be ready to write risk management plans or have risk management specialists on staff. If that is the case, use the whiteboard.

Gather a couple of smart people at the whiteboard and ask, "What could possibly go wrong next week?"

Write all the answers on the board. Most of the potential problems will not hurt the project much. If they occur, you will work through them in a day or two without expending many resources. Write these risks on a piece of paper (never throw away information) and erase them from the board.

Some of the potential problems can hurt the project significantly. Give these more thought and scribble these extra thoughts on the board. Ask, "What could we do to prevent these from happening?" and "What would we need to do if these potential problems occurred? What resources would we need?" Scribble these on the board and start gathering those resources. If the problem does not occur, you will not need to spend those resources. If the problem does occur, you are ready for it.

Ask, "What will indicate that the potential problem is happening? What will be our early warning or trigger?" Write that on the board and have your people watch for those indicators.

In 30 minutes at the whiteboard you will have performed risk management for a week. That did not hurt much. You have done the necessary activities and have done it openly. Everyone realizes that talking about potential problems is fine and that you want to know what is happening.

CONCLUSIONS ABOUT FACTS AND RISK

In all projects, the facts overrule the theories. If we do not admit this, and we do not work with it, the facts will mug our theories. This brings us to the prin-

ciple of facts, theories, and risk: The data are the data.
Watch out for:

- "That can't be right, let's go on anyway."
- "Joe always brings bad news; that's just his personality."
- "Don't bring me problems without solutions."

Try to do some things that help create a good situation:

- Admit that potential problems (risks) exist.
- Measure twice, then think.
- Welcome the messenger.
- Post all data in public.
- Practice whiteboard risk management.

Don the buyer fell into a trap in which he could not wish away a small problem and did not tell anyone else about it until it was a big problem. A big part of risk management is to write a personal rule that says, "If I have a problem for X days, I will be confident and strong and tell my supervisor." That is the simplest and most difficult part of risk management. We also recommend it as the top priority.

Don's story is all too familiar to me. I fell into the same predicament while working on a Y2K project (see Chapter 25). The builder ran into unexpected problems that grew each month. I was the only buyer working on the project, so no one else knew that things were not going well. The project, however, was relatively simple, and my theory was that the problems would go away. Each month the facts pounded my theories into the ground. Late in 1999, the builder brought in just the right people at just the right time and saved the day. I did not practice risk management, I did not gather the courage to tell others what was happening, and I avoided disaster only because of the fine work of others. I did, however, learn some of the lessons discussed in this chapter and I hope I never forget them.

Part 4

The next four chapters look at different aspects of working with people. Chapter 11 discusses a high-profile person on a project—the project manager. Chapter 12 is about people trying to communicate with one another. We find that most problems in projects stem from people not communicating well. Chapter 13 discusses making decisions in projects and how "just knowing" what to do instead of formally deciding causes problems. Chapter 14 delves into recognizing people for their performance. It seems strange, but doing something good like this often causes problems.

It Sounded Good When We Started. By Dwayne Phillips and Roy O'Bryan
ISBN 0-471-48586-1 © 2004 by the Institute of Electrical and Electronics Engineers.

Chapter 11

A Charlatan in Sheep's Clothing: The Right Project Manager

The project manager is responsible for the execution of the project. In a situation like Delphi, there are several project managers. The obvious one is the builder's project manager who manages the work done at the builder's facility as well as all products delivered by vendors and subcontractors for a given project. The other project manager is the lead person from the buyer's side. This person manages the contract and the relationship between the builder and buyer. These two project managers have different jobs, but they have many of the same tasks and responsibilities.

Delphi had four different project managers on the builder's side and three different ones on the buyer's side. Some did well in good and bad circumstances while others did poorly. This chapter relates some of their stories as well as lessons learned during the project.

THE PROJECT MANAGERS ON DELPHI

The builder had four different project managers on Delphi in four years. The story of these four different project managers says much of the tribulations and importance of the project manager.

The first project manager, Oliver, was a terrible fit for the job. Oliver came from the manufacturing side of the business and was a good project manager on production contracts. He could guide a project in which a group of assemblers would build a thousand copies of a single complex electronic system. That is a difficult job, full of its own kind of challenges.

It Sounded Good When We Started. By Dwayne Phillips and Roy O'Bryan
ISBN 0-471-48586-1 © 2004 by the Institute of Electrical and Electronics Engineers.

Delphi, however, was not a production contract for a thousand copies or even a hundred. We were only going to build nine systems. Before the assemblers came in, the engineers had to design, prototype, test, and repeat these steps several times. Only after the engineers had proved the design to be correct would a short production run occur.

Oliver was lost from the first day. He did not understand how to plan those types of activities much less how to find out how well the engineers were progressing with the design work, and he certainly did not understand how to report this to the buyer. These failings led to a bad relationship between Oliver and Don, the lead on the buyer's side. Communications failed as neither side knew what information they wanted from the other. Poor communication led to mistrust in a downward spiral.

The builder's management removed Oliver after six months. The buyer's management had hinted that this is what they wanted. This hint was conveyed through a zero award fee six months into the contract (more on awards and award fees in Chapter 14). Don left the project three months later. He was not happy with how his management was handling the situation.

The second project manager for the builder was Fred. Fred was experienced in this type of contract. He knew the type of information the buyer wanted and how to gather it. Fred, however, was also put in a bad situation. First, Fred was a "new hire" and really did not have any "chips" to play. Fred had come to the builder's company from a competitor. Although his resume was impressive, no one in his new company knew him, and he did not have time to establish his credentials.

The project was six months old when Fred arrived, but no one was sure of its status. Fred spent the first few months trying to find out what was ordered, what was designed, what was tested, and what was where. He was looking for a needle in a haystack on the back of a speeding bobsled.

It was about this time that I came in as the lead for the buyer. I did not know much about the project, the product, or the people. I spent my first couple of months also trying to learn everything.

In the meantime, Fred was working himself to a frazzle. He was doing everything, everywhere, all the time. In his efforts to do so much, Fred did not track the schedule well. This project was large enough to have had a full-time person gathering status and updating the schedule. This person did not exist, and Fred, instead of obtaining such a person through his management, attempted to do the job on top of all his other duties.

In addition, Fred did not adjust the project's plan. When events do not occur as planned, a project slips. The only way a project can regain the lost time is to determine what went wrong and fix it. This means looking at the project's plan and making changes as they are needed. In our case, this meant updating the plan every couple of weeks. Fred did not have time to do this as he was working more than six days a week doing everything else.

The biggest problem Fred faced was that he did not have the full endorsement and support of his management. After all, Fred was an outsider brought in from another company. Fred needed some helpers for a few months to gain control of the schedule. The help did not come. Fred needed a few extra engineers for a few months to bring the designs back on schedule. That help did not come, either. The people working on the project were not sure about Fred, his ability, or how secure he was in the company. Upper management did not help with any of these questions of job security. Action speaks louder than words, and inaction speaks even louder.

All the above led to one thing that almost always dooms a project—Fred became discouraged. One of the project manager's chief duties is to keep up the morale of the project team. When the project manager is discouraged, everyone else becomes discouraged, too.

To his credit, Fred kept the project going through 18 difficult months. He was honest and open, so no matter the nature of the news, Fred passed the news on to us.

Fred led his team through several major planning sessions detailed in Chapter 6. His final plan was the one that brought the project to a successful conclusion. Fred, however, was not on the project at the end to see this.

Fred's upper management removed him after 18 months. They also removed Fred's direct supervisor as well. They finally realized that without good support from above, the project manager did not have a chance. The buyer's upper management also got into the act and handpicked Fred's replacement. They wanted someone who had led successful projects in the past.

The third project manager was Peter. Peter turned the project around with the help of many people. He was project manager for 18 months and during his tenure the engineers proved their designs, the short production run began, and the first couple of systems were delivered.

Peter did about everything well that his predecessors did poorly. For example, Peter left the technical work and decisions to the engineers. He only stepped in when the engineers were overengineering. Peter also let others do much of the status gathering work. He did his share, but he called on team leaders to watch their schedules, report on progress, and suggest corrections when things did not go well.

Most important, Peter always had a positive attitude. He maintained this through some difficult negotiations and plenty of technical failures. Peter always looked for the good in any situation and he passed that along to everyone every day. People believed that they could build the product and finish the project. Much of that belief came from Peter's attitude. One of the ways Peter showed his positive attitude was by going home on time every evening. The engineers followed his example. They rested, came to work with more energy, and did a good job.

The fourth and final project manager was Bruce. Bruce followed Peter's example. He brought his own personality to the job and continued the good practices that Peter began. Bruce presided over the final nine months of the project. The team delivered the remaining systems during Bruce's tenure. It was not easy, as there were plenty of technical and managerial problems to overcome. Nevertheless, Bruce continued through to the successful end.

WARNING SIGNS OF TROUBLE WITH THE PROJECT MANAGER

The project managers on Delphi had major influences on the project. Oliver misguided the project for the first six months. Fred worked hard to keep the project going in spite of problems (many of which were beyond his control). In retrospect, we saw warning signs of some of this trouble. We, however, did not notice these and take action in time. The following sections discuss these and other signs that point to impending trouble with project managers.

Hour After Hour

Many project managers want to stay busy so they do everything they can find to do all the time. To some project managers, busy means hard work, and many project managers mistakenly feel that hard work is always good. One of the problems a project manager can bring to a project is the desire to be busy.

There are two basic tasks the project manager should do. These are (1) manage the project and (2) lead the people. Managing the project means having a plan, gathering status, and acting when necessary. Chapter 6 describes planning and we discuss leading people in many places throughout this book. Therefore, in this section we will only discuss gathering status and acting when necessary.

Gathering status involves many time-consuming and tedious details. It is bad when the project manager attempts to take care of all these details. These include making spreadsheets, entering data, and making charts. Other people should do those important but time-consuming tasks. The project manager has other duties that must be performed and only he can perform them.

Acting means changing what people are doing so that the project stays close to the plan. Most projects fall behind plan and, without action, they stay behind. Acting requires thought, and thought requires time. A project manager busy with tedious details does not have time to think and act.

A warning sign of the busy manager problem is when the manager is working too many hours on the project. We saw this sign with Fred. He was working every Saturday and part of most Sundays. Fred was too busy to be an effective project manager. Fred was conscientious, honest, and hard working. We saw him bury his head in spreadsheets in status meetings. He penciled in the latest status of every detail and then spent hours in his office putting the numbers into the computer. His zeal for details and hard work, however, did not allow him the time to take action to keep the project on track.

Peter was not too busy. He did his job and worked hard, but he let other people do their jobs. Peter had the advantage of better support from his managers. They left Fred on the project for a few months to track the details of parts, testing, and assembly. This gave Peter the time to take actions that kept the project on plan.

I Can Still Out-Engineer Any of You

The problems that occur daily on projects bring stress. When under stress, people often revert to what is comfortable. Since most project managers came up through the technical ranks, this means that if they feel stress they will revert to technical work.

Sometimes the project manager delving into technical details is good for a project. In most cases, however, when the project manager does this, it is bad for the project. The project manager already has plenty of things to do. If the project manager is trying to do the job of an engineer or programmer, no one is doing the project manager's job.

The technical people can provide the warning sign of this problem. Listen to how they talk about the technical work. If they mention the project manager's influence on designs, test setups, and other technical details, then the project manager is spending time on technical tasks instead of managing the project.

Peter was a good example of a project manager who kept out of the technical details. Peter did not ignore everything that was technical. He rightfully stepped in when the engineers were overengineering. The Delphi engineers found a number of ways to improve the product. On many occasions, they wanted the product to far exceed specifications. Peter was able to overrule them. The product met the specification, and the user and the buyer wrote the specification. It was possible to do better, but meeting the specification satisfied the buyer and user.

Technical people can always find reasons for another test, another experiment, and another whatever. The project manager should be able to see beyond one more whatever. If the project manager is trying to be an engineer, he has lost his perspective, and the project can quickly become a science project. It can be great fun, but the project will fail.

Living at Work

This book is about people working on engineering and IT projects. This is intellectual work, and people can only do it six to eight hours a day. If we work more than that, and we make mistakes that take extra hours to correct. Some people want to be appear tough by showing others that they can work forever. That does show some sort of endurance, but it is shortsighted. The hours at work catch up with us one way or another.

Many project managers spend extra time and extra days at work. They are the epitome of the company man (or woman). Some rose through the ranks to project manager by working the extra hours. Others feel obligated since the company promoted them and now pays them more money. They feel that they owe the company the extra hours.

Working long hours for long periods of time is a problem for projects. This is especially true when the project manager is working long hours, as the project manager sets the example for the team. When he works long hours, others follow his example.

The warning signs of spending extra hours at work are easy to notice. Phone conversations with the project manager often give hints about being at work. Hints like, "Well, we were in here all weekend, so we are ready for your visit next week," and "Lee has worked night and day to get this filter working."

Other tips are when the project manager doesn't walk out to his car when you do during a visit. The project manager seems to have "one more little thing" to do before going home.

Fred spent too many hours at work. He was the project manager of a troubled project, and hard work was required to bring the project back on track: At least that is what Fred and a few others thought. When you are behind schedule, you have to catch up somehow. Working smarter requires time to think, and that steals time from other work. Working longer just requires staying longer.

I cried one Father's Day. Fred had four wonderful daughters—all grown, several married, with several grandchildren. Fred worked ten hours that Father's Day. He did not see any of his daughters or grandchildren that day. That was terrible.

We noticed this warning sign on Delphi. Our efforts to convince Fred to cut back on hours were in vain. We spoke with Fred's management about this sign and the problems that were occurring because of long hours. They were either unable or unwilling to change the situation. The problems on Delphi continued.

Woe is Me

The project manager has the most influence on creating and maintaining the work environment. If the project manager is discouraged, many problems follow.

Being discouraged is one way we may choose to react to an event. For example, when a part does not arrive on time, that causes disappointment, and disappointment is an emotion. The key is how the project manager reacts to the event and handles the emotion. Being cheerful and resolute is one reaction; being downcast and discouraged is another.

One of the problems with being discouraged is that it consumes energy. People who are discouraged dwell on failures longer than necessary. This is one of the warning signs of the project manager being discouraged. He will dwell on past events. This surfaces in meetings with statements like, "We would be in good shape this month, but that shipment of parts was late a few weeks ago. If only they had arrived on time. We were ready to put the parts into the system."

Another problem with being discouraged is that is leads to blaming. Blaming often begins with a problem event. No one wants to bring the news of the event to the project manager because the news will cause more frowns and anxiety. Therefore, people try to hide the event. If they cannot hide the event, they try to blame it on someone else. In these situations, people concentrate their energies on hiding problems and creating a way to blame them on others. Little or no energy is expended on solving problems. Troubles persist much longer than needed, and the project slowly falls farther behind.

The blaming culture is another warning sign of discouragement. To notice this, look for people asking about "who" instead of "what." In a problem-solving culture, people will ask "what" questions like, "What happened? What did we do wrong? What should we do now?" In a discouraged blaming culture, people will ask "who" and "you" questions like, "Who did this? Who was supposed to do this? Where were you at the time? Why did not you do something?"

The problem of being discouraged caught up with Fred on Delphi. He was overworked and undersupported. Hard work and persistence were not enough to pull the project out of its troubles. Fred became discouraged, and the project slipped into a blaming culture.

When I came on as the lead for the buyer's team, overcoming discouragement and blame were my major tasks. I found it hard not to lash out when the builder gave me more bad news. Lashing out, however, would have only spread blame. It would help neither the project nor the people working on it.

I found that it was fine to voice disappointment. When a parts vendor failed to deliver, I could say, "Oh, that is terrible, I am sure your guys are as disappointed as I am. We had so much hope for them. Well, what do we do now?"

This told the builder that the problem was a disappointment. It also told them that they, too, could be disappointed. The final question was "what do we do now?" instead of "who screwed up?" The "what" question leads to problem solving. The "who" questions always lead to blame.

CREATING A GOOD SITUATION

Peter and Bruce were good influences on Delphi. Peter especially did things that helped create a good situation. The following sections discuss several of these as well as other methods we have seen project managers employ. We hope you will be able to use these on your projects.

What Three Things Need to Happen?

One good thing a project manager can do is ask people, "What three things need to happen for this to be a successful project?"

First, the project manager should ask the buyer. This is as simple as, "Let's ask the buyer what they want." The project manager should know what is important to the buyer. Take care when asking this and acting on the answer. There are many things the project manager is supposed to do for the buyer. The buyer's answer does not relieve the builder of all these responsibilities. It does, however, provide the builder's project manager with important and powerful information.

The project manager should also ask this question of the builder's team. They know much about the project and product, and have their own perspective. The engineer's perspective can teach the project manager much about his own perspective, his blind spots, and his biases.

Asking this question reveals much about the project manager. First, the project manager is proactive and is seeking information. He wants to do well for the buyer and have the builder's team look good by providing such information. Second, the project manager is being humble. Asking such a question is an admission that the project manager doesn't know everything. If he knew all, he would not need to ask. Since he is asking, he wants others to be smart and contribute to his understanding.

We have seen many project managers on both buyer and builder sides assume what was important. They mistakenly worked hard on things that did not matter to anyone. Asking someone what they want helps focus your efforts, your team's efforts, and shows the buyer you are concentrating on what they want.

Peter did this often on Delphi. Most times, he did not ask straight questions of us. One thing he did was to find our answer in the documents we provided to him. When he came on the project, the first thing he did was read the Statement of Work (SOW)—the specification for the project. (See Chapter 3 for a discussion of the SOW and the part it plays in a project.) Peter came on the scene 24 months into the project. Many people on the project had become so involved in the details that we had forgotten what we were supposed to deliver to the user. Many of us "knew" what would happen, what we had to do, and what was going to be impossible. We were afraid of all sorts of monsters out in the hallway.

Peter's reading showed that these monsters did not exist. His simple inquisitiveness and desire to please showed us what we wanted. He also provided ample opportunity for us to change our mind. His actions gave us a well-known, straight path to project success.

Public Endorsements

The project manager is the appointed leader of a project. This person should have responsibility, authority, and support from upper management. Most project managers have responsibility pushed on them. If the project fails, it is their fault. The second and third items, authority and support, are critical but not as common as responsibility. Oliver did not have authority and support, and neither did Fred.

These things come from upper management. The managers should provide them and provide them publicly. It is good for upper managers to stand in front of the builder and buyer and say, "This person is the project manager. We selected him because we believe in him. He is responsible for the project, has the authority to move resources, and we will support him." The upper managers should then do what they have said.

It is also important for the upper managers to monitor the project manager. They have said, "This is our person," and they are responsible for their choice. If the person they appointed as project manager wreaks havoc, it is their responsibility. The upper managers should supervise the project manager. They should also talk with the people on the project to learn what these people think of the project manager.

There are several reasons why the public endorsement is important. First, a key job of the project manager is to act. The project manager cannot act without authority and support. Second is the topic of longevity. People on the project will ask themselves, "will this guy be around long?" If their answer is yes, they will follow directions and work toward a successful project (or leave the project now). If their answer is no, they will wait out the project manager by doing what they want regardless of his direction.

A good thing that happened on Delphi was the endorsement of Peter as project manager. The buyer's and builder's managers met and discussed who would be the project manager of this troubled project. The buyer's managers were adamant in their belief that Peter was the person for the job. He had managed several successful projects for us before. Once Peter became project manager, people knew management's commitment to this project was real. Their message was, "Okay, we messed up, but we are serious now. Let's all go forward."

The builder's management also kept Fred on the project for several months with Peter. Fred was an immense help to Peter. If Fred had left, Peter would have had to try doing two and three jobs, and the project would have continued to be a failure. Keeping Fred on the project was further commitment from management.

Talk with Everyone Every Day

A good practice for a project manager is to talk to everyone on the project every day. This provides a couple of benefits. The first is that the project manager will learn about the project. People know how tasks are going and what the quality of the product is. If the project manager talks to them often, they will share this information.

The second benefit of talking to people every day is that it helps the project manager know what he or she is doing. Many people lose focus and drift while working on a project. Instead of doing what they are supposed to do, they find interesting things on the side that occupy their day.

Talking to everyone will also help the project manager know how people are doing. Morale is important to a project (refer to the earlier discussion on being discouraged and blaming). Daily conversations help the project manager know if people are happy or sad at work. Happy people do better work, and depressed people need help with what is troubling them. Being depressed now and then is normal for people. Helping depressed people is the right thing to do for the person, and it helps the project in the long term.

Talking to people every day is not a gimmick or a slogan. The phrase "management by walking around" has been abused in many places. Nevertheless, it works. It shows people that the project manager is human too, maybe even a caring human.

Fred did this on Delphi. Fred was a caring person who took an interest in people and how they were doing. It was unfortunate that Fred had too much else going against him. Peter and Bruce also walked around and talked to people. The engineers liked them, and liked working under their leadership.

Fred, Peter, and Bruce were all engineers by training. None of them had a dynamic personality, which is not necessary and are often a hindrance when working with technical people. They all had caring attitudes. They all wanted to know what people were doing and how they felt. Their personal attention helped people work through a difficult project.

What, So What, Now What?

Whenever something happens on a project, the project manager should ask three questions about the event. These are What? So what? and Now what? These relate to the event, implications, and adjustments needed because of the event.

The "what" question asks "what happened?" What is the event that occurred or failed to occur today?

The "so what" question asks "so what does this mean to me?" I want to know the implications of this event. Should I care? What does this mean to the project? What does this mean to the product? Is this a small thing or a catastrophe?

Finally, the "now what" question asks "now what are we going to do?" This event affects the project. What can we do to make up for it? It is nice to have at least three options. What are the options? What are the advantages and disadvantages of the options?

If a project is to finish on time, an event must occur the week before. For that event to happen on time, another prior event must occur the week before it. This continues back to the start of the project. If a task in the first month finishes several weeks late, this has implications for the remainder of the project. Fred, struggling with everything else, was not able to trace the implications of nonoccurring events. There were too many events not happening as planned for Fred to chase.

When I first arrived on the project, there were many things that I did not understand. Fred would tell me what had happened recently. He did not, however, tell me the "so what" and "now what" of the event. Since I did not understand the event, I did not understand its implications. I struggled with asking Fred for the "so what?" information. This extra question usually consumed a day, so the two of us were always trying to work yesterday's problem while today's problem was waiting to be solved. Since we were always behind, we frequently did not reach the "now what" question. Hence, we never had good ways to react to problems. They kept piling on top of us.

Peter was able to correct this situation. He recognized that I was always asking him the same three questions. With time, he asked the questions of himself and came to me with a complete description of the situation. When Peter called, he told me what had happened, what that meant to the project, and three possible actions we could take. He also summarized the advantages and disadvantages of each possible action along with his personal recommendation. Peter went through all this with his team. Delphi went from reacting while retreating to acting ahead of problems. This was a major step in turning Delphi from a failure to a success.

Use a System Engineer

One of the best things to help create a good situation for a project manager is to have a system engineer on the project. Some organizations call this position the chief engineer or lead engineer. Whatever the title, this person is responsible for the technical aspects of the project—the product. The system engineer delves into the technical details with the engineers and other technical people. Key tasks of the system engineer include tracking the technical performance measures (TPM) and the technical budgets.

The TPMs are the critical technical requirements for the product. If execution speed of software is important, that becomes a TPM. Other TPMs may be memory usage or power consumption.

Technical budgets relate to how requirements are allocated to different parts of the system. Consider a software system that must fit inside 1 MByte of memory. The system comprises five software subsystems. It does not matter how much memory each subsystem consumes as long as the total is under 1 MByte. The system engineer monitors the memory usage of each subsystem.

At first, the system engineer probably allows each subsystem one-fifth of 1MByte each. Some subsystems will need more and others will need less. The system engineer ensures that the more and less balance so that the entire system meets its requirements.

The system engineer works the details of the product. This allows the project manager to work the details of the project. A system engineer helps create a situation in which the project manager can succeed.

We did not have a strong system engineer for the first two years of Delphi. This was one of our big problems. Fred struggled with many technical details because the system engineer assigned was new to that position. Fred tried to do the system engineer job as well as the project manager job. This had two effects. In his efforts to do at least two major jobs, Fred was unable to do either well. Second, we had many technical problems and no one to work on the TPMs and technical budgets. The problems grew, caused us to redesign many parts of the system, and set us behind schedule and over budget.

Peter and Bruce had a good system engineer working for them during their time as project manager. They could concentrate on the project manager job, so the project benefited. The system engineer concentrated on the technical work, so the product benefited.

The Power of Positive Thinking

Just as a discouraged project manager can doom a project, an optimistic project manager can help one. There are many bad things that happen during a project, unexpected things that throw the project off track. A project needs a project manager who has a positive demeanor and tries to encourage everyone.

One of Peter's best attributes was his positive attitude. There were times when he drove us a bit crazy with his attempts to find the positive side of the situation. He, however, kept at this and it proved to be a large part of the successful turnaround of Delphi.

Being optimistic does not mean being overoptimistic. We had much of that during the early months of Delphi when people refused to see the problems. They felt that if we just kept working, all would be well. Those good feelings had no basis in fact.

Peter was grounded in reality. He told us when things were going badly and how much time and money it would cost to correct problems. He would then tell us that, given those resources, we could do it. He always ended with a smile and suggestion of success.

Having a positive attitude is not a Pollyanna concept. It is the idea that we have problems on projects, and that is normal. We solve the current problem and move on to the next one. People respond to that type of attitude in a project manager. They bring problems to the surface and solve them quickly.

CONCLUSIONS ABOUT THE PROJECT MANAGER

The project manager may be the single most important person on a project. This is not because the project manager is the smartest, the highest paid, or the one anointed by upper managers. The project manager does not make the product, but creates the environment that enables others to do so.

This leads to our principle of project managers: The project manager creates the work environment and thereby influences the people on the project and the chances of success.

Watch out for:

- The project manager is working too many hours.
- The project manager is trying to be an engineer.
- The project manager is living at work.
- The project manager is discouraged.

How to create a good situation:

- Ask, "what three things need to happen for this to be a successful project?"
- Have the project manager's management endorse him publicly.
- Have the project manager talk daily with everyone.
- Every day, the project manager should ask "what," "so what," and "now what?"
- Use a systems engineer.
- The project manager should have a positive attitude.

The project manager can doom a project staffed with excellent people. The project manager can also create a place where people thrive and do wonderful things. We hope that you choose your project managers wisely and provide them with the simple things they need to succeed.

While working on Delphi, I had a manager in my office named Chuck. He was responsible for my work on Delphi as well as the work of other lead buyers on other projects. Chuck's great contribution to our group of project leaders was the concept that work is important, but it is only work and not our entire lives. He showed us this principle by keeping his work and personal life in balance. He also demonstrated this principle in his actions. For example, I had a beeper with me at all times while working on Delphi. The builder would call me to discuss issues when I was in the office, at home, and on vacation. While on one vacation, Chuck called the builder and told them stern-ly that I was on vacation and they were not to contact me until I came back to work. Chuck was telling the builder to take care of their issues themselves. He was also giving me two messages. First, when I was with my family I was to be with them and not my job. Second, he had confidence in my ability to create a situation in which the builder could take care of things without me. Chuck created an environment that allowed me to succeed on Delphi and succeed in the rest of my life, and for that I am thankful.

Chapter 12

But You Didn't Ask— Communicating with the Customer

People talk to one another on projects. At least that is what happens every day on the projects we have experienced for dozens of years. Given all this practice we have talking, we would think that we were good at communicating. The trouble is, talking is not the same as communicating. Hours and hours of talking can produce little if any transfer of useful information.

This chapter discusses some of the trials and triumphs we have had with communicating. We have learned a few things that indicate failing communication. We have also learned a few things that make communicating a little easier.

THE $80,000 BRIEFCASE

We needed transit cases for the equipment on Delphi. A transit case is a small suitcase that has foam padding in it to protect the equipment. We needed 18 transit cases for our nine sets of equipment. The builder estimated the cost of the cases at $80,000. A little math shows that we would be paying about $4,000 per case. How in the world could someone try to charge us that much?

We held a two-hour meeting with four representatives from our office and six people from the builder. The builder showed us the type of cases they would buy (American Tourister luggage), the type of foam padding they would use (it was good quality), and drawings of how they would put the dif-

It Sounded Good When We Started. By Dwayne Phillips and Roy O'Bryan
ISBN 0-471-48586-1 © 2004 by the Institute of Electrical and Electronics Engineers.

ferent pieces of equipment in the different cases. We talked in a healthy manner and decided on a smaller package.

Everyone was satisfied. We had answered all the questions and cleared up all the confusion. Two weeks later the builder came back with a second estimate of $50,000. How in the world could someone try to charge us that much?

We had another two-hour meeting on the subject. The builder showed us the drawings that came from the previous meeting. The builder understood just what we wanted, but how could they try to charge us that much?

The builder explained that they were using a skilled craftsman who had a workshop about a mile from their facility. They would take the suitcases and drawings to the craftsman. He would cut foam and insert it into the suitcases. Then he would use their drawings and cut out the holes for the equipment.

Now we agreed on exactly how the cases would appear, what equipment they would hold, and how the builder and the craftsman would do the work. We were sure the next estimate would be in line with our thoughts.

The builder came back with a third estimate of $40,000. How in the world could someone try to charge us that much?

We did not have any more meetings on this subject. Instead, we cancelled the transit case portion of the contract, and high-level managers from our organization and the builder had heated exchanges on the telephone. We might have cancelled a $30M contract because of these cases. Some cooler heads prevailed, and we continued with the rest of the contract. We made the cases ourselves for about $150 each.

What was the problem here? Why did the builder want to charge us $2,000 a case for something that cost us $150?

First were the drawings. The builder was having a draftsman make top-quality drawings. The first job was to measure and draw within 1/100 of an inch the suitcases they had bought at Sears. Next they would measure our equipment to within 1/100 of an inch. Finally, they made the drawings of the foam cut-outs to within 1/100 of an inch. A team of senior draftsmen reviewed each drawing. These seniors would ensure that the draftsman had followed all drawing standards. Each time the draftsman made one change to one drawing, the seniors would review the entire package. Quality was important to them.

We spent about $10,000 on the draft drawings we used in the meetings. The meetings cost us probably $20,000 when we included the time and expense of cross-country travel.

Second was the review process the builder was going to use while watching the craftsman fit the equipment into the foam-packed cases. He would cut out one hole for one piece of equipment per the drawings. The builder would take the case back to their facility and try to fit in one piece of equipment. If it fit, they would repeat the procedure for each cutout on the first case. If the equipment did not fit in the cutout precisely, they would start over with a new piece of foam. They budgeted to have at least three restarts.

Our idea was to buy some foam, cram it into the suitcase, draw lines around the equipment, and cut the foam. We always cut the holes a little smaller than the equipment so we could jam the equipment into the holes. The foam tore a bit each time, but after a year of use we would throw it away and start over.

See the big mismatch? We finally did, months later. The question was why couldn't we communicate at the time?

This builder made its living producing items. Once they had their design in good shape, they would usually make 10,000 items. Top quality drawings were essential. Without them, they would have large variances in their 10,000 items. Therefore, they reviewed their drawings with great attention to detail and they would make things only when everything was just right.

We were accustomed to making 10 items. Grab some materials, cut it, tape it, and jam it in.

The past experiences we both brought to the meetings overshadowed what each of us said. We saw and heard everything in the framework of our vastly different ideas of production.

WARNING SIGNS OF FAILING COMMUNICATION

The story above illustrates some of the difficulties we encounter when we do not communicate well. All we needed were some simple carrying cases. We, however, failed to convey that concept to the minds of the builders. The builders were not trying to gouge us for more money and we were not stupid. Yet, the two of us could not communicate.

In addition to our failure to communicate, we failed to see the signs of poor communication. The next paragraphs discuss some of the signs we should have seen in the above story and in other stories from other projects.

Assumptions

We make assumptions and use them in communication. If nothing else, we assume people are all speaking English (or German, or French, or some standard language). We assume "one" means one, "black" is black, and so on (although there are cases when even these simple assumptions can hurt).

The trouble with assumptions is they are often wrong. When a person makes an incorrect assumption, they usually proceed in an incorrect direction and consume resources. In projects, this can mean cost overruns, schedule delays, poor quality products, or all three. There is an old saying about assuming things, "If you assume (ass-u-me) something, you make an 'ass' out of 'u' and 'me'." This is a crummy old saying, but it is true.

In the story of the transit cases, the builder assumed we wanted transit cases that were of the quality to hold $3M devices. We assumed the builder knew we wanted simple and cheap cases.

If we had said something like, "We are assuming simple, inexpensive cases—not expensive, high-quality cases. What are you assuming?" we could have avoided our problem.

It is difficult to detect when others are making assumptions. One warning sign is the use of absolute words. These are words like "require," "need," "never," and "always." These words indicate that the other person is certain of something—so certain that they did not give it much thought, so certain that they probably assumed it. When hearing these words, ask "why?"

For example, had the builder said, "We need to make detailed drawings of the cases." We could have asked, "Why do we 'need' detailed drawings?" This would have led to a discussion that might have uncovered the miscommunication we were having. We might have seen our trouble, communicated with one another, and avoided our troubles.

'He's Not Here Right Now, But ...'

Another problem in communication is triangulation. This is when we say something to person A. Person A then goes to another room and says something to person B. Person B then goes to another room and says something to me. The three of us are corners of a triangle. We always talk in pairs, and we usually talk about the person who is not present or about something that involves the person who is not present.

We often see this happen on projects during meetings. A topic comes up for discussion, and someone blurts out the warning sign, "That topic involves Joe. He's not here right now, but we all understand it well enough to discuss it anyway."

The group then discusses the topic at length without Joe. A couple of days later, Joe meets with one of the meeting participants to discuss the topic. The group did not quite understand the topic well enough, so Joe enlightened this one person. This group then discusses the topic with the rest of the group.

Triangulation hurts projects in a couple of ways. First, it wastes resources. All these meetings and incomplete conversations take time. People are pulled off their jobs to waste this time. In addition, they become frustrated and are not able to work well for a while after the meeting.

The second problem is that these meetings often lead to decisions. Since the decisions are made with incomplete and incorrect information, they are bad decisions. People leave the meetings and build the wrong products or use the wrong processes. These mistakes eventually come to light, but they are expensive to correct.

Puzzled Looks

People need to understand one another when working on projects. When we do not understand, we build poor products, waste time, and sometimes simply freeze. We sit in our cubicles and do nothing because we do not understand what it is we are supposed to do.

A sign that warns us when others do not understand us is a puzzled look on their faces. It is as if they were eating a lemon or we were speaking backwards. They tilt their heads to the side, wrinkle their noses, open their mouths, and stop breathing. These looks mean that they are hearing something they do not understand or do not expect, or both.

Be careful when people have these funny looks and the speaker continues without stopping to ask about the looks. When trying to communicate, we try to observe the listener. What type of look are they presenting? Are the nodding yes and smiling or making one of those faces?

We remember the builder's engineer explaining to us his design for the transit cases. He was focused on the sample case that he brought with him. His eyes were fixed on the case as he pointed out all the features. He was not looking at us, so he did not notice any of our expressions. In addition, the builder did not notice the look on our face when they told us the price for the transit case. Surely we must have given them a look of disbelief. In addition, we did not say anything to explain the looks on our faces. We assumed the builder saw and understood those looks. We both failed to communicate, and the project suffered.

"Heeeeere's Johnny!"

There are occasions in a project when the project manager has information that the team members need. Sometimes, the team does not receive that information. They are left wondering, so they start wandering.

A warning sign of failing communication in these occasions is the monologue. One definition of a monologue is "a long speech monopolizing conversation." This is when someone starts talking and is able to talk for a long time without anyone else saying anything.

I once worked on a project in which the project manager would deliver a monologue at every meeting. The project manager thought that while he talked everyone else listened. They all heard all his words, understood them, and would proceed to do as he had said. He was disappointed, as the project wallowed in trouble for months.

Several things happen during a monologue. First, the speaker is full of himself. I've done this. It is a good feeling to be in a room full of people and I am the only person talking. It is like I am king holding court. All listen and all will obey, or so I think.

Often the speaker assumes that "silence is agreement." No one interrupts, no one raises any objections, so all agree with him. This, like most assumptions, is dangerous.

Instead of agreement, the usual reason that people do not interrupt the speaker is that they are afraid. They do not want to upset the king, so they sit quietly. The result is no questions, no interactions, and no communication.

After sitting through a monologue, people talk. They cannot wait to leave the throne room, breathe, and talk. Their talk is rarely positive. The usual is, "What is wrong with that guy? He really likes to hear the sound of his voice."

Finally, people fall asleep. Well, they do not close their eyes and bang their heads on the table. Nevertheless, they do not hear anything the speaker says. Afterward, they go do what they would have done anyway.

Fear of Fear

The monologue inhibits communication from the top down in an organization. A problem that inhibits communication from the bottom up and horizontally is fear. A culture of fear is one of the worst things that can occur on a project. People do not communicate necessary information because they are afraid.

We notice this fear when someone says, "I'm afraid to tell them." Less obvious signs of fear are when people hesitate to answer yes–no questions like, "Did the tests pass last night?" They will answer, "Well, um, I am not sure, maybe."

People are afraid to say things that relate to projects. These range from, "I want to take off next Friday," to, "I do not think this design will work," and, "The overnight test had 100 failures."

The result of fear is the same bad news as above. People do not communicate information that others need. Hence, people continue to work on things they should not be working on instead of stopping and changing direction. Other people stop working and wait instead of continuing to make progress.

Call it a Day

Communicating with people is hard work. Trying to communicate complex information like the kind encountered on technical projects is really hard work. If we attempt to communicate too much in a day, fatigue conquers our bests intentions.

One warning sign of fatigue in communication is when someone says, "I understand." This may sound curious. We want people to understand, but this reply is insufficient. What we want people to say is that they understand, and then tell us what they understand. The simple, "I understand," with nothing following it is not good communication. It lacks feedback and interaction.

We often heard "I understand" in the story of the transit cases. The builder told us they understood what we wanted. We told the builder that we did not understand why their cost estimate was high. Neither of us really understood the other. Both of us were tired physically, tired of the subject matter (transit cases—who cares?), and tired of each other.

It would have been a different story had we stated, "I think I understand what you are saying. Let me state it back in my own words to see if I have it right." That would have caused some discussion and maybe some real understanding.

The best thing to do when people tire of communicating is "call it a day" and go home. People rarely do this. We feel that we are high-paid professionals who should be able to do our jobs. We do not "get tired," or at least we do not like to admit it. Judgment is better than false pride, so call it a day, go home, rest, come back tomorrow, and communicate.

Cultures

Communicating with people from a different culture is difficult and has dangerous traps. The difficulty is that people from different cultures use the same words differently. They often think they are communicating and agreeing, only to discover later that they had different ideas in mind.

Our transit case story has several instances of this. In our culture, we never built more than ten copies of any one thing. The builder always built 10,000 copies of everything. We understood that the purpose of drawings was to give someone a rough idea of what items we would put in a case and about where they would go. The builder understood the purpose of drawings was to allow workers on an assembly line to make thousands of copies with each copy being within 1% tolerance of the drawing.

Another culture clash we had was that we represented a government agency and the contractor represented a publicly held company. A good project for us is one that yields a product that works for us. We work toward the product. A good project for the builder is one that is profitable now and in the future. The builder works toward profits for stockholders.

We also clashed in terms of geography and weather. We talked about how the cases would need to hold up in hot, humid weather. I grew up in Louisiana and my coworkers from the east grew up in Virginia. Hot and humid meant 100°F and 90% humidity to me. My coworkers thought about 85°F and 55% humidity. The builders from southern California dropped down to 80°F and 40% humidity.

There are various warning signs of different cultures clashing. One is dress. We wore sport coats and ties to the meetings, whereas the California builders did not. That should have flashed red lights in my eyes: "WARNING: Different cultures about to clash."

We missed these and other warning signs of differing cultures. Therefore, we assumed they were using words the same way we were. That was a mistake, and the project suffered for it.

WAYS TO COMMUNICATE BETTER

There are many potential and real failures of communication in projects. We have found a few items that help us communicate. The first item below is a discussion of the Satir interaction model. This explains one view of the process of communication. It has helped me understand good and bad communication. Following it are several ways we have seen that help create a good environment for communicating.

The Satir Interaction Model

Human communication is a fascinating topic. It is not, however, just something to discuss on cool evenings on the front porch. It makes a real difference on projects and in people's lives.

There are countless discussions between the buyer and the builder during a project. We state something and the builder replies. Most of the time, the discussion proceeds well and we do not notice anything wrong. Sometimes, however, one side replies in a way that startles, confuses, irritates, or even enrages the other. People dismiss the other side and communication, now and forever, suffers. No one performs well because we stop speaking.

Let us look back at our fiasco with transit cases. We said, "We need 18 transit cases for our nine sets of equipment." The builder responded with, "That will be $80,000." What happened? What did we do wrong? How could we have done better?

The Satir Interaction Model [1], named for the family therapist Virginia Satir, can help us understand. It is a model that can help us see what we are doing and guide our actions.

The four basic parts of interaction are intake, meaning, significance, and response. The following describes the steps and how our transit case situation collapsed.

This communication model begins with intake. The first step is not input, as in "I input all the correct information, but they weren't listening and did not understand." The first step in intake as in "I do not think their intake was what I intended." The key is not what I send, it is what they receive.

It is the responsibility of both parties to understand the difference between intake and input. The sender cannot assume that the receiver heard what was said. I must ask the receiver what they heard and I must look at the receiver to see if they are puzzled or if they act in any way other than what I expect. If I think the receiver heard a different message than the one I sent, I must do something to correct the situation (that I caused).

As a receiver, I should tell the sender what I heard. I must admit to myself that I do not hear perfectly. Acting otherwise would be overestimating my abilities.

Intake is an action, not a state of being. My ability to intake well depends on how hard I try. I can listen attentively or I can listen while reading, typing, or listening to many other things.

Let us go back to the example given earlier. We said, "We need 18 transit cases for our nine sets of equipment." The builder's intake was, "The customer wants me to provide transit cases for the equipment."

After intake, the receiver assigns meaning. In technical work, we understand that data have no meaning, as they are simple numbers. Data become useful after we assign meaning to them. The same is true for conversation. What we hear has no meaning until we give it meaning.

We often take this step for granted. We assume that the other person will assign the meaning using the literal words we send. Communication rarely works this way, as we communicate via words more than numbers. The words have different meanings to different people.

It is good to apply the rule of three interpretations to each message I intake. I should think of at least three different meanings for what I heard. If I cannot think of at least three, I have not thought enough.

It is also good to use the data question when assigning meanings. This question is, "What did I see or hear to cause me to think that?" This is a good question to ask others when they respond in surprising ways. Walk through the steps of the model. Ask what they heard and ask how they interpreted it. If this was not the intended message, start over. Communicating is not a battle of wits, it is something we need to do to succeed on projects.

Understand that people bring history with them to a conversation. This history (past conversations, childhood, marriages, the workplace, their education, etc.) can overshadow what is happening in the current conversation. Consider when someone says, "We're just one big family here." They probably mean that the people in their organization are close and often see one another after work. If, however, the word "family" floods my mind with past and painful experiences, I will apply a bad interpretation to what I heard. I will become angry and respond with anger. The other person will not know what hit them or why.

Let us continue with the exchange between the builder and us regarding the transit cases. We said, "We need 18 transit cases for our nine sets of equipment." The builder's intake was, "The customer wants me to provide transit cases for the equipment." Their possible interpretations are:

"The customer wants me to throw together something to carry the equipment."

"This sounds like a job for our packing and shipping people."

"A set of equipment costs $3 million, the customer wants transit cases of relative cost."

The next step is significance. Significance is how I feel about the meaning I assign to the intake. Is this conversation important to me? Does it anger me? Surprise me? Amuse me?

Note that these are all emotions. If I feel upset about the conversation, it becomes fairly significant to me and I will act in anger. If I feel calm, I will act calmly.

Feelings and thoughts work together in this step. Anger causes me to think about angry things and reactions. Amusement causes me to think of humorous things and try to think of humorous responses.

This step moves into the realm of "touchy feely stuff." Please stay with us on this one. It can make or break communication, and communication can make or break a project. The meaning we assign to our intake triggers a feeling. This gives us significance, and significance will drive our response.

The running example now looks like this: We said, "We need 18 transit cases for our nine sets of equipment." The builder's intake was, "The customer wants me to provide transit cases for the equipment." The builder interpreted this as, "A set of equipment costs $3 million, the customer wants transit cases of relative cost."

The builder's feeling about the interpretation was, "Wow! They think a lot of me and I will not let them down. I will design the best possible transit cases and do it in a way that each case has consistent, high quality."

Now the receiver responds to the sender. All of us have internal and external responses. Filtering our internal response before we let it out may be good. That tends to provide a courteous and professional response. Too much filtering may be bad and lead to a response that does not connect with the other person. The other person should know how we feel and what we think.

Too little filtering can be just as bad as too much filtering. Anger can lead to venting or exploding. While this may be a true representation of how we feel, it can overwhelm others. Explosions can shut down people, communication ends, and troubles follow.

Emotions are present in communication. As much as we might like all communication to be technical and predictable, that is not reality. Emotions often hurt thinking. Weak thinking hurts the product and the people producing it.

We have emotions present during communication, but what is important is how we deal with emotion. We all need to understand that when emotions swell in us during a dry, technical conversation, there is nothing wrong with us. We are having normal responses. We need to feel our emotions, understand what they are, and deal with them. Stay in the present and think. If necessary, stop, take a break, and think.

The running example concludes with: We said, "We need 18 transit cases for our nine sets of equipment." The builder's intake was, "The customer wants me to provide transit cases for the equipment." The builder interpreted this as, "A set of equipment costs $3 million, the customer wants transit cases of relative cost."

The builder's feeling about the interpretation was, "Wow! They think a lot of me and I will not let them down. I will design the best possible transit cases and do it in a way that each case has consistent, high quality."

The builder responded by using their highest quality process to produce the highest quality product. At the end they told us, "That will be $80,000." Looking through the individual steps in the model, the builder's response makes sense.

The Satir model gives us a way to think through communication. It, however, requires effort. We need to ask people what they heard and tell people what we heard. We cannot give ourselves more credit than we deserve ("some people do not hear well, but not me"). Next, we ask people about the meaning they assign to what they heard. Next, what type of significance does this have for them? Are they angry, bored, or tickled? Allow everyone, especially yourself, time to work through emotions. Ask people to explain their response. The response wraps around the Satir model and starts a new communication.

We encourage people to use the Satir model and explain it to others on the project. Communicating well is important. Had we done better, we would not have wasted $10,000 talking about transit cases only to cancel the whole thing.

One Room at One Time

A simple, practical tip to aid in communication is to bring all the people together in one room at one time. People sit face-to-face, talk about one subject, and make decisions. This helps stop triangulation. The meeting does not end with, "As soon as we can find Joe, let's have another meeting."

A possible problem with these meetings is that they can be difficult to manage. The topics can go in many different directions with the meeting ending with no conclusion. We recommend using a trained facilitator to lead the meetings. A facilitator steers the meeting to keep it on track. The facilitator has an agenda and goals for the meeting, but he is not concerned with the content of the conclusion. That means he is able to concentrate on the process and the communication.

We held many meetings on Delphi related to the transit cases. One of our problems was that we did not discuss what we were willing to pay for the transit cases in these meetings. Suggesting or proposing a price for services is a delicate subject with a contract like the one we had on Delphi. It is sort of like "gentlemen do not discuss money."

The builder sent us their proposed price in a facsimile. We did not have everyone in the room to discuss the price and the reasons behind it. We guessed at the reasoning and held several meetings of different parties at different times. Our failure to gather everyone together in one room at one time kept us from understanding the situation and acting in a productive manner.

Give Me an Example

Something that helps people communicate is pulling information from other people. It helps to shift thinking from abstract to concrete. One way to do this is to say, "Give me an example." For example, in the transit case story, we never asked the builder to give us an example of a similar case they had built. We did not tell the builder to give us an example of the tolerances they used in building carrying cases. Looking at the other side, the builder did not tell us to give them an example of the types of carrying cases we used with other equipment. We all had ideas in our heads, but that is where they stayed—in our heads.

The "give me an example" statement fuels discussion. It causes people to think of real things they have done and relate them. Examples often lead to stories. Stories are a good form of communication as people listen to stories. They seem to be less work-related, more fun, and more entertaining. When someone hears a story, they often remember something and tell a story back.

Many of the statements and questions people make put others on the defensive. Statements like, "Show me how this works," are often heard as, "Prove to me why your idea works." The other person must now gather evidence and present it in a convincing manner.

The same is true for the common question, "Why did you do that?" The other person must defend their actions. Defending actions often upsets people. They ask themselves, "Why must I defend myself? Don't they trust me? What are they trying to pin on me?"

A simple statement that helps pull out information and improve communication is, "Help me understand this." This statement puts me on the defensive. I lack something and need someone else's help so I, too, can understand. The other person is in a superior position. They understand the subject and will now teach it to me. It is good to preface this statement with, "Everyone here seems sure that this will work. I do not have much background, so I do not understand it yet."

Be Assertive (but Not a Bully)

There are times in communication when people need to say what they feel they need to say. Often, however, we are afraid to say something or think that it is inappropriate in a professional discussion. People attempting to communicate should be assertive.

Being assertive does not mean being a bully. We have been in many meetings where people said things that hurt and embarrass others. Pain and embarrassment was their intention, and they succeeded in destroying communication.

For example, being assertive is stating facts like, "The overnight test had 100 failures."

Being a bully is saying something like, "Whoever wrote the software that we tested overnight should be fired. It had 100 failures."

Being assertive requires a degree of confidence. The speaker should not be afraid to tell others the facts. If challenged, the speaker comes back with,

"These are the facts as I found them. I would be happy if someone else checked this."

Being assertive does not require being a public speaker or having an extroverted personality. That is the fallacy that keeps many people from being assertive. They lack training as a public speaker or they have always been quiet. Therefore, they do not talk in meetings.

I have struggled with being assertive during my entire career. When I assert myself, my pulse quickens, my temperature rises, and I have a difficult time thinking and talking. When I want to say something assertive, I have found it helpful to write what it is I am going to say ahead of time then read it aloud in the meeting. This ensures that I "get out" everything before my emotions shut my mouth.

Small Words and Short Sentences

Technical projects are complex. To worsen our plight, we in the technical fields have invented vocabularies of long words. To help communicate, we suggest using small words and short sentences. This advice sounds too simple, but it works. Short statements provide other people a chance to talk. I make a statement (a couple of seconds long) and stop. The other person now has a chance to say something. Their statement gives me a much better idea of what they heard and understood from me. Now I can make another statement along the same line of thought.

Long statements have cause problems. For one, by the time I reach the end of a long statement, the other person has forgotten what I said at the beginning. If I cover six subjects in one statement, no one will remember the first three. They will forget them, and not comment on them. Their lack of comment often leads me to believe that they agree with me.

Using short words means using as simple terms as possible. English is a rich language, and there are places for saying, writing, hearing, and reading the unusual and little-used words in the language. We feel that a meeting conducted during difficult technical projects is not one of those places.

We also recommend using direct statements instead of talking in circles. Consider the statement, "We need to distribute the plans." People can interpret this in many ways. First, who is "we?" I do not want to do this task, so "we" sounds like someone else. It must mean some other people in the room.

Next, what is "need?" I certainly do not need to do something. I will be able to feed and clothe my family without doing this. There must be some mistake here with this "need" business.

Next, what is "distribute?" Does that mean put it on the bulletin board? Isn't that something secretaries do?

Finally, what are the "plans?" Are these the schedule, the production plan, or the quality assurance and configuration management plans? I have not seen any plans on this project. What is this?

Now consider, "Joe, please give the paper drawings to John." I understand this. First, it is Joe who must do something. I am clear here as I am not Joe. Second, Joe should give something to someone. That means move it from his hand to someone else's. Next, the object to give is the paper drawings. Finally, John is to receive the object. This is John and no one else.

This statement is simple and direct. People have a much better chance (not a 100% chance) of understanding it than understanding the first example.

Precise, Concrete, and Specific

A final tip is to be precise, concrete, and specific. In technical projects, we try to have specific terms for specific items. A system is not the same as a subsystem, to integrate is not the same as to compile.

Consider the statement, "Integrate the system." What do "integrate" and "system" mean is this?

Now consider, "Connect and test for four hours the input system." There is still some ambiguity in this statement, but it is much more precise, concrete, and specific than the first statement.

Being precise, concrete, and specific is the responsibility of the listener as well as the speaker. If the speaker is vague, the listener should start asking questions. Good questions include, "When you say integrate, do you mean. . . ." "When you say system, are you talking about X or just about Y?" "Which specific tests do you want me to run?" "How long do you want me to test?" and so on.

The goal of this tip is to remove ambiguity and vagueness. Listen to the words we use. Write them on paper and examine each word. We find that we often use words that carry many meanings. This is fine in conversations but, again, we feel that this is not fine in meetings in complex technical projects. Being precise, concrete, and specific is aggravating at times. It does, however, bring rewards in the end.

SOME CONCLUDING THOUGHTS ABOUT COMMUNICATION

In our experience, 90% of the problems in troubled projects are caused by failures of people trying to communicate. People assume the other person understands them, so they move on and do what they think they agreed to do. After a while, people reconvene only to learn that something else entirely has been happening. Accusations start to fly about integrity and intent, and the project starts spiraling downward.

This leads us to the principle of communication on projects: Clear communication is difficult but possible.

Watch out for:

- Assumptions.
- "He's not here right now, but . . ."
- Funny looks and puzzled expressions.
- Monologues.
- Fear.
- Fatigue.
- Groups from different cultures trying to communicate.

How to create a good situation for communication:

- Run through the Satir interaction model with people.
- Bring all interested parties together in one room at one time.
- Say, "Give me an example."
- Be assertive, but not a bully.
- Use small words and short sentences.
- Be precise, concrete, and specific.

We conclude with the thought that we should treat everyone else as a smart caring person. If we can only understand one another's thoughts and intentions, we can succeed in most projects.

Just recently, I wrote a plan for a new project. I visited a group that would play a key role in the project to learn what they thought of the plan. Their first statement was, "We do not agree with this plan!"

Though immediately disappointed with their statement, I understood the Satir model better than I did while working on Delphi. I took a deep breath, paused, and started working through the situation with them. My plan stated that this group would "oversee a contractor" on the project. This group read these words and assigned the meaning "pay for the contractor" to the phrase "oversee the contractor." This was significant to them because they did not have the budget to pay a contractor. Their response ("We do not agree with this plan") was understandable. I explained that I meant "oversee a contractor" to mean "watch the contractor perform the work" and not "pay the contractor." We changed the words accordingly, and everyone was satisfied. Understanding a model of communication and treating others with respect is not just a nice theory. It really works in real life.

REFERENCE

1. *Quality Software Management, Volume 2, First-Order Measurement,* Gerald M. Weinberg, Dorset House, 1993.

Chapter 13

A Penny Saved Is a Penny Earned: Maximum Reward versus Minimum Regret

One of the problems we have stumbled through on projects is how we make decisions. Every project has problems; every problem has alternative solutions, and every alternative solution has its good and bad points.

As simple as this seems, we often forget these principles and fail to use them. Instead, we usually "just know what to do" and try it. Sometimes that works, but often it doesn't. The stories that follow are about a couple of projects where "just knowing" hurt badly. The remainder of the chapter discusses warning signs of trouble and techniques that help us make clear decisions instead of just knowing what to do.

THE DROP TEST

All manufacturers of quality electronic consumer products use some form of environmental test screening to ensure that their product will operate reliably in the real world. This test includes burn-in, turning the product on and off thousands of times, over- and undervoltage tests, temperature shock tests, and vibration tests. Part of the shock and vibration tests is to drop the product to see if it will withstand some abuse from the user. A product should not break when dropped from a reasonable height. The word reasonable depends on the product. A calculator, telephone, or pager should still work if you bump it off your desk. Hence, a drop of three feet onto concrete is a reason-

It Sounded Good When We Started. By Dwayne Phillips and Roy O'Bryan
ISBN 0-471-48586-1 © 2004 by the Institute of Electrical and Electronics Engineers.

able test. A television is not built for that type of drop, but should survive a four-to-six-inch bench handling drop. This is where you lift a corner of the television and drop it on a wooden workbench.

A colleague of ours named John related the following story of a drop test on one of his projects. John was the buyer. The builder was trying to make a box full of electronics that would weigh 60 pounds. The final package, however, weighed 100 pounds. It was common practice to perform some type of drop test during the development of such a box. The builder knew this and designed the structure of the box to withstand the appropriate drop.

For some reason, the original buyer failed to specify a drop test. John was not the original buyer. John came into the project, learned of the absence of a drop test, and wanted to perform one. The drop test had been a part of John's previous projects, and he could not understand why it was not in this project.

John convinced the users that a drop test was necessary. He wanted to do a "packaged" drop test. This is where the system was put in a shipping container and dropped on concrete from three feet. This test would show that the system could withstand a drop that might occur while shipping the system.

John's explanation to the users was one-sided. Everything John told the users showed that the drop test was a good thing. When we want to do something, we tend to look at the positive side of it.

John's explanation was, "What if we drop this system during its first shipment to a field site? It would break and we would never be able to use the system. Do we want that to happen?" Of course, the users did not want that to happen. They wanted to be sure the system would survive shipment.

Everyone seemed to assume that performing the drop test would mean that the system would pass. John neglected to tell the users that the system might break during the drop test. In that case, the users would need to pay extra money and delay delivery to fix any damage. This is a tendency of optimistic people. We tend to think that systems will pass tests that we perform.

Armed with only evidence in favor of the drop test, the users agreed that the builder should perform it. The builder reluctantly agreed and performed the drop test. The builder's fears prevailed, as the system did not survive. Several circuit boards in the system cracked, and structures inside the system bent out of shape.

We had to spend an extra $500K (about 15% of the total cost of the project) to remedy the failed drop test. This included funds to replace the damaged circuit boards, redesign the chassis to withstand more drop force, and repeat the drop test (it passed the second time). This also delayed delivery six months. The project was already having some difficulty meeting cost and schedule, and this mechanical failure pushed everything over the edge. This almost destroyed the project at the last minute.

John and the users, however, were happy to see this failure at this time. It was good that the system broke in the builder's facility instead of in the field. Almost everyone involved was happy with the outcome.

There was another side to the drop test question. Most people on the project, however, did not consider the other side. First, this project was only building two systems, not 200 systems. If the builder was producing 200 systems, the drop test would have been absolutely necessary. It is common to destroy one or two systems in qualification testing on projects where a large number of systems will be built. The automotive industry does this on every car model every year. People who build calculators, toaster ovens, and electric drills do the same. The idea is to ensure that the basic design is good before building several hundred or several thousand copies.

People who only build a couple of systems do not do this type of destructive testing. This is because of how the users use the systems. Users of unique systems do not treat them the same way they would treat mass-produced systems. They do this because they know their systems are unique. If they drop or break a system mechanically, they know they cannot buy a replacement. Hence, they take care not to harm them.

John subjected the system to a packaged drop test to simulate what might happen during shipment. The system being built, however, would only be shipped twice a year. The nature of the use and shipment indicated that people would take special care during each shipment.

In the final analysis, John conducted the drop test because we always do that. He "just knew" it was the thing to do. He repeated the standard arguments for doing the drop test. He did not analyze how the system would be used to see if the standard arguments applied in this case. The result almost killed this project during its final month.

FILTERING POWER LINES

John is not the only person we know who had problems considering alternate solutions. We had a similar problem on Delphi. The power supply portion of the hardware took in 12 volts DC and generated a half dozen different DC voltages for the rest of the system.

At the start of the project, we encouraged the builder to place filters on all the power supply lines. That would provide better power to the system and probably improve performance. We thought this was necessary, but the builder disagreed. They felt the power supply would generate voltages that were "clean" enough. The extra filters would cost design time, make the systems harder to build, and take up precious space and weight. The builder had the choice on this issue and did not filter the power lines.

Three years into the four-year project, the builder changed their mind and filtered the power supply voltages. They had hit a point where several other parts of the system were not performing as desired. They had tuned those parts of the system, replaced components, added software, and done everything they could imagine to bring the performance to the desired levels.

They accidentally discovered the benefit of filtering the voltages. While working on another part of the system, they used a power supply that they had on the test bench. This power supply was a large box that provided clean voltages. When used in place of the power supply housed in the system, the system parts under test began performing better than desired. The builder put in the power filters they had rejected three years earlier. The system performed better than specification, and we were all happy.

We were happy that the system was performing well, but we were not happy with other things. We had wasted a large sum of money in the three years because we did not have filtered power lines. The noisy power caused us to spend extra time tuning circuits, replacing components, and scratching our heads trying to find ways to have the system perform to specification. If we had filtered the power originally, we might have saved six months and $5M.

In hindsight, we had good excuses for not filtering the power lines. The builder wanted to work on the interesting parts of the system, and the power supply was not interesting. It seemed mundane compared to everything else. We all admitted that it was the foundation for everything, but building the power supply was like pouring concrete. People "just knew" how to do it, so we did not need to pay close attention to it.

In the end, it took us several years before we filtered the power lines because we did not think about the situation. The builder only saw the disadvantages to doing that—spending time and money on a mundane part of the system. The builder and we had failed to look for advantages to filtering the power supply lines. Our discussions were one-sided, and we decided to go with that side. We neither saved nor earned a penny. Instead, we lost $5M.

WARNING SIGNS OF TROUBLE IN MAKING DECISIONS

The above two stories showed how projects ran into trouble because people failed to consider alternatives before making decisions. That situation happens often in projects. There are a number of warning signs that indicate people are not following a good process for making decisions. The following subsections discuss some of these warning signs.

Time Is Not on Our Side

Considering alternatives requires time. People on projects often feel rushed and, regardless of what someone wants to do to assist, rushed people feel as if they do not have time for that assistance. Considering alternatives can fall into this category. A warning sign we have noticed is when someone suggests one technique or another only to be shouted down with, "We do not have time for games!"

The ever-present schedule pressure pushes people to forego thinking and make snap decisions. There are times when the pressure of moving quickly is real. There are other times when people fall into analysis paralysis and take too long to consider the situation. In our experience, those two cases are not the norm. The problem we usually see is that the schedule pressure is not as great as people think.

Decision making takes little time when compared to the time needed to implement the decision. One hour of discussion leads to a decision that may take weeks and months to implement. That is 1% thinking and 99% doing. In light of this, schedule is a poor reason for not thinking.

Schedule is often an excuse for people doing what they want to do. They have their favorite alternative to a problem and do not want any discussion because that might change the minds of other stakeholders. Schedule becomes a tool to frighten people out of thinking.

A typical statement is, "If we do not do this now, we will fall weeks behind schedule." When given this statement, we suggest asking, "Please show us the schedule and how a one-hour discussion will lengthen it by several weeks."

In the story of Delphi, the builder felt rushed before the project started. We had several problems on the buyer side that delayed the start of the project. The budget process took longer than planned, and we were late in preparing contractual documents. The builder was losing people they had planned to use on the project. Every several weeks of delay cost the builder a person as people moved to other projects.

It was during this rushed period that the builder decided quickly to forego filtering the power lines. We urged them to spend more time considering this issue, but they did not have the time to think. If we had been on schedule with our part, maybe they would have used the time. The combination of wasting time (the buyer) and not using it (the builder) hurt the project.

How Many Sides Does a Coin Have?

Considering alternatives is a major part of good decision making. Each alternative to a situation has at least two sides to it. For example, John was faced with deciding about a drop test. One alternative was to conduct the drop test. There were others like simulating a drop test, analyzing structures with models, and so on, but let us just discuss the first alternative. There are good and bad aspects of conducting a drop test.

A warning sign in decision making is when people only look at one side of one alternative. There are two general cases to this troubling situation. One is that people will not consider the bad in an alternative. The other case is that people only consider the good in an alternative. These sound the same but, as the following will show, they are different.

Let us first discuss the "no negative" case. This is usually voiced as, "We do not need negative thinking here." This statement usually comes out when trying to elicit what is wrong with an alternative. Every alternative we have seen had something wrong with it, and we should look for that.

Some people see looking for the bad in an idea as an insult to their ability to implement an alternative. They often growl back, "Don't you have confidence in us? Do you think you could do this job better?"

It is important to let people know that listing the problems related to an alternative is not an affront to someone's ability to implement it. We are trying to list what might go wrong. This relates back to Chapter 10, which discussed risk and risk management.

Sometimes, attempts to find problems are taken as an attack on the idea and the person who suggested it. People may shoot back with, "Well, what is your idea that is better than this?"

Looking for problems with an idea is not the same as deciding against it. It is only a step in the process. We can avoid this conflict and the hurt feelings it brings by first stating, "We have an idea under consideration. We haven't decided about it yet. One step we'll use while considering it is to list some of the negative things about it."

Looking for problems with an alternative is also not an attack on the person who suggested it. That situation comes up when the idea originator says, "Well! Do you have any ideas better than mine?"

Note here that the conversation has shifted from ideas to people. Avoid saying, "I see a problem with Dave's suggestion. It is. . . ." Instead, phrase the statement as, "One possible downside to suggested alternative number two is. . . ."

The other general case is when people only consider the benefits of an alternative. This is usually not a conscious choice of the people involved. They are not denying problems as in the previous discussion. Instead, they just do not think to think of bad things. They think of good things and then stop thinking. This is what happened with John and the drop test discussed earlier. John and others could only think of reasons why they should perform the drop test.

Considering only the benefits happens in moments of optimism. Such optimism often occurs when people are young or inexperienced. This was the first project on which John served as the lead buyer. John thought of alternatives and reasons why they would work. He did not want to think of bad things because we worked in a culture that prized "can do" people. John's desire to "do good" lead him to only "think of good." He did not think that anticipating and preventing failure was "doing good."

"We Know What to Do"

Experience can be great. We have enjoyed projects where we worked with people who knew what they are doing because they had done it many times before. Experience, however, can cripple people when trying to make decisions. A warning sign of experience dominating a decision is when people say, "We know what to do." In such cases, people are overconfident of themselves and their abilities. They feel that processes, such as formal decision-making processes, are a waste. The thought goes that people are paramount, and anything that diminishes the role of people is a hindrance.

This "we know what to do" attitude can be a problem for projects when it is time to make decisions. First, the people tend to go on autopilot and stop thinking. In intellectual work such as engineering and IT, stopping thinking is not good.

Process—the creation of procedures that handle every situation—is not everything, either. It does, however, have its place. Most processes can be written as checklists. Smart people created these checklists after many years of forgetting things and making mistakes. The checklist helps people overcome the frailties of being people.

The story of John and the drop test was one such instance. All the people involved were smart and had reason to have confidence in their judgment. They did not use a good process when they decided to drop the system. They did not consider the possibility and consequences of failure. They did not consider how the users would ship and handle the system. They, like all of us do from time to time, made a mistake. Our mistake on this project was not pointing out their overreliance on themselves and underreliance on some process.

This Time Is Last Time or Vice Versa

The above section dealt with how a person's experience can cause problems with making a decision. A similar problem is when people depend on a single past event to determine what to do now. The warning sign we hear is, "This is just like the last time." This is never true. There are at least three reasons why it isn't. The first reason is time itself, because today is not yesterday.

People who work with digital systems may argue against this. A system running the same program with the same inputs will produce the same result as running it any day in the past or future. That may be true, but it does not occur as often today as in the past. Many systems today interact with outside systems like the physical environment or the Internet. Running a program today on the Internet is not the same as running it a week ago on the Internet because the Internet changed in the interim.

The second reason why this time is not like the last is technology. Technology is changing at a rate faster than ever before. We can be working on the same problem today as we did six months ago, but it is unlikely that we are using the same technology or the same components today.

The third reason why this time is not like the last is people. The people are different today than they were the last time. Firms are experiencing turnover at much higher rates than in the past. It is unlikely that the same people are working on the situation this time as worked on it last time. Even if we have the same people today, people do not remain the same. We have greater and more varied knowledge today than a year ago. Sometimes, however, we forget things we knew last year. The addition and subtraction of knowledge in the same people changes the situation.

The "just like the last time" thought brings many of the same problems as overrelying on experience. The major problem is that people stop thinking. People make the assumption that things are the same, so they do the same things they did last time.

This "just like the last time" situation plagued both the drop test and power filter stories discussed earlier. John convinced people to do the drop test because we had always done the drop test. This system was just like the last dozen systems we had built, but only in some respects. One of the differences in John's case was that the builder was only building two systems. In prior cases, builders had built a couple dozen systems. Destroying one during testing was acceptable. With only two being delivered, destructive testing was not a good idea.

The power line filter situation has occurred in almost every system ever built. We always relegate the power supply to a second-class status. Power supplies, the builder contended, are always the same. They did not need to think about them and certainly did not need to add extra circuitry to them.

In both cases, the thinking started and stopped on one statement: "This is just like the last time."

HELPING TO MAKE DECISIONS

We have struggled over the years to make good decisions on projects. We have also learned several decision-making techniques. Mingled in the next few sections is a description of one such technique. We call it the maximum reward and minimum regret technique. It is a simple process that helps make a difficult task a little easier. A good attribute of the technique is that we can apply the first few steps mechanically. This gives us some progress while reserving our energy for the thinking that is necessary.

Every question, issue, or problem has alternative solutions or answers. It is a mistake to think that there is one, and only one, answer to a problem. There is always one more possible answer.

Each alternative has good and bad sides to it. It is important to acknowledge at least three good and bad points to each alternative. That shows that we are thinking about the alternatives. If we have not found three good and bad points, we have not thought about it long enough.

Now we are starting to outline our technique. We have a question or issue, we have several alternatives (again, at least three), and we have at least three good and bad points about each alternative.

Time Is on Our Side

It should be evident that the technique we are describing will consume time. As discussed earlier, many people do not like spending time thinking about problems. Instead, they like to jump into an alternative as soon as it comes to mind.

We have found that a good way to enable thinking is to plan ahead and allow time for it. People are often rushed on projects because tasks seem to come from nowhere. Problems occur in projects, and people need to think about them. Good thinking consumes time, so plan now and put time into the schedule for thinking.

The final couple of years of Delphi went according to schedule. One reason is that the builder planned for problems and allowed time for thinking about them. Peter, the project manager who helped reverse the fortunes of the project, did not allow his team to rush into solutions to problems. They used the large whiteboards in their project room to think and work through problems. We saw the results of their working sessions when we visited. The time and effort Peter had his team expend paid off well.

Draw a Line

Now let us delve into the details of the maximum reward versus minimum regret technique. First, write the question or issue on a whiteboard or at the top of a large piece of paper (flip chart paper, newsprint, poster, etc.). Phrase the problem as a question such as, "What are the alternatives to ensuring that the system will not be damaged during shipment?"

Write alternatives as they come to mind and put the alternatives in the same large space as the question. List at least three alternatives.

Now write each alternative at the top of the piece of paper. Draw a vertical line down the center of the paper. On one side of the centerline write, "What's the most that we could gain if we choose this alternative?" This is the maximum reward for the alternative.

On the other side of the centerline write, "What's the most that we could lose if we choose this alternative?" This is the minimum regret for the alternative.

Put these pieces of paper on the wall next to the question under consideration. We want to see everything at once because making our thoughts visible is a key part of this and any decision-making technique. We can move close to the wall to study one alternative and move back to see and consider everything.

An advantage of this technique is that it helps us think. The first few steps are mechanical—write this and write that. They create places for us to put our thoughts when they come to mind. Having a place to put thoughts is a big help in developing and maintaining them.

The key part of this exercise is the first question. The suggestion above was, "What are the alternatives to ensuring that the system will not be damaged during shipment?" This is the question John and his team should have asked. Alternatives could have been (1) perform drop testing to ensure the design prevents damage, (2) package the system with extra padding and a strong case, and (3) train users in how to handle the system carefully.

John and his team thought only of option (1)—the drop test. Their decision making centered on justifying that option. They asked themselves, "What is good about doing a drop test?" They listed the answers to that and repeated them to themselves, the users, and to their managers. The decision process involved no decisions, only justifications. This mistake on the first step prevented John and his team from using the rest of the technique as described below.

Both Sides Now

Now we are ready to write the good and bad points of each alternative. Work through both sides of the centerline. Bounce back and forth instead of trying to list all the good before looking at the bad. Also bounce around among the different alternatives. We have placed everything on one wall to make it visible, so use that visibility.

Ask about each point written on the paper. For each good point for an alternative, ask, "How can this be a bad point? How can this upset someone or something?" For each bad point for an alternative, ask, "How can this be a good point? How can this improve something or make someone happy?" These questions help us to think of the other side of any alternative.

Keep working until the wall contains at least three good points and three bad points for each alternative. With a little practice, it is easy to find three things. We usually find at least half a dozen.

Sometimes, the good and bad lists are lopsided. There may be twice as many items on one side of the centerline than on the other. In such cases, stop and ask the people involved how they are feeling. Are they happy today? Are they sad today? Optimism or pessimism may be dominating the day and clouding the thoughts. Work around these things if possible.

Outside the Lines

This technique involves looking at a situation and thinking. As with any such technique, one thing that improves the environment is to bring in an outsider to look at the situation. Outsiders bring a fresh perspective. Their preconceptions differ from those of the team that has been working on the problem. This fresh perspective often opens new lines of thinking.

Such an outsider helped us see the benefit of filtering power supply lines on Delphi. Those of us working hard on the project had forgotten about that idea. It only came to us when someone used a big power supply that was sitting on a workbench and noticed the improvement in system performance. That someone was a test technician. He did not know much history on Delphi and certainly did not know the possible implications of using a different power supply to run tests. Grabbing such a power supply was something that was natural to a person with his background and perspective. That move turned out to be brilliant. Outsiders often bring different perspectives and solve problems when they do not know there is a problem.

CONCLUSIONS ABOUT MAKING DECISIONS

It appears that the old saying "a penny saved is a penny earned" has some merit. Time and effort making a decision is a penny saved. They prevent us from "just knowing" and "just doing" on projects.

This brings us to the principle of making decisions: There are at least two sides to every alternative, and we need to consider them.

Watch out for:

- "We do not have time for little games."
- Considering only one side of an alternative.
- "We know what to do."
- "This is just like the last time."

How to create an environment for making decisions:

- Allow time to think.
- Draw a line down the center of a piece of paper.
- Acknowledge both sides to every alternative.
- Bring in an outsider

We have not seen this much thought given to situations often, to our dismay. There are many reasons why we rush through a decision-making process, but these reasons are only weak excuses.

All too often when we make decisions, we concentrate on the virtues of the alternatives and neglect the potential consequences. We often say, "If we do A then B will occur." We put the Bs into two categories—desirable and undesirable—and concentrate on the best possible outcomes or the maximum benefit. We do not spend much time on the worst that could happen or the maximum regret. We should understand that in the real world, things can go wrong.

When Roy's (coauthor Roy O'Bryan) daughter Stacey was in the second grade, she was selected to attend a program for gifted and talented students from third through sixth grades. She could stay at her current school where she would continue to receive special attention. If she decided to go, she would have to leave her friends at her current school to participate in the program at another school. This also meant that she would leave all of her friends in the neighborhood, too. She would neither be standing with them waiting for the bus to go to school nor be coming home with them after school. Roy and his wife Lynda decided to let Stacey make the decision.

Since Roy and Lynda had decided to let Stacey decide, they had to help her frame the important factors. They went to the other school to meet the teachers, visit the classroom, and talk about what she would be doing in the third grade. They repeated this at Stacey's current school and went home and helped her write down all the good things she remembered about the two schools. On another sheet of paper they helped her write down the negatives, if any. She had a list of the good things and the bad things about each school.

They then discussed in detail how she felt about each thing she had written. They tried to help her determine which were most important and least important—like not being with the neighborhood kids at the bus stop. They then told her to sleep on it because she had plenty of time to decide. After a week or so, Stacey came home from school and said that she had decided to attend the other school. So, in the fall, Stacey left behind her friends at the bus stop and entered the third grade. A few weeks after school started Stacey told Roy and Lynda how much she had appreciated them helping her arrive at the big decision.

Then Stacey revealed that the iguana was gone. It seems that there had been an iguana in the classroom at the other school. They remodeled that school and the iguana could not be left in the dust and debris so they found a new home for it. The iguana was the real discriminator for Stacey, but the iguana had never been mentioned in any of the discussions. Sometimes you just have to know the right questions to ask.

Chapter 14

Punish the Innocent Bystanders: Award Fees, Bonuses, and Other Rewards and Punishments

Rewards and recognition are part of the workplace. Different forms of recognition can be quite rewarding and motivating to some people. At the same time, we can make a big mess of the workplace with a recognition program.

THE AWARD-FEE CONTRACT

We misused an award system on Delphi's contract. We wanted to communicate, but we abandoned other means and instead tried to communicate through an award (or lack of award). We turned a bad situation into a really bad situation.

We used a cost-plus award-fee contract on Delphi. The government often uses this type of contract when building a difficult or unique system. The cost-plus part is where the buyer pays all the costs the builder incurs. This may sound like a great deal for the builder—keep running up the cost and the buyer will keep paying. Such contracts, however, have checks and balances so that the buyer knows (to the dollar) what the builder is spending each month. It is the buyer's responsibility to monitor cost and progress closely so we know when trouble may be coming.

The award-fee part of the contract comes into play every six months. The buyer judges the builder's performance and awards a percentage of an award-fee pool. The buyer does this at an official award-fee presentation. The buyer's managers meet with the builder's managers, and the buyer's team lead shows

It Sounded Good When We Started. By Dwayne Phillips and Roy O'Bryan
ISBN 0-471-48586-1 © 2004 by the Institute of Electrical and Electronics Engineers.

viewgraphs that state the percentage of the award-feel pool granted. The builder wants to receive 100% of the award-fee pool. The buyer wants to award 100% of the pool as that indicates a contract where things are proceeding to plan.

The first six months of Delphi were a catastrophe. The builder was having problems, and we all needed to address them. One problem was that the builder was understaffed. They were supposed to have twenty people working on the first day of the project, but they only had ten. They fell behind schedule and made a number of technical mistakes while rushing to catch up.

The builder's managers failed to address the staffing and other problems. They were hoping people would come to the project when other projects ended, and the new people would correct all the problems. That was all wishful thinking, and wishing things to happen rarely makes them happen.

The biggest problem was poor communication between the builder's project manager, a gentleman named Oliver, and Don, the buyer's lead (see the Chapter 11 for more details). Each assumed that the other knew what they were thinking, but they failed to state clearly what was on their mind. They fell into something that is common early in projects. Each was not sure about the other. Since this was a new relationship, they wanted to "be nice" so they did not come on strong for fear of offending the other. That fear caused them to err on the side of keeping quiet and hoping things would work.

This shortage of communication and surplus of hoping led to a disaster six months into the project at the first award-fee presentation. Don was unhappy with the builder's performance. They were behind schedule and over cost. In addition, the communication between him and Oliver was growing worse instead of better. Don's managers were also unhappy with the builder. Previous contracts with the builder had similar cost overruns and schedule delays. They were "sick of this" and wanted to put a stop to it. These managers decided to award the builder 0% of the fee available.

A zero award is unusual. In our organization, it occurred in about one of five award periods in one of every ten contracts. In many contracting organizations it never occurs.

The zero award was a shock to the builder. A senior manager from the builder had been on vacation in Europe and came to our East Coast office for the award-fee presentation. He had heard from his people that "things were going fine" on the project.

Don showed the viewgraphs and said the words. The builder, in the opinion of the buyer's managers, was doing a terrible job. The buyer had no recourse but to slap a zero award on them. The builder's expectations and the buyer's feelings could not have been farther apart. This was an obvious failure to communicate.

The reasoning for the zero award seemed faultless to the buyer's managers. There were three themes in the discussions about why a zero award was justified. First, it was the buyer's duty to "send a message" to the builder. The builder had failed to manage projects in the past. All attempts to communicate our displeasure had failed. It seemed that the only way to send a message that the builder would hear was through the pocket book.

Second, we were justified in "punishing" the builder. They had failed to perform time and again. We rewarded "good" builders and punished bad ones. This was a bad builder, and we were to punish them by withholding the award fee.

Finally, we had to "get their attention." Oliver was not paying attention to the things Don was telling him. The builder's upper managers were also not engaged in this project. It was time to do something so they would pay attention to our project.

Our faultless reasoning for the zero fee award was full of faults. First was "send a message." It was as if other ways of sending a message did not exist. We both had telephones, and daily phone conversations occurred, but the people were speaking different languages.

Second was the idea of "punishing" the builder. Adults punish children; adults do not punish other adults. The punishment theme spoke volumes about how the buyer's managers viewed the builder's managers. We were the experts in all things and were trying to teach the builder how to do everything. They were children who needed such teaching. They weren't learning their lessons properly, so it was our duty to punish them. Somehow, the partner and teaming concepts had gone away.

Finally, we had to "get their attention." There are ways to do this. Talking to people usually works. If it does not, talking to their managers is the next step. If that does not work, we could have continued up the line. If none of that worked, we could have canceled the contract.

Several things resulted from us giving our builder a zero fee award. First, we embarrassed our partner. The builder was our partner, not our adversary and not our hireling. We entered into a contract because we needed them to build a system. We agreed to pay their expenses, and they agreed to "open their books" so we could see how they spent every dollar.

A second result of the zero fee award was we punished innocent bystanders. We were upset with the builder's managers. We wanted them to feel pain, embarrassment, and financial loss. The people we hurt most, however, were the engineers working on the project. They were working long hours and weekends on a difficult technical problem and they poured everything they had into their tasks. Staff shortages, parts problems, etc. were out of their control. A zero award hurt the engineers in their salaries because their corporation based much of the annual salary reviews and raises on the profit of the projects on which they worked. Working on a zero award (low profit) project showed poorly in their annual salary review.

The engineers were demoralized. People lost their desire to work hard and build good products. We heard lots of "who me?" reactions from the engineers in the succeeding months. They felt they were working hard and doing well on the things that were in their control. They were bewildered as to why were we punishing them.

A final result of the zero fee award was that we almost killed an important project. We entered into this contract because our users needed the product. We chose this builder because they were the most qualified to build it. Our actions almost led to canceling the project. Had we done that, we would have had to restart on a five-year learning curve.

THE BOTTOM TEN PERCENT

Back in the early 1990s, I worked in an office with 500 people where we were to identify the bottom 10% performing people at each grade. We were to list the bottom 10% of the junior engineers, the bottom 10% of the journeymen engineers, and so on. This was not an awards system, but it was a recognition system fraught with many of the problems of awards systems.

The concept of the bottom 10% program was simple: identify the people in the bottom 10% of each grade and have them improve themselves. Panels of managers were to implement this program. These panels reviewed each person in each grade and listed them from one to N as far as performance. The bottom 10% was the people at the bottom of the list. If we had 50 junior engineers, the 5 at the bottom were on the 10% list.

The second part of the program was to work with the people at the bottom and help them climb off the list. No one was quite sure how they would do this step. They reverted to the tried and often untrue method of "we'll work this on a case-by-case basis."

The first part of the program followed the concept well enough. Panels of managers met and worked through lists of people. They ranked people from one to N at each grade. Those at the bottom of the list were in the 10%.

The trouble in this step was how to rank the people. The panels comprised five or six managers who did not know all the people they were ranking. They used bits of information from different sources and did the best they could.

No one outside the panel had any insight into how the panels did what they did. The information compiled in the meetings was confidential. Managers above the panel saw the notes, but no one below the panel did. We, the ranked, were in the dark.

The program continued to fall apart in the second step. A senior manager, someone a couple of grades above the person found on the 10% list, would speak privately with the person on the list. Instead of trying to help people improve, the conversation became a case of trying to convince the person to leave the office and find a job elsewhere in the government. Leaving the office would take care of the person's performance issues as far as the managers were concerned.

The program's affect on people was predictable. At least it was predictable to the rank and file engineers once we learned what was happening. Somehow, the people who created the program were quite surprised to learn how the program was affecting people. The people who were put on the bottom 10% list were demoralized. They did not understand why they were listed as poor performers. We had used a system of annual fitness reports for years, and most persons in the office were described as performing above average in the vast majority of their fitness reports. Some of these above average performers were now listed in the bottom 10%.

One problem was that they were not really told that they were in the bottom 10%. The senior managers kept the lists confidential. People guessed that they were in the bottom 10% when a senior manager had a private talk with them and hinted about finding jobs elsewhere. When people asked directly if they were in the bottom 10%, managers would not answer yes or no, only that those lists were kept confidential.

Although most people identified were demoralized, some were angry. They were fed up with the system of secret meetings, confidential lists, and being labeled as failures. They lost interest in their work and spent their days meeting with coworkers in gripe sessions.

After the program ran its course, we finally learned its real agenda. Our office managers had been told they might need to downsize because we had too many people for our budget. The lists of bottom 10% people were what senior managers would use if the order came to cut people.

Laying-off Federal government employees seemed quite improbable to most of us. Besides, it seemed easy to downsize without layoffs. The reason was that a large percentage of the people in our office could retire in two years. Downsizing would occur naturally if we did not hire new people as older people retired. If we needed to push things along, the office could have created cash incentives for people to retire. That would have cost money, but holding meetings to create lists of bottom 10% people cost more money.

In the end, we did not need to lay off anyone. People retired as they usually did, and the office did not hire any new employees to replace them. We reached our smaller workforce in spite of the bottom 10% program.

The bottom 10% program did, however, have its affect on the office. First, people distrusted the senior managers of the office. The workforce saw the entire program, touted as important to the office and to the individuals who would improve, as a lie. We stopped believing what these managers told us. The managers themselves retired as usual in a few years.

Second, we distrusted all secret management meetings thereafter. Our managers held such meetings twice a month. These meetings were a normal part of government, at which empty positions were filled with people wanting new assignments. Most managers saw them as such and did their job. Many of us, however, saw them as meetings at which we were labeled falsely and our careers damaged. We were wrong most of the time, but we knew that this had happened once and had reason to believe that it would happen again.

WARNING SIGNS OF TROUBLE IN AN AWARDS PROGRAM

The above stories are of two cases where a recognition program wreaked havoc on a workforce. It is easy for something that should boost morale to end up destroying morale instead. Most of the problems with recognition programs come from actions of managers. This is not to place blame on a single group of people, but the managers usually make the decisions regarding recognition, and managers, like the rest of us, make plenty of mistakes. We have learned that here are things that warn of impending trouble with awards programs. The following discuss some of these things.

'It's Lonely at the Top'

Projects need teams of individuals to build all but the simplest products. People come with different skills, have different experiences, and move on and off a project in its phases.

One problem that many managers have is a distorted view of how individuals work in teams. Let us illustrate with a story related to Delphi. One thing that helped us on Delphi was a secure communications link between our facility and that of the builder. This link allowed us to transmit proprietary and classified computer files from coast to coast. This may not seem like much today, but it was a significant accomplishment and aid on Delphi in the mid-1990s.

One sister government organization sent a technician to the builder's facility to install equipment. The technician returned stating that all was well. A technician in our building, however, spent dozens of hours configuring the link so that it would work reliably. Our sister organization briefed us of their accomplishment, at every opportunity. I happened to sit in one of these briefings and mentioned to my supervisor about the technician in our building who did a great job but never seemed to receive any recognition for it. My supervisor shrugged the whole thing off as a little technical trick that did not matter. He felt that the "real stars" would be the people who managed the ensuing projects, like Delphi.

We feel that these managers had a bad view of individuals in projects. The manager of our sister organization felt that his technician was the star; other people played minor roles. My supervisor felt that program managers would be the stars; other people played minor roles. We believed that everyone played essential roles.

A warning sign of the simple view of individuals and teams is in a recognition program. Most of these programs give awards to individuals. Deming, the leader of the most successful quality programs of the 20th century, felt that there should be no individual awards. Singling out individuals meant that there were bright shining stars surrounded by a large area of dark. The large area of dark doomed an organization in the long term.

The vast majority of the people in the workplace contribute to the success of a good organization. The classic case is the award winner who wants to thank all the "little people." There are many people who enable the individual to do well. Their only reward is to be lumped into a group of "little people." Is that supposed to motivate them to continue contributing? People labeled as little will probably stop performing well on projects. When people stop performing, the projects are doomed.

The story of the bottom 10% was one distasteful example. The managers designated individuals to be on the dreaded list. These individuals became demoralized, and this showed in their work. The usual case was that a project that had a "bottom 10% person" working on it starting having problems.

Managers might explain that as, "Well of course, they had a poor performer on it."

Another explanation was that the person on the list was demoralized. That person had low self-esteem and spent a large part of the day grumbling about the entire bottom 10% list program. Complaining takes time and is contagious. The project suffered because the (un)awards program selected individuals.

Cause and Effect

Individuals are complex, and motivating individuals is a complex endeavor. A problem many managers have is that they have a simple view of motivating people.

A warning sign of this simple view is when managers discuss basic cause and effect relationships in recognition programs. The two stories at the start of this chapter were instances of this. The award-fee contract was simple: pay people more money if they do a better job. The bottom 10% list was also simple: discourage poor performers by putting their name on a list.

Simple cause and effect rarely exists with people. For example, cookies almost always motivate five-year-old children. We, however, work with adults who are complex and resent it when others assume they can motivate them the same way they might motivate a five-year-old child.

Consider the bottom 10% story. Putting people on the dreaded list would cause them to feel bad about their performance. They would work harder to improve their performance. The effect would be a better performing office. What could be simpler, and yet what could be farther from reality?

Simple cause and effect ideas ignore side effects. These are all the things that happen in our lives besides the "big things." Plenty of side effects occurred in the bottom 10% story. People had hurt feelings, did not understand what was happening, resented secret meetings, and stopped believing anything managers said.

We're Out of Control

As stated earlier, projects need individuals to build all but the most simple products. Given this, it would seem that managers would always remember the individual people. It is sad, but there are times when managers forget about people when they recognize them.

A warning sign of forgetting about people is when managers recognize them for things that are outside their control. There are things we cannot control—the weather, the state of the economy, government research dollars going into telecommunications technology, and so on. If someone were to base awards on the weather, almost everyone would protest. Many managers, however, base awards on the corporation's profits. It is true that the combined efforts of all employees have an affect on the corporation's profits. Often, however, the biggest factor on profits is the economy in general. As we saw in September 2001, a handful of terrorists can influence the economy beyond our control.

It is common for managers to award bonuses when the economy is good and withhold them when it is not. Such a practice completely removes the person from the situation. The manager is denying the individual by basing awards on things outside the control of the individual.

The story of the award-fee contract illustrated this problem. The zero award-fee affected everyone. The engineers who were working long and hard and producing good results in their areas were punished because of factors beyond their control. They had nothing to do with staffing levels, parts availability, logistics delays, etc. In the end, however, their salary reviews for several years were hurt by the zero award.

Events outside our control happen. When we give or withhold recognition in such cases, the best policy is to be candid in our explanation. If we give many and larger awards in a year when the economy is good, we should say, "This has been a good economic year. Therefore, we are able to distribute more and larger monetary awards."

If we give small awards in a year with the economy is bad, we should say, "The economy has been bad this year, and we have less money to distribute as part of our recognition program. People will receive less this year, but that does not mean they have contributed less to our group."

Substitutions

Recognition has a place in projects as most people like someone to appreciate their efforts and results. Many managers, however, take this to an extreme. They expand the thought that recognition is nice to the thought that recognition is everything.

When recognition is everything, managers substitute it for other things. This sign of coming problems is difficult to see. We have to ask questions at a deeper level such as, "Why are we giving this recognition? What do we want people to do? What could we do, other than give this recognition, that would accomplish the same thing?"

Most of the time, recognition is a substitute for clear communication. A manager wants to say something, but instead of saying it directly, uses a regular (annual, semiannual, employee of the month, etc.) award to try to say it.

The trouble with this is that the message becomes confused with the recognition. People think about the recognition, who received it, who did not receive it, why, why not, etc. They usually have strong emotions about the circumstances surrounding the recognition and the recipient. All the questions and emotions cloud their ability to hear the intended message.

The award-fee contract story is one example of substituting an award for something else. What we needed to do was have senior managers from the buyer and builder discuss the problems on the project. We could have communicated our concerns, the builder could have communicated their challenges, and maybe we could have come to a resolution. Instead, we gave a zero-award as our managers felt that would be the message in itself. They were wrong.

The bottom 10% story is another example of substituting a recognition program for something that was needed. We needed a program to reduce the number of employees. We could have done this via natural attrition, but we chose the bottom 10% recognition program. It did not work, and it produced a number of bad, unintended effects.

Here Comes the Judge

An inherent problem with any recognition program is that someone must decide who is recognized and who is not. Most of the problems we have seen with recognition programs come back to this impossible position for these "judges."

We have seen three main problems with people judging others for recognition. First, the judges are usually not qualified to judge the performance or results of others. The judges manage others for a living. They have lost most of their technical skills and lost touch with the work itself. They cannot judge the quality, quantity, difficulty, or importance of a person's work.

Second, the judges only see the surface of the situation and often miss who is really performing the work. Recognition often goes to someone who is sitting in a particular chair.

Third is how the judges judge. This is often done in the secret meetings. There are no notes sent out of the meeting, and no one outside knows what people say and consider. I was present during a number of award panels and was amazed at the ignorance of the judges. I was able to correct some of it with simple facts that were in the personnel folders in front of the judges. Those folders and the facts they contained, however, seemed to be of no interest.

The all-knowing managers were present in the story of the bottom 10%. These people were the judges who somehow, to date I still do not know how, labeled some people as being in the bottom 10%. Those people were shocked, they were not pleased, and their displeasure hurt their projects.

WHAT CAN WE DO TO MAKE AWARDS BETTER

Recognition programs are difficult. The stories and situations described above relate some of the problems we have seen. We have also seen techniques that create an environment where it is easier to reward people for their efforts. The following describe some of these techniques.

Communication

Good communication helps people in many situations, and recognizing people is one of those. We suggest striving for constant, clear, and consistent communication. Chapter 12 discussed communication at length and the Satir model of communication. We will not repeat that here.

Constant communication means speaking with every person every day. We should not have any gaps of months or weeks when we do not speak with a person or an organization.

Clear communication is having the other person receive the exact message we are trying to send. This is difficult, but we can approach this goal. We recommend using small words and short sentences. We deal with complex topics and issues, and explaining these with long, complicated sentences does not communicate them well. Think, break the topic into background, topic, and summary, and say it. Follow this with, "Please tell me what you heard."

Consistent communication is stating the same information every day. It does not work to tell one person that punctuality on the job is important and then present an award to someone else for "thinking outside the box." The first person will feel betrayed, and once trust is lost, it is almost impossible to regain.

Constant, clear, and consistent communication has much to do with improving a recognition program. People should know what is expected of them in terms of the cost, quality, and timeliness of their work. They should also know how well they are doing per the standards. If and when we give recognition, no one should be surprised.

The award-fee contract story is an example of terrible communication. The builder was shocked to receive a zero award because they thought "things were going fine." Failure to communicate expectations and status shot the builder's engineers through the heart.

The bottom 10% list was also a case of failed communications. Managers gave an inconsistent story on the program (was it intended to improve people, or was it a downsizing program?). People who received private visits from senior managers were shocked. They had always received good reports on their performance and had no indication that they were poor performers. The surprise visits demoralized people and caused lost productivity from those people and their coworkers.

Teamwork

We discussed earlier the importance of teams of people to projects. One way to create a good environment at work is to recognize teams instead of individuals. Emphasizing individuals is inconsistent with the praise given to teams.

We are not advocating eliminating individual recognition. We are advocating that we emphasize team accomplishment. The key word is "emphasize." We can recognize individuals, as there are times when that is warranted. These, however, should come after team recognition.

One technique to emphasize teams while recognizing individuals is team celebrations for individual success. Consider the case where two individuals, John and Bill, are part of a successful team and we want to give them individual recognition. We take the entire team to lunch and give them the afternoon off. John and Bill receive a few good words and a little round of applause. Everyone receives something (lunch and an afternoon off), and John and Bill receive individual recognition.

The lunch is one type of team celebration, but there are many others (dinner and overnight stay at a fancy hotel, company picnic, a day at the bowling alley, etc.). What works for one team may not work for another. Talk to your team and learn what is best.

Clear as a Bell

People often receive mysterious recognition. Several times in my career I have received awards with no clue about what I did to deserve them. I went to managers to learn the reason for the award only to be met with mumbles and generalities.

When someone receives recognition, it should be clear why. The person giving the award should state the specific time, place, situation, and action. A good guide is the WWWWWHH model. State who did what, when they did it, why they did it, where they did it, how they did it, and how much it contributed to the group.

Mysterious recognition produces mysterious behavior. If not stated clearly, people make wild guesses at what earned recognition. They act randomly trying to emulate that behavior.

The bottom 10% list is one example. People did not know why others had been placed on the dreaded list. In reverse, they did not know what they did to keep off the list. Was it working on the right project, doing the right extracurricular activities, giving briefings, going to the right office parties, etc.? No one knew, everyone made guesses, and many people started acting strangely trying to implement their guesses.

What Do You Want?

Giving a person or a team recognition can be difficult. It's like the Christmas gift quandary of what to give someone who has everything. It is good to give a person or team something they value, but what? The best advice we have on this issue is to ask the person what they would like.

Some people balk at this advice because asking a person what they want for recognition "ruins the surprise." We can think of two things here. First, why surprise the person? Surprises are often for the benefit of the person giving the recognition. The recognition is supposed to be for the benefit of the recipient. It may be fun to surprise someone, but that is not the objective of the exercise.

Second, "surprise" the person with the honor and give them the recognition they desire later. We advise congratulating the person on their accomplishment with kind words and a pat on the back (handshake, hug, whatever is appropriate). Tell them they will receive well-deserved recognition, ask them what they would like, and give them time (a few days, a few weeks) to decide.

Again we suggest using the WWWWWHH model. Ask them what they want, when they wish to receive it, with whom they wish to receive it, where they wish to receive it, how they wish to receive it, and how much they wish to receive. The "how much" may be a surprise. Most people will not say that they want a million dollars. They know what types of awards people usually receive for the type of work they performed. They will probably ask for less than you intended to give.

Different people want different recognition. Some want cash, others time off, and others a handshake and photograph with a person they admire. Standard gifts (office paperweight, plaque for the wall) say little about the person and the act they performed.

The Daily News

Several times in this book we have encouraged managers to talk with everyone every day. Here we go again, this time in regard to recognizing people. A basic recognition program is to award people daily with appreciation. The concept is to notice the person, notice their contribution, and show them that we notice.

We often have trouble saying nice things to people. If you think not, make a point today to tell five people (one at time) that you think they are doing a good job. Notice your feelings. We are not sure why we have trouble with this, but most of us do. It takes a little practice, but we can all become accustomed to it.

Here are some examples, "I appreciate that you took care of the meeting this morning, thank you." "I appreciate how you finished the test procedure on time and up to our standards, thank you." "I appreciate that you organized the office party, thank you."

Avoid the old cliches that do not make sense. Examples include, "I would like to thank you for . . ." (do not like to thank someone, thank them). "You have all done a good job on this . . ." (do not lump everyone together, thank them individually). "We appreciate how you . . ." (who is we?).

We want to mention a side topic here on a contribution to a project. We usually notice extroverted people, tall people, pretty people, people who stand in front, sit near the front office, give briefings, and other traditional things. We, however, do intellectual work often in front of a terminal or in a corner workbench. Discovering a new algorithm that optimizes a key attribute of a system is not always noticeable. This is especially true if the person doing that is quiet, humble, and does not tell anyone about it. We need to expand our definitions of leadership, contributions, and notice more.

Keep It Cool

A final note on recognition programs is to keep the monetary value of recognition at a relatively low level. If an award is 10% of a person's salary, they may press so hard to receive it that they make stupid mistakes. If they do not receive it, they may become destructive to themselves and those around them. They may become a substance abuser or person abuser.

The military gives medals that have little or no monetary value. They are purely symbolic, and the honor goes to the recipient. Recognition should be of a similar nature. People show the recipient honor and appreciation. Money has its place, but the appreciation of people is quite pleasing. Put the money into the everyday salaries of people.

SOME CONCLUSIONS ABOUT AWARDS AND RECOGNITION

People are an important part of projects. It is a tradition to recognize people who make outstanding contributions to projects. We have, however, seen recognition programs tear teams apart and destroy projects. This leads us to the principle of rewards: Recognition usually has unintended consequences.

Watch out for:

- Awards for individuals.
- Simple cause and effect relationships.

- Basing awards on things people cannot control.
- Substituting awards for other things.
- Who does the judging.

How to create a good situation:

- Use constant, clear, and consistent communication.
- Reward teams instead of individuals.
- Make clear what is being rewarded.
- Ask people how they want to be rewarded.
- Encourage people daily.
- Keep bonuses at a relatively low level.

People deserve appreciation from their colleagues and managers. There are ways to do this without damaging everyone and everything else.

The strangest recognition I ever received was when I was promoted in 1994. My division chief, a manager two levels above me, called me into his office for a private discussion. During our meeting, he leaned forward, spoke in hushed tones, and had this look on his face like he was about to tell me a deep dark secret. "I asked you here to tell you," he said in the most serious voice he ever used with me, "that you were promoted."

A few days later, I met with another manager one level above the division chief. He told me in a loud but stern voice, "There are a lot of people here who do not like you and did not want to promote you, but we promoted you anyway."

I felt like I had been praised and chastised at the same time. These contradictory feelings helped convince me to leave that organization and work elsewhere. I do not think that is what these managers had in mind when they went through all the trouble to promote me. Such are the side effects of recognition.

Part 5

The next three chapters discuss what happens when people do not work together as well as we would like. Chapter 15 discusses how one person working alone on a tough problem can dig into the problem so much that they lose track of where they are. Chapter 16 looks at the situation in which people respect or fear one another so much that they do not review each other's products. Chapter 17 discusses the problems we have when supervisors do not supervise adequately.

Digging Yourself into a Hole: Put Down the Shovel and Seek Outside Help

There comes a time in troubleshooting a problem when we believe that one more hour or one more day will yield a solution. The trouble is, we wake up one morning to see that we have dug a 20-foot hole and cannot climb out.

This chapter discusses an aspect of problem solving that really hurts. This is when we "get hooked" by a problem and cannot stop working on it. We work and work, but do not find an answer. We step back from our work and discover that we have lost track of time and everything else. This is tough on people and wreaks havoc on projects.

THE MEMORY BOARD

Once I was watching a technician who was replacing a memory board on a large computer. I needed to be with him while he worked (a long story that I will skip for now). It took the technician four hours to replace the memory board. This job usually took 15 minutes.

The technician inserted the board into the computer in about five minutes, but he could not bring the computer back to life. He ran diagnostics over and over again; he used the troubleshooting guide his company had written; he made a dozen phone calls to his local office and to the plant on the West Coast, and nothing worked. Time moved on. After an agonizing four hours, the computer was working again. I asked him about the solution.

It Sounded Good When We Started. By Dwayne Phillips and Roy O'Bryan
ISBN 0-471-48586-1 © 2004 by the Institute of Electrical and Electronics Engineers.

"Well," he said with a big grin on his face like he had just solved one of the universe's greatest problems, "you have to put the connector on just right."

I stopped breathing for a few moments. I had sat and watched a man work for four hours because he did not attach the connector cable correctly in the first five minutes. If he had checked that simple matter twice before he had turned on the power to the machine, we would have both had half a day to do something productive, and a dozen users could have used the machine. Instead, I sat and twiddled my thumbs. He went round and round and wasted not only his time but also the time of technicians in the field office and engineers in the plant.

He could have asked me what I would check. He could have asked other technicians in our lab what they would check. No one in his company asked him to check the cable connection because he told him that everything was connected correctly.

He spent the four hours digging himself deeper and deeper into the troubleshooting procedure. Had he put down his shovel, climbed out of his hole, and surveyed the situation, he might have seen the crooked connector.

THE CRACKED SOLDER

Toward the end of Delphi, the builder was having trouble with one circuit board. This board was complicated as it contained thousands of components and performed dozens of functions.

The board had an intermittent problem. These are the worst kind to find and fix because the board worked on some days and not on others. When it did not work, the trouble showed itself only under certain combinations of inputs.

The builder assigned the board's designer, Nate, to work on the problem. Nate was smart, hardworking, and sure to find and fix the problem.

Nate worked on this board for two months. That sounds extravagant and wasteful, but it was not. The components on the board were installed by craftsmen using 60-power microscopes and special machinery. The board contained thousands of components with tens of thousands of connections. We could not throw away the board and start over (we did think about that, though) as we did not have the time and money to do so.

The problem was related to temperature. It only showed itself after moving the board from room temperature to cold and then hot temperatures. That temperature cycling required several hours. Because of this, Nate could only run a few tests each day as he spent the rest of the time cooling and heating the board.

Since the temperature affected the problem, Nate looked at everything that might change its state with changing temperature. He analyzed the design and the parts used to build the board. He considered the materials in the components, the solder, and the board itself.

Nate created a flow chart of possible problems and the tests needed to investigate each problem. He worked his way through each test diligently, took detailed notes, and kept all test data organized. Every result gave Nate new theories and led him to create new possible problems and tests. Nate chased down every theory that came to mind.

After two months of digging into the problem, Nate did not have the answer. He knew many things that did not cause the problem, but he still did not know what did.

The rest of us tried to help. We sat with Nate while he raised and lowered the temperature of the board. He told us his theories and the tests he would run. We suggested new theories, he took note of them, and he designed and conducted tests for our theories. Nate dug deeper and deeper into the problem.

We started to notice that we were having a more difficult time talking to Nate about the problem. He was so wrapped up in it that nothing else seemed to matter. He was down deep into the hole he had dug trying to find the solution.

Finally, Nate took off a week for a long-planned vacation. Nate did not want to go on the vacation, but instead wanted to keep working on the problem. He had conducted a few special tests and was certain that he had found a new path to the problem's cause. All he needed was a few more days. Maybe he could work Monday and Tuesday, find the answer, and then take a three-day instead of five-day vacation.

We forced Nate to take his full vacation. He could find the answer in two days when he came back. One more week would not matter that much.

While Nate was on vacation, a young engineer named Steve walked into the lab and looked at the board. That is all Steve did; he looked at the board under a microscope. Steve did not know how the circuitry worked and he did not really understand what the board was supposed to do. Steve did, however, know how boards were supposed to appear under a microscope.

Steve noticed tiny cracks in the solder on the board. These cracks would expand and contract as the temperature of the board fell and rose. The resistance of the solder changed as the cracks changed. The solder in question connected a series of capacitors. Everything was falling into place. A fundamental of electrical engineering is that combinations of resistance and capacitance changes the timing of circuits. The board was experiencing timing problems.

Steve really did not understand all that. He did not know that timing was the problem as he had not participated in any of the troubleshooting meetings. Steve knew almost nothing about the problem compared to the rest of us. Steve, however, saw the cause of the problem in a couple of hours while the rest of us, Nate in particular, had spent a couple of months looking in vain.

The manufacturing people mended the cracks in the solder, we cycled the board through temperature changes, and we ran the tests. The problem was solved, and the board worked.

WARNING SIGNS THAT SOMEONE IS DIGGING A HOLE

The two stories above illustrate a situation we often find on projects. We have a problem, someone works on it, they work on it some more, they continue to work on it some more, we allow them to work on it yet some more, and we do not find the solution. Then someone wanders in, looks at the problem casually from a different perspective, and finds the solution in five minutes.

It is not surprising that someone can find a solution quickly when they approach it from a different perspective. The perspective of the investigator is often the most important attribute they bring. What is surprising is that we allow someone to dig and dig into a problem until they cannot climb out of the hole they have dug. At that point, the only approach seems to be to allow them to dig some more.

There are many things we have noticed that indicate that we are allowing someone to dig themselves into a deep hole. Most of these are things that people say. We have not always noticed these in time to stop the digging, but we are learning.

"I'm Sure"

One problem with a person troubleshooting a problem is a false sense of optimism. The person feels that a solution is near and they want others to stay back while they solve the problem.

A warning sign of false optimism is when the person says, "I'm sure it's in this area." There are two chilling things in this statement. The first is the word "sure." How can someone be sure about the problem that has frustrated them for so long? Sometimes there are clear indications of a problem and its cause, but we are not discussing those situations. Here, we are discussing problems in which a person has dug and dug in vain. A person in this case is sure of nothing. If they were, they would not have dug themselves into a hole.

The second problem with the statement is the phrase "it's in this area." We learned that when someone says that, we should look everywhere else but that area. Again, this person has a difficult problem. Everything indicates that they do not know where the problem lies. If they announce it is in one place, it is probably in another place. Look in those other places while the person looks in that one sure place.

Early in working on Delphi's circuit board, Nate told us that he was sure he knew where the problem was. He was wrong. He stopped using the "I'm sure it's in this area" statement. Unfortunately, he started using other statements that should have warned us of other troubles.

"One More Experiment"

People working a problem for days on end easily lose their way. There are a couple of states of being lost. One of them is losing track of where you have been and where you are now.

A warning sign of losing your way is the statement, "I want to try one more experiment." Sometimes this statement makes sense. If the one more experiment is the last in a sequence of logical and planned experiments, do it. This experiment may locate the problem and lead to a solution. This only works if it is part of a logical sequence.

More often, the one more experiment is something that just popped into the head of the person down in the hole. It is a slight variation of the experiment the person just finished. Sometimes the one more experiment is a repeat of something performed much earlier. The person repeats it because they did not keep a record of that earlier experiment.

This often happens to people in holes. They are looking for a solution so frantically that they do not do the things they know they should. Keeping accurate records of test setups, error indications, test results, etc. seems to go away. The person is sure they will find the solution quickly, so they do not waste time with paperwork.

We do not know how many experiments Nate performed on the circuit board. Under normal circumstances, he kept good records of his tests and their results. Looking for a problem for two months was not a normal circumstance. Therefore, Nate did not keep good records about everything.

Nate had a few more experiments he wanted to perform. He would have missed his vacation and performed these had the project manager let him. We are grateful that Nate postponed these until after his vacation. Steve had found the problem and the assembly people corrected it before Nate returned.

The Land that Time Forgot

Another way that people digging a hole lose themselves is they lose track of time. The hours, days, or weeks they have been digging all run together. They have no idea of how long they have been digging.

The next two statements are warning signs that the person down in the hole has lost track of time. These are, "I thought I had a couple more days to finish this," and "When do you need this?"

Time is not the most important thing in the world, but it is important in projects. There is a schedule, and there is a customer waiting for a product. When people have forgotten about time and schedules, they have lost the context of their work. The project is in trouble as this task, this problem, this hole they have dug for themselves fills all the time of their life.

Nate never went this deep into his hole on Delphi. He was aware that time was slipping. We knew this because he could talk to us about days on his vacation and the number of days to perform more experiments. That was a good sign, but we still had big problems on the project.

"He's Always Come Through"

Many of the people we have seen dig themselves into deep holes had lab fever. This is a malady in which a person lives physically and mentally where they are working on the unsolvable problem.

There are several warning signs of lab fever. One is that people with lab fever are true believers. First, they believe in their ability to solve problems. They have solved so many problems in their life that they become "a problem solver." This little title becomes their life, and they feel that they must live up to it.

True believers also believe in the rightness of the solution they are seeking. The problem is important, and finding the solution is important. These are good characteristics when kept in perspective, as we want to work with people who dedicate their energies to the project. We must, however, draw the line when people dedicate their lives to the project.

Finally, true believers believe that everything will come together. It has always been this way in their lives, and they are in their position of responsibility because of past successes.

People talk about the true believers with phrases like, "He's always come through." This is terrible because people are assigning a person's value to a circumstance in which they were given a problem and the resources to solve it. Sometimes, we have problems and do not have the resources to solve them. This has nothing to do with our value as a person.

The "always come through" statement should be fed back as, "He's always had the resources for the problem given him up to now. This time, we haven't yet given him the resources necessary. Let's do that now."

Another warning sign of lab fever is when a person who usually helps others with their problems stops helping. Some people on projects are known for their expertise. Other people go to them for advice, and the expert usually stops her own work and helps others.

All that stops when lab fever takes over. The problem has the expert's full attention. Other problems being worked by other people become far less important, so the expert turns down requests for assistance from other people.

Pay attention when an expert refuses requests for help. The expert may have lab fever.

Another warning sign of lab fever is when a person's home and family go away. We all work with people who spend long hours at work. We like this in some instances as it shows dedication to the project and it usually gets things done.

Such long hours at work become a bad situation if they continue past a couple of weeks. Healthy, happy people work well on the job; people suffering mental and physical exhaustion do not. More importantly, they are miserable people. Projects should not ruin lives, and lab fever can do that.

Lab fever is an addiction. The person becomes so attached to working a problem that the problem becomes their life. If they walk away from the problem, they have walked away from their life.

There are various reasons why a person with lab fever cannot walk away on their own. One is they do not want to be a quitter. They do not quit working on problems because they would disappoint others on the project and disappoint themselves. Quitting is also an admission of weakness. People know they are not perfect and they know there are problems they cannot solve. They know these things intellectually, but admitting them is difficult. Another reason they cannot quit is they do not know they can take a break. No one has approached them and told them it would be fine to stop for a while.

Many people with lab fever will not stop and seek help because they do not think anyone can help them. There is some logic to this reason. A person who has spent weeks on a problem knows much about it. If a "helper" arrived, the person would have to spend their time and energy teaching the helper all they know about the problem. It would take them weeks just to catch up to the current situation. How could the project wait for them to learn?

This all assumes that everything done to date was done well and in a logical manner. That assumption seems correct to the person with lab fever. It never enters their mind that maybe some of their digging was misguided because they were too close to the problem.

Finally, the person digging the hole may feel that it is not their job to take a break and ask for help. That is the manager's job. This is half-true, as the manager does need to do things, and we discuss those later. The problem solver, however, is also responsible for asking for help.

STOP THE DIGGING

A person digging himself into a hole is in a bad situation for himself and the project. It is almost impossible for the person to realize his situation and extricate himself. This is where we, the project manager or the buyer, must act. We need to stop the digging and pull the person out of the hole.

More important than helping people out of holes, we need to prevent people from picking up a shovel and starting to dig. We have learned a few things over the years that can help with all this needless digging. The following sections discuss a few of these lessons.

An Example Is Worth a Thousand Words

I have dug myself into holes in my career. On several occasions, I started to write a small and simple software utility that became a crater. A "couple-hour" task took two weeks. My biggest mistake on those occasions was not that I wasted my time. My mistake was that I did not tell my coworkers about my folly. They did not know that I too suffered from hole digging.

A project manager should set an example. We should admit that we, too, dig and dig until we are too deep to climb out. When we stumble, we should bring in help and let everyone know about it.

Setting an example is a good way to prevent others from digging holes. We are all human with finite resources, and some problems we face are bigger than our resources. There is no shame in admitting this and accepting help from others. If the project manager can do this, it is easier for everyone else to do it.

The computer technician trying to install a memory board was digging a fine hole. He would not admit his plight and ask me for advice. I could see he was struggling, but I did nothing to ease his fear of asking for help. Had I told him of some of my troubles, maybe he would have asked for help. That would have benefited everyone involved.

Talk is Cheap, but Worth a Lot

Time is an enabler for people who are digging themselves into holes. With little time, a person cannot dig a very deep hole. To keep time short, the project manager should check with everyone every day. The project has a plan that states what people should be doing. The project manager must gather status and learn what people are doing. By comparing reality to the plan, the project manager can see when someone is digging a hole.

The project manager should ask how people are doing on their tasks. The previous section discussed several things we hear when someone is digging a hole ("I'm sure it's in this area," "I just need one more day and I'm sure I'll find it," etc.). We need to listen for these and similar statements.

Checking with people every day helps keep any holes shallow and helps keep the project moving. When people leave me alone for several days, I begin to feel that I am alone. If I am having a problem with my work, I am on my own, so I start digging. In my experience, I rarely dug holes when people talked to me about my work daily. Their frequent chats convinced me that they cared. When I hit a problem, I usually went to them because I knew they cared.

We checked with Nate on Delphi regularly. The trouble was our regular checks occurred every two weeks. That was not often enough. We gave Nate the impression that we wanted him to solve the problem but were not ready to help him. We cared about the result, but not about him.

Triggers

Even with daily visits, it is difficult to tell someone they are in a hole and need help climbing out. One thing we have found that helps with this is to plan ahead. Before someone starts a difficult task, we need to set triggers. If they work X extra days without finishing, we should act.

Setting triggers helps the project manager in at least three ways. First, a trigger helps the project manager decide to act. The trigger set ahead of time removes some of the gut-wrenching decisions the project manager faces in the heat of a project. We hate to tell someone that we are bringing in help for them. We want to believe along with them that a solution is imminent. Making the decision while looking at their stern face is difficult. That is why we need to set the trigger point before the task begins. When things do not go as we would like, we must abide by the decision we made beforehand.

Second, the trigger helps the project manager act. Bringing in help is necessary if the project is to become "unstuck" and move forward again. Often, the project manager has a bigger problem than the person who is digging a hole. The person in the hole is working furiously. The project manager is paralyzed with the fear of telling an expert that they did not have the answer this time. The trigger helps the project manager overcome this fear.

Finally, the trigger helps the project manager say the words he should say. The trigger allows the project manager to say something objective like, "Nate, you had 10 days for this task and have worked 20 days. Per project policy, we are bringing in some people to look at this." That may be easier to say than, "Nate, I do not think you can solve this problem, so I am bringing in someone to do this for you."

The project manager did not have a trigger set with Nate on Delphi. He let Nate work and work for weeks. Nate set his own trigger—his vacation. Had Nate not had a vacation trip booked, we would have let him dig for who knows how long. Nate's trigger allowed us to bring in Steve, and he solved the problem in a couple of hours.

Bring in the Reserves

All the suggestions so far lead up to bringing in someone to help with a tough problem. Those suggestions mean little if the project manager does not have someone to call on for help. To do that, the project manager needs to keep people in reserve.

The project manager should keep these reserves out of the problem until needed. If he involves them early, they will be in the hole digging deeper and deeper themselves. Keep them out of the problem so that if the project manager calls, they will be fresh. They will bring a new perspective, new ideas, and new energy.

It is difficult to have reserves on a project. Someone has dug a hole because they did not have the resources they needed. If they did not have the resources, why should the project manager have resources on reserve? The reason the project manager should have reserves is that he is the project manager. Part of the project manager's job is to keep a list of outsiders who can help if needed. These outsiders need not be working on the project at this time. They are probably busy working on other projects. The trigger helps the project manager activate these resources. If someone is one-third the way to their trigger point, the project manager pulls the list of reserves out of the drawer. If someone is one-half the way to their trigger point, the project manager starts making phone inquiries. If someone is two-thirds the way to their trigger point, the project manager bangs on doors and asks upper managers to release people to him.

We did not have any list of reserves to help Nate on Delphi. Steve came in to look at the circuit board almost by accident, and no one expected him to solve the problem. We do not know what we would have done had Nate returned from vacation and had to face the problem. We did not know because we had not planned, set triggers, or had reserves.

And Now for Something Completely Different

The final suggestion we discuss here is that when bringing in help, do something different. A smart person has been working on the problem. They have tried many things, and none of them have worked. Do not repeat their steps. Too often, we do the opposite. If something has not worked, we try the same thing again.

The project manager should have the help try something different. They should look from a different perspective and try a different approach. If the first person tried a debugger, have the second use test scripts. If the first person tried a noise figure test, have the second try a timing test.

Steve solved the problem that plagued Nate by doing something different. Nate knew the functions of the board well. He tested it every way he could imagine to find the performance flaw. Steve knew nothing about the circuit board, so he just looked at it. Nate did electrical testing; Steve did visual testing. Nate looked at the performance of the board; Steve looked at the board itself.

CONCLUSIONS ABOUT DIGGING HOLES

Sometimes, we dig ourselves into a hole so deep we cannot climb out. We have allowed entire projects to sink into holes that were almost impossible to escape. A little help can stop this.

This leads us to the principle of putting down the shovel: Sometimes we accomplish more and faster by stopping and asking someone else to start.

Watch out for:

- "I'm sure it's in this area."
- "I want to try one more experiment."

- "I thought I had a couple more days before this was due."
- "He's always come through."

Try to:

- Set an example; get help now and then.
- Check with everyone every day.
- Set triggers ahead of time for stepping in.
- Hold someone in reserve.
- Do something different.

I have had the pleasure of working with many fine people in my life. Many of these people were able to do things that amazed me. Such accomplishments gave me confidence in their ability and gave them much self-confidence. I do myself, them, and our projects a great disservice when I allow their past success to convince me that they will always succeed. Smart people are stumped sometimes and dig themselves into deep holes. If we truly admire them and their ability, we need to stop them, pull them out of the hole, and let someone else look for loose connectors or cracks in the solder.

Knowing a few things about digging inescapable holes helped me while writing this book. Some chapters flowed easily from my mind into the keyboard. Most, however, did not, and some chapters were a monumental struggle. The lessons we shared in this chapter helped me with these especially difficult chapters. Instead of digging away, I stopped and went on to another chapter. I would come back to the troublesome chapter and pick up the shovel with new energy and a different perspective. Sometimes, the second attempt was much easier. If it was not, I would put down the shovel again and go on to yet another chapter. If I tried in vain three times on a chapter, I decided that it was a hole not worth digging. I filled in the hole and deleted the chapter from the book.

Chapter 16

Fear of Stepping on Superman's Cape: Not Holding Meaningful Internal Reviews

One of the few practices that most people agree are good for engineering and IT projects are internal reviews or peer reviews. In such reviews, people look at the products created by their peers. Those extra sets of eyes find defects that the creator missed.

Internal reviews are simple but, like most things that involve people, they can be difficult. We have seen organizations avoid internal reviews because of fears of all sorts, poor management, improper emphasis, and other problems. The result is that errors linger in the product. This chapter discusses some of the problems we have seen with reviews and ways to create an environment in which reviews are welcome.

WE DO NOT DO REVIEWS HERE!

We once worked on a project called Sigma in which the system contained a large software element. The application involved scheduling, equipment control, communications, and a large graphical user interface. This was $4M worth of software. The software project leader for the supplier was named Zeke.

About two-thirds of the way through the project we as the buyer visited for a regular monthly meeting. One of the standard questions we asked was whether Zeke and his team used internal code reviews.

"Oh, no," replied Zeke, "not on this project. We do not have that much time and money." Zeke was certain in his opinion. Reviews were for someone else on some other project, but they had no place on Sigma.

The months went by as Zeke and his team built the software and prepared for a full test. They coded and performed unit tests on small pieces of the software. This was all in preparation for one day integrating and testing the software system.

The project was not going well. Zeke's team and the other teams on the project were behind schedule. The hardware was not working, and people did not have much hope for the software working either. Morale was low.

The day arrived for testing. The result was not surprising; it was disappointing, but not surprising. Testing required six weeks and experienced over 200 failures. We were not sure how many defects we had in the software—at least 200, maybe more.

Zeke's management brought in some extra help to look at this situation. After a couple of months, they felt there were 240 defects in the software. They used some corporate history and financial information and estimated that it would cost $4M to correct the errors. The cost to fix the errors would equal the cost to create them.

Our upper management had a number of meetings with Zeke's upper management. We considered where we were, what we had promised our users, and what it would cost us to start over with another supplier. We decided to stay with Zeke's company.

One of the agreements made by upper management was that the supplier would use better software practices. Among the list of better practices was internal reviews. Zeke was not too happy with this, but he would do as he was told.

REVIEWS WORK GREAT HERE!

Zeke and his team went to work fixing the 240 defects. There were a few significant changes on the project, including a new project manager. The new man, Peter (the same Peter who was a great project manager on Delphi; see Chapter 11) was good at his job. He planned well, tracked progress closely, and reported the situation to us monthly.

Zeke and his team started using internal reviews. At first, these required hours of preparation time and several hours for the review itself. People were not sold on the idea of reviews. Few people are sold on an idea when management dictates it to them.

The project slowly turned around. Instead of a mess with 240 defects, there were 239 defects, then 238, and so on. The people on the project were starting to think that things might work. They had a long way to go, but they were on schedule. In fact, they were a little ahead of schedule. They were able to find and fix nine out of ten defects faster than anticipated. This was the first time they had been ahead of anything since the project started several years earlier.

There is something about success that breeds success. People feel better about themselves and what they are doing. They are happier when they come to work, their minds are clear, and they do better work.

The internal reviews started to work. Zeke and his team prepared for and performed reviews more quickly. They found errors on paper in the reviews and saved time in testing. This was a surprise at first, as none of the team members had ever seen reviews work.

Soon the reviews almost became unnecessary. Each person was able to think ahead to the review. They saw their errors before going to the reviews and corrected them on their own. The reviews went faster, there were fewer errors, and testing the individual fixes went quickly.

We saw the change in attitude during a routine visit when we asked Zeke how the reviews were going. He praised their value. They saved time, found mistakes, prevented waste, paid for themselves, improved morale, and on and on. This was the same person who nine months earlier told us, "Oh, no, not on this project. We do not have that much time and money."

The months went on, and the work proceeded. Zeke's team found and fixed all 240 errors. In the process, they found several dozen more errors and fixed those, too. The total fixes took less time and money than estimated.

The project ended as planned with the integration testing being almost a formality. The testers found a few more defects that were corrected quickly.

Reviews were not the only thing that turned around this project. The new project manager brought a new attitude to work every day. A couple of excellent maintenance programmers joined Zeke's team, too. Attitudes changed, and that means so much on software projects.

SIGNS THAT REVIEWS ARE NOT WORKING

Internal reviews work. Nevertheless, Zeke and his team avoided them during the first part of Sigma. Their reluctance was in spite of a corporate policy requiring everyone on all projects to use internal reviews.

There are signs that indicate trouble with reviews. We have also seen signs that people are conducting internal reviews in name only. The following relate some of these signs that we have seen.

Reviews Cost Too Much

Reviews have a positive return on investment as they save more money and time than they cost. If reviews are costing more than they save, people are not conducting them properly or not using the results properly. The problem is that people are attempting techniques for which they are not trained. A warning sign of people attempting reviews without proper training is what Zeke told us when he said, "Reviews cost too much." Zeke was right. He and his team had not been trained in how to conduct reviews. Therefore, they had many of the problems and lacked many of the benefits discussed in this chapter.

Poorly run reviews spell coming trouble for a project. Defects in the product, and there are always defects in the product, will linger. The team will find them long after they were introduced. This delay will mean that the defects will be harder to correct. The project will fall behind schedule and overrun its budget.

This was the story of the early phases of Sigma. Reviews were tried and dropped by the team because they were wasteful. The defects in the code went undetected until the software integration testing. The tests showed that the software was full of defects (over 200 of them). What is worse is that the team spent the entire project budget to reach that conclusion. The buyer had to double the project's budget to correct the defects and deliver a working product.

"Reviews Are Meetings"

Most people in technical fields hate meetings. We are in technical work because we enjoy the work, and much of it is one-on-one—me working along with the problem. Meetings only take time away from real work.

Reviews are not meetings. The most common meeting is the status or staff meeting. Everyone on the project gathers in a meeting room and first listens to the project manager talk for half of the allotted meeting time (the standard meeting is one hour long). After the project manager finishes, we "go around the table" and allow each person to say something. These things are usually one-on-one conversations with the project manager while everyone else appears to be interested. Eventually, it is my turn to talk with the project manager. I have to think of something significant to discuss or I appear insignificant. These are painful and wasteful meetings.

Staff meetings bear no resemblance to a review that is conducted properly. Reviews concentrate on the quality of the product. There are many excellent books that discuss this subject in depth [1, 2], and the final section of this chapter provides some tips. It is our choice whether we conduct them well or poorly.

A warning sign of trouble on a project is when people are referring to reviews as meetings. They do not see the difference between the basic staff meeting and a review. This means the team is not conducting the review properly.

Zeke and his team conducted reviews properly in the second story about Sigma. The reviews found many defects in the product, and after each review, the producer would improve the product. As they gained experience with reviews, the team members were able to create better products before the reviews.

All-Day Reviews

An important part of a good review is the preparation. The reviewers study the product individually before the review. This may involve reading a document, studying a set of design drawings, or reading source code.

Many people dislike the preparation part of reviews. This is especially true of some programmers, as they hate to read other people's source code. They feel that their job is to write code. Reading code is for someone else.

A major problem that can plague reviews is when people are not prepared for them. Ask people directly, "Have you spent X hours reading this code in preparation for this review?" If the answer is no, stop. Do not hold the review until everyone is ready.

One warning sign that people are not prepared for a review is when the review degenerates into an all-day meeting. What is happening is that the group is studying the product together. A review should only last about one hour. A team can hold two or three reviews in one day, and that is the limit because reviews require high levels of concentration. People cannot do this for more than three hours in a day. Any more, and the effectiveness of the review drops drastically.

The project manager should always watch for people grumbling about preparing for a review. It takes a while to learn how to read code just as it takes a while to learn how to read anything. Most programmers do not participate in enough reviews to learn this skill. Make sure that part of the review has the code writer walking through the code explaining it to everyone else. This makes the reading easier and helps people learn how to read code.

"Let Them Find Their Own Mistakes"

In a review, people spend time looking at products created by their peers. The purpose of the review is to find any defects in the product. After the review, someone, usually the person who created the product, removes the defects. This works well for the team as long as the project has a team. When the project has a collection of competing individuals, reviews have big problems.

A warning sign of competition instead of cooperation is when people murmur, "Let them find their own mistakes."

Engineering and IT work is knowledge work. The products come from the minds of people on the project and, in good teams, people share their knowledge and experiences. Reviews are one of the best places for such sharing. Some people, however, do not want to share their knowledge. They feel that it belongs to them and others are not privileged to it.

Few projects can succeed when people are allowed to be on the team roster without playing a part on the team. This form of elitism prevents any synergy on the team. If one person will not share knowledge, why should anyone else? If no one shares knowledge, the project team is only as strong as the weakest member, and the project is doomed.

This happened to an extent in the first story of Sigma in this chapter. People did not want to participate in reviews. If they helped improve someone else's product, they would be giving that person an edge in competitive salary reviews. Note the words "someone else's products" and "competitive." The words "our products" are missing and so are the words "cooperative salary increases." Sigma did not have a team working on the project. Instead, it had a group of individuals who happened to sit near one another and whose products happened to (only sometimes) integrate into a system. The desire to avoid reviews showed that the team was not a team and the project was doomed. We failed to notice that in time to prevent a disaster.

"You Don't Step on Superman's Cape"

Most projects have a team member who stands out because of their expertise, productivity, quality of their work, and other desirable qualities. That person is the "superman" or star performer of the project. Along with the desirable qualities that the superman brings, he also brings something that pushes people away from reviews. This is summarized by the phrase "do not step on superman's cape."

Sometimes we hear, "Joe is working on that part. He always comes through, so we are not concerned about that part." What usually follows from this confidence in Joe is that the project team does not examine Joe's product in an internal review.

There is some logic behind this. Suppose Joe has a long record of success, and his products have had no or only small defects. Why should we "waste time" reviewing them? We probably will not find any problems. The product will have the same quality after the review as it did before the review, which brings lots of pain and no gain.

Not using reviews on Joe's product misses a key benefit of reviews—education. People learn when reading and discussing code written by others. If Joe is a superhuman programmer, the project manager should want everyone to read and discuss his code. That is the quickest way to teach everyone the programming art of a master.

We have found other reasons why people avoid reviewing the code written by Superman. One is that people may be afraid to embarrass Joe. He has the reputation of carrying the team, and if someone hurts his confidence, he may not carry the team anymore. What will the team do then? Will the team be able to carry on and succeed without a confident leader?

In addition, if I embarrass Joe while reviewing his product, what will he do to me when he reviews my product? He does have x-ray vision. He could see right through my products, find all my mistakes, and show them to everyone in the review. This is starting to sound a little silly. It is, however, what people do on occasion.

Another reason to avoid reviewing Superman's code is that I may be wrong when I think I see an error. Suppose I find what I think is an error and mention it in the review. Joe may look at it and show me (in front of everyone) that I was mistaken. His code was correct all along. Now how do I look in front of everyone? I took a shot at Superman only to be proven wrong. I think next time I will just keep my mouth shut.

Finally, people may avoid reviewing Joe's work due to a mistake of optimism. They want Joe's product to be in great shape because someone on this project needs to do something right. Therefore, the team should not waste resources looking at his work. The team should move forward, being confident that Joe never makes mistakes and his product is fine.

The problem is that Joe isn't superhuman. He may have a record of building good products in little time at little expense. That is great, but, Joe, like everyone else, is only human. It is not right for anyone to treat him as something else. If people depend on him for performing some magic in difficult circumstances, they are being unfair to him and belittling their own abilities. They need to regard and treat Joe the same as they do themselves. We are all fallible people working on a project. We review one another's products to improve the products and educate ourselves.

HELPING REVIEWS

Reviews were one of the practices that helped turn around Sigma. As the preceding discussion showed, there are many things that keep people from using reviews effectively. We have seen a few things that help people and projects work around these difficulties. The following discuss some of these.

The Blame Game

Fear inhibits good reviews. Some people are afraid to have their peers look at their work, and other people are afraid to point out mistakes that their peers have made. We cannot remove all the fears of all our people. As a project manager, however, we can reduce fears by working to remove blame from reviews.

We all make mistakes frequently. If we had people who did not make mistakes, they would not work with us for long. They would leave and start a one-person company. Removing blame means that we do not point fingers at people. When someone makes a mistake that the review team catches, make note of it, assign someone to fix it later, and move on.

Some may argue, "So what. We work with adults. Professionals will not pout about it when I point out their mistakes. They'll work harder next time to avoid a little temporary embarrassment." That may be true with a few people. Nevertheless, it is our experience that most people do not take well to, "Hey, you messed up big time, stupid. Now we will fall behind trying to fix your mess!"

Removing blame is especially important when trying to use reviews for the first time. The first few reviews may be rough because people are not sure what to expect. This happened in the second story of Sigma in this chapter. People did stumble, and the first few reviews were longer than desired. The project manager, however, kept people at ease by keeping blame to a minimum.

The Product and the Producer

Reviews look at the quality of products. People create these products, but people are not the subject of reviews. Products are things and people are people. People have lives, families, and other people who depend on them. Things are just things and are replaceable.

We should keep reviews in perspective. Sometimes, in a review where we are finding one error after another we become tired and frustrated. All perspective is gone, and we lash out at people.

We have found it best that when tired we say, "we are tired." If that is the case, stop and try again tomorrow. Reviewing products is difficult work that requires fresh minds. If you or others are tired, do not hold the review today. The results (the product) will be bad. The side effects (crushing people) will be worse.

A way to help keep the product and producer separate is to keep the results of reviews anonymous. Most people in technical fields observe and record data. Internal reviews are one place where we need to change the norm. We record the number and type of defects found in a product during a review, but we do not record who found what and who created the defects. Keeping score on people destroys reviews.

If a review finds ten defects in module A, record it as, "We found ten defects in module A." Do not record it as, "Tom found five defects and Bill found five defects in module A, which was written by Dave."

Another way to keep products and producers separate is to prevent managers from attending reviews. Some managers want to attend reviews to observe how they are done. If that is the case, hold a mock review so they can see. Other managers want to see how the people perform under pressure. Let them walk around during the day and talk to people.

There are many bad things that can happen with managers in reviews. Some people are afraid to say anything in front of their manager, and other people are afraid to stay quiet in front of their manager. Jumble up six people with these two tendencies, and chaos rules. The review turns into an acting festival with the result that people forget about it while they are busy "acting right" in front of the manager.

A final way to keep the focus on the product is to have and use standards for the products being reviewed. Some people do not like coding standards as they stifle creativity. Standards can be written and used incorrectly, but they make it so much easier to review products and not people. Standards help keep the focus on the product and they also give people a way to point out defects without being too personal. A later section on how to talk in a review will discuss this point further.

We Are All in This Together

The projects in our careers that were both successful and fun had great teams. Someone in the team, sometimes the project manager and sometimes someone else, was able to instill in everyone the idea that we were working as a team. This concept of the team is a key to creating a good environment for reviews.

Reviews will show time and again that we all make mistakes. Products going into reviews have defects, and those defects did not climb into the product by themselves. People (our coworkers) put them there. With a good team environment, however, someone's mistake is merely a defect in our product. Tomorrow, the team will review a product I created, and I hope they find the mistakes I made. That attitude for reviews helps improve our products.

A good technique the project manager can use is to have people review his work. The project manager makes products (schedules, task descriptions, plans, etc.). These products contain mistakes, and if the team can find and fix the mistakes, everyone benefits. Hold internal reviews on the project manager's products. Present the materials to the team, tell them the standards for such products, and allow them to find the mistakes. The project manager should let the team see how he reacts when people find mistakes and improve the product. Do not be defensive during these reviews. People will follow the project manager's lead when it is good and when it is bad.

The project manager on the second part of Sigma was able to do these things. He first created a schedule for the project and put this up on the wall for the team to review. They made drastic changes to it, and he reacted with a good attitude. He preceded to create an environment conducive to teams. Once the individuals felt comfortable as a team, they worked well in reviews.

Speak with Care

The words people use in reviews can cause many problems. The next few paragraphs provide some suggestions on how to talk in reviews. Most of us "techies" give little thought to what words come out of our mouths. As shown later, it does matter. The three tips we have are (1) talk about things not people, (2) use inclusive language, and (3) qualify your statements.

First, talk about things, not people. This relates to the idea of keeping the review about the product and not the producer. A good statement to make is, "This construct violates standard ABC." This statement is all about things. It relates the product to the standard.

A bad way to say this is, "You violated standard ABC." Here we are talking about the standard and the producer. The producer will not appreciate this and can become defensive quickly. Now the review degenerates into people defending themselves against other people. The quality of the product is no longer in the discussion.

Try to use inclusive words. The "you" word used above is an exclusive word. It points to "you" as someone not associated with "me." The team is broken. Inclusive language sounds like, "We have a problem here in that we've violated standard ABC." We created the problem, we wrote the standard, and we found the defect. We are a team working together to build a product. Any mistake by any of us affects our product.

Finally, we need to qualify our statements. An example is, "I do not understand how this will work." This starts to sound like we are breaking the inclusive language rule, but we are not, because we are talking from ourselves about the product.

A poor way to say this is, "This will not work." That is a declaration that the producer has made a fatal error. We have also declared our omnipotence because we are certain this will not work. We may be wrong. In my career, I have seen many things that I thought could not possibly work, but then I saw them work.

Another qualified statement is, "I've never seen this approach work in a situation like this before." This is a true statement about my experiences and me. The product may work fine, and I may learn something new. On the other hand, the product may have a defect. I have stated my ignorance and my question without attacking the producer.

We have met many engineers and programmers who want nothing to do with these three tips on talking in a review. Many people feel that their peers are adults and they should not have hurt feelings. We hear things like, "I do not have time to tread lightly. We have work to do here. If he cannot take it he should get out."

We urge you to remember that we are working with people. Few of us have enough people to do the work we have to do. How many people can we waste? How many people can we hurt and cause to sulk?

Another way to look at this is that people care and take pride in their work. If we destroy these qualities, we have people who do not care and do not take pride in their work. Which would you rather have in your workplace? We can influence this situation with a little thought and care.

CONCLUSIONS ABOUT REVIEWS

The point of reviews is to improve the quality of the product. We said that a number of ways in this chapter, but we wanted to state it one more time as plainly as we could. As managers, we must remember that, say it all the time, and act like we believe it.

Reviews have helped project after project to create good products. It would seem that something so beneficial would be practiced universally. The trouble with reviews is that they depend heavily on people, and people can sometimes act against their best interest.

This brings us to the principle of reviews: Review everyone's work.

Watch out for:

- "Reviews cost too much."
- "Reviews are just another meeting."
- All-day reviews.
- "Let them find their own mistakes."
- Superman's cape.

Help reviews by:

- Remove blame.
- Review the product, not the producer.
- Remember that "we are all in this together."
- Speak with care.

The essence of reviews follows from their origin. That is, "To err is human." We all fail from time to time. We all also seem to be able to see the errors of other people easily. This means that other people can see our mistakes easily. If we can see beyond "my" and "your" mistakes and concentrate on the quality of the product and the success of the team, we can employ reviews effectively.

I recently led a team that wrote a policy for an organization of 10,000 people. Much of our efforts went into writing the policy and creating a presentation to convince people the policy was the right one for us. I wrote a report that contained the details of everything we did and what we recommended. I also wrote a presentation that summarized our activities and gave our recommendations. These two items required about 100 hours of my time. I went through them again and again, being as sensitive as I could to find errors in logic, presentation, and basic typos.

Once a week, the team met to review what I had created. I hated those team meetings because everyone picked on what I had done. I had to put on my thickest skin so their criticisms would not hurt me. By the way, their criticisms improved the quality of the product dramatically. Without them, our recommendations would have fallen flat. Given the review of the team, the recommendations were adopted and became official policy quickly.

Such is the plight of the person subjecting themselves to reviews. We have to be sensitive to many things to create our product. When the review occurs, we have to be insensitive so the comments of others do not hurt us. This switch between sensitive and insensitive is difficult. The resulting product, however, is much better.

REFERENCES

1. *Handbook of Walkthroughs, Evaluations, and Technical Reviews,* Daniel P. Freedman and Gerald M. Weinberg, Dorset House, 1990.
2. *Software Inspection,* Tom Gilb and Dorothy Graham, Addison-Wesley, 1993.

Chapter 17

Not Providing Adult Supervision: Do the Junior Team Members Really Need Mentoring?

We all have a first time for everything. After the first time, there may be a second time, third time, and so on. Each time is an experiment, and experiments build experience.

Most project work is performed by people who have less experience than we want. In addition, the supervisors, managers, and team leaders have more experience than those doing the work. The supervisor's job is to supervise or watch the workers perform work. To those who have not supervised, this may sound easy. To those who have supervised, we know that sometimes it is not an easy task. We often wish we were back "just banging out code."

One of the supervisor's tasks is to teach or coach the less-experienced workers. The workers make decisions each day on how to implement a subroutine, perform a test, design a circuit, etc. Often they make good decisions, but sometimes they do not. Their mistakes or poor choices are part of experiments that build up experience. The customer, however, is not interested in how much the worker learned while building the product. The customer wants a good product, not one filled with many lessons to be learned.

The supervisor needs to perform a balancing act. He or she should let the worker make decisions, but should also step in and "correct" the worker when they make a poor decision. This is not easy. The supervisor can step in too often and too harshly. This causes them to be labeled micromanagers (one polite label—there are many others that are not so polite) and can cause people to leave the team and search elsewhere for a supervisor who is not so heavy-handed. The supervisor can also stay too far back and allow too many

It Sounded Good When We Started. By Dwayne Phillips and Roy O'Bryan
ISBN 0-471-48586-1 © 2004 by the Institute of Electrical and Electronics Engineers.

poor decisions to ruin the product. This brings dissatisfied customers and workers who are not learning.

This chapter discusses some of our experiences with supervisors who did not mentor less-experienced workers quite enough. The result was wasted effort, much rework, and projects that had cost overruns and schedule slips. We also try to balance this with problems that micromanagers bring.

THE PORTABLE CONTROLLER

We told this story in the Chapter 7 while discussing requirements. The moral to this story is the lack of adult supervision that Ronald had. His supervisors were there, but they did not provide sage counsel. They did not apply their perspectives and experiences to the situation.

A key part of the system we were building on Delphi included a laptop computer that would attach to the system's main unit. While attached, the laptop computer would enable the user to program the main unit similar to programming a VCR at home. The user could then detach the laptop computer and the main unit would perform as programmed.

It was also possible to keep the laptop computer attached to the main unit. In that configuration, the user would control the main unit like controlling a VCR by pressing the front panel buttons. This allowed the user to experiment with the main unit and run diagnostics on it.

Our anxious engineer named Ronald found a palmtop computer to use as an alternative to the basic laptop computer. This was not like the Palm PDAs of the late 1990s. The palmtop machine had a complete QWERTY keyboard and a text-based screen (80 × 25 characters). It opened like a laptop and fit in the palm of your hand.

Ronald discovered this computer at a trade show. This was really neat and it was new. So new, in fact, that the salespeople at the manufacturer's booth did not know about it. Ronald found it at the Japanese booth of that manufacturer. The Japanese branch of the manufacturer was building it, and the palmtop computer was not to be sold in the United States.

Ronald had to have it. Ronald had the project buy two dozen of these (Japanese keyboard and all) so we would have plenty in case some failed in a few years. No one had any idea what the Japanese characters or symbols on the function keys meant, so we had to build a template for the users. The project moved along as planned and we worked the palmtop computer into the system. In those days, the basic laptop computers ran MS-DOS. The palmtop ran MS-DOS, so it was compatible.

During the next few years, laptop computer technology moved forward. Laptops started using 386 and 486 processors, whereas the palmtop computer used a variation of the 286 processor. This did not cause problems. The processors and system architectures were similar enough so that the software environment needed for the palmtop worked on the laptops.

As we moved into the mid-1990s, laptop computer technology kept moving forward. MS-DOS slowly gave way to MS Windows. The palmtop would not work in that environment. We stayed with the palmtop computers and we stuck with the MS-DOS environment.

The laptop computers we were using had worn out (because of a tough environment and heavy use). We bought new laptops, but the laptops had advanced so much that it was difficult to find ones that would still work with the old MS-DOS environment needed by the palmtop. The builder had to search hard to find a backward-compatible laptop. They had to rework the software so it would function in both the new laptops and the old palmtop. All this software rework was costing us a lot of money.

After several years of keeping the palmtop and the laptops running the same software, we dropped the palmtop. Ronald left the project, and other people arrived who were not enamored of the palmtop. This had something to do with the serial cable that connected the controlling computer to the main unit. The serial cable we used was extra heavy and extra thick—like an elephant's trunk. There were good reasons for the large bulky cable, so it had to stay.

Dropping the palmtop computer from the system did not end our problems. We were stuck in the "286 protected-mode" software environment of the palmtop. We had to continue in that mode because we had invested so much money and time in it. Now the builder had to find laptop computers that would work in that old software environment. This continued to cost a lot. We were wrestling with this problem years after Ronald discovered that cute little palmtop computer.

The root of the multimillion-dollar problem was that Ronald had lost sight of the essence of the controller. The large, bulky cable that connected the controller and the main unit was a project constraint that was nonnegotiable. Cute little computers did not help any. The limiting factor was that elephant's trunk cable.

The disappointing thing about this story is that Ronald had supervisors on this project. No one gave Ronald absolute authority to do anything he wanted and take the project in any direction he wanted. He had to take his ideas to his supervisors before he implemented them. After all, our organizational structure was a classic hierarchy.

What were Ronald's supervisors thinking? They did not see the problems the palmtop computer could bring. They did not see the folly of a computer smaller than the interface cable. They did not see the problems that a COTS computer could have in the future. They did not stop Ronald from going down the garden path. By not stopping Ronald, one can only assert that his supervisors did not have the technical background, experience, or education to mentor or were so distracted by other matters that they chose not too become involved. Not getting involved is a conscious decision, deferring is a conscious decision, and having no decision is a conscious decision

It appears that they fell into a hands-off style of supervision or deference managing—no mentoring. If Ronald had looked at the situation and recommended something, they would approve it carte blanche. Supervisors often do this. They do not have the time to look at all the details and they do not want to micromanage. They spend their time avoiding things instead of supervising.

YET ANOTHER CONTROL INTERFACE

We had a situation later in Delphi in which we were able to provide some supervision and assistance. Our users had received a couple of the systems and they were performing experiments. One experiment was putting a wireless control interface on the product. This would remove the big, thick interface cable. This was a neat idea that could add useful capability to the product. The builder had thought about this idea, but had not worked on it because they had plenty else to do.

The users thought they had the wireless interface working just fine. The product, however, was more complex than they knew. It had many necessary features that the users had neither learned nor used. They overlooked these features and they did not know how to test them with their wireless interface.

The users were so proud of themselves that they wanted to show off their new control interface. The users were about to embark on an important business trip and they wanted to demonstrate Delphi using only the wireless interface. They had decided on their own that they would demonstrate the utility of the wireless interface on this trip.

We learned of these plans via hallway conversations. A number of questions came to mind. How did the users know this would work? Had the users rehearsed everything they would do on the trip? Had the users repeated the complete system testing on the wireless interface? Had the users told anyone about their intentions? Why did the users want to use this interface on this trip? Was it necessary? Was it fun? Was this an excuse for taking the trip?

This put us in a puzzling position. We could inform upper management that these users were putting the organization at risk by trying unproven technology on an expensive and important trip. Upper management would then reprimand them for their risky actions. We could also let these users go on their trip and fail miserably. They would be caught in the postfailure investigation. That might teach them and others like them a "good lesson."

After some thought, we decided to try to provide some adult supervision. We arranged for these users to take their wireless interface to the builder for a demonstration. That demonstration showed the perils and pitfalls of this experimental interface. The builder worked with the users and they modified the system to work in the limited modes needed for the trip with the experimental interface. They also performed enough system testing to ensure the trip would succeed.

This all worked well. We were fortunate in that someone heard about these experiments and the planned trip in the hallway. We were also fortunate that we did not act rashly but, instead, worked with the users to improve their chances of success. These two users also displayed good, rational thought in accepting our offer of assistance and working with the builders. They decided correctly that a little supervision and assistance might help them.

SOME ADULT SUPERVISION REQUIRED

The previous two stories related how sometimes a lack of supervision allows people to run amok with a bad idea and how sometimes just enough supervision produces good results. We have had more cases of poor results from lack of supervision than from too much. We have noticed warning signs that indicate that poor supervision exists. Below we discuss some of these.

Hide and Seek

There are many fine engineers who love to work in quiet. They toil away in their cubicles and labs for hours on end and much of their work is neither seen nor heard. This lack of sight may be a side effect of working diligently and quietly. It may, however, be a result of hiding things deliberately.

Buyers and project managers tend to trust these strong and silent people. We have every reason to do so because they usually do good work and build good products. Another reason is that we have enough problems facing us each day. There is little reason to go hunting for more trouble.

Some hunting is part of being a supervisor and of providing some needed supervision. There is an important tension between trust and supervision happening here. Trust is a belief we hold. We trust our engineers and believe that what they are working productively. When they tell us something, we believe them. Supervision is a job we do. We are responsible for the resources expended and products produced on a project. Therefore, we supervise. This includes talking to people, checking on products, and asking plenty of questions.

We trust people and supervise them at the same time. This is not "I trust you, but cut the cards." It is, "I trust you, but we know that you and I both make mistakes, so we look at one another's work and play our cards face up. Since I am being held accountable for your work, I need to see what you are doing while you are spending project resources. Other people look at what I am doing, too."

When people hide things, it is a warning sign that the supervision is causing trouble for the project. The person may have some aversion or fear of the supervision. Two possible reasons are (1) the person does not like supervision and (2) the person does not like my supervision.

If (1) is the reason, the person needs plenty of supervision and consultation; in other words, the project manager needs to talk to the person about supervision. Supervision is part of working at work instead of a hobby at home (all nagging aside). Almost everyone in almost every work situation has a supervisor. This is a responsible task that project managers and others perform. It is not a personal assault on a person's character.

If (2) is the reason, I have to work on how I supervise people, and the two of us need to work together to help the supervision work for both of us. I may be doing something that frightens the person into hiding their work. That has never been my intent, but I cannot say that it has never been the result. Supervising is difficult work, and different people need different types of supervision. We discuss several tips for improving supervision later in the chapter.

In the story of the wireless controller, the users were not hiding; at least we think they were not. They were not volunteering information to us, so maybe they were hiding. Whatever the case, we were fortunate that we learned of their plans, that we were able to offer help, and that they were willing to listen to us.

Plan? What Plan?

There are many tasks to perform on a project. Those tasks are planned with a start and an end date. They have preceding and succeeding tasks with products flowing into and out of each task. Sometimes, however, we have found people performing tasks out of sequence. The people were working hard and producing high-quality products. Nevertheless, the products did not feed into anything in the project.

When people work outside the project plan, that is a warning sign that the supervisor has not been supervising. The supervisor has let the person doing the work "go dark." This means the person has figuratively if not literally gone off in a corner and worked on something that was interesting to them. Maybe it related to the project, but probably it did not.

The work they did wasted resources. The money spent on that work was charged to the project, but did not add to it. The time was also lost. The person was supposed to be doing something for the project. Instead, they were doing something else. The project is now behind schedule and over cost.

The supervisor failed the project and the person. Had the supervisor supervised, he or she would have discovered the person working on other things. A quick chat could have brought the person back into the project where he was needed.

One of the worst aspects of this situation is that the supervisor has to tell the person that he is throwing away the product of their efforts. Nothing hurts more to a person who takes pride in their work. Nevertheless, that is what must happen.

Experiments

Many people we know love to perform experiments. Experiments increase the level of experience, increase knowledge, and lead to better products. Experiments also increase the satisfaction that people have in their jobs. They enjoy the exploration and knowledge that comes with experiments.

Like the tasks discussed above, some experiments fit in the current project or they help with an upcoming project. People have considered the situation, discussed the experiments, and obtained approval.

It is unfortunate, but many experiments people perform are not related to a project. They are done with all good intentions, but they do not connect to current or upcoming projects. Like unplanned tasks, they waste resources, with the most precious waste being the energy of the person performing the needless experiment.

Experiments that do not fit are a warning sign that supervision is lacking. If the supervisor were supervising, he would ensure that the experiment had a purpose. Supervisors sometimes allow random experiments because they want to let people have some fun at work. This is good if kept in its proper place. Experimentation because supervisors are not supervising is not good.

The users trying to create a wireless interface for Delphi's system were performing unsupervised experiments. We still have no idea how much time, money, and other resources they consumed on their experiments. The users performed many iterations of trial and error before they reached something that worked to an extent. The builder's engineers had been thinking of such an interface for several years. They had a good idea of what would and would not work. We were fortunate that we were able to arrange for the two groups to work together.

"I Did it the Hard Way"

When I was in graduate school, the head of our research lab rarely offered his experience as an aid to new students trying to find their way around the lab. He viewed our stumblings as a type of intelligence test. If a student could learn the systems on their own well enough to write a small but useful program, they would be "in" the group. This was his method of "weeding out lesser students." He would not spend his time supervising students until they proved themselves to him.

I disagreed with the head of the lab regarding his method of supervision. This was a university, and people can debate how to supervise students in a university. Nevertheless, choosing not to supervise people is a problem in the workplace.

A warning sign that the supervisor chooses not to supervise is the statement, "I did it the hard way, let them do it the hard way, too."

The first part of that statement may be true, but the last part is wasteful and harmful. One reason for having supervisors and supervision is that we hope to learn from our past mistakes. We know more about engineering, IT, and project management today than we did 20 years ago. We can use this knowledge to improve our projects and the lives of the people who work on them. We can also choose to hide this knowledge and watch people struggle while repeating previous mistakes.

Some people who make the above warning statement were shouldered with terrible supervisors when they were young. Both authors lived through such episodes. We, however, see no good reason to pass along those bad experiences.

The bitter supervisor attitude hurts projects in several ways. The first is that the people working do not have the benefit of the supervisor's experience. They are working on their own and probably will make many mistakes. The second way this attitude hurts is that the people are working for a supervisor who does not want them to succeed. He wants them to experience pain and make plenty of mistakes. These mistakes may impart knowledge, but the product will have poor quality and the project will suffer.

School Days

The classic form of "supervision" is the boss telling people what to do and standing over them while they do it. Another form of supervision is mentoring. Mentoring and coaching occur when a more-experienced person shares their experiences with a less-experienced person. Age or standing in an organization has little to do with this. I have benefited from the mentoring of college students working for course credit as well as countless lessons from 11-to-14-year olds in recreational sports programs.

The mentoring or coaching form of supervision is beneficial to people working on projects. Many people, however, shy away from this. A warning sign that people refuse to mentor is when they say, "Hey, I'm not a mentor. I'm an engineer. I deal with technical problems. Go hire a school teacher."

This begs the question, who is a mentor? If I do not help a less-experienced engineer, who will? This comes from a basic misunderstanding of mentoring and helping. These are not professions, but are things that people do when they know something that a colleague does not know yet. When a person helps another with something, they qualify as an experienced mentor and helper. It is that simple, yet it is complicated. Discussions later in this chapter offer some tips.

ON BEING AN ADULT

The previous tales and lessons show that providing proper supervision is helpful but not always easy. Most of us in the technical fields were not trained to supervise and provide knowledgeable assistance. The following are a few things we have learned that may help.

Talk to Everyone Every Day

On several occasions in this book we have advised talking to everyone every day. We do so again here in the context of providing supervision to those who need a little help now and then.

I once worked for a supervisor who supervised only when something was wrong. He darkened the doorway of my office when something bad happened. If I looked up from my desk and saw him, I knew I was in trouble. I did not like it when he stopped in to talk and I did not like his supervision.

Several times in my career I have worked for supervisors who came by my office and chatted almost everyday. We chatted about the weather, news, sports, our families, and everything else. I enjoyed their daily visits and I like their supervision.

One result of these conversations is that I felt comfortable talking to these supervisors about anything. I cannot overemphasize the importance of that last statement. I could ask them about my current struggles in the job. They could then supervise and mentor me. Since I was comfortable and asking, they could answer and help me with things that I did not know "up to now" (see the next section about these three magic words).

The comfortable feeling that allowed me to ask them for supervision did not come in one day. It developed over time by talking to my supervisor every day. Relaxing chats about the weather do not solve the complex problems on difficult projects. They do, however, relax people so they can ask for and receive some help.

Safety Zone

One of the root causes of people not receiving supervision is they do not feel comfortable with it. They do not like someone "looking over their shoulder." One way to help people feel comfortable is to provide a safe work environment. When people feel safe at work, they are more likely to be open to others. They let people see their work, they tell people what they are doing, and they feel at ease letting others guide them. Supervision is someone showing them another way, not punishing them.

I worked in an unsafe, toxic environment for four years. I was afraid of everyone except a few close coworkers. The competition for advancement was fierce. Every little misstep was recorded and discussed at performance reviews. People in management were looking at everyone closely and recording things daily that they might use against me. Maybe that last statement was not correct; maybe it was only in my mind, but that was the kind of thought that filled my mind while working in a place that was not safe. I had no desire to be supervised because that would only give my enemies more chance to hurt me. Do you hear the fear in these statements? In an atmosphere of fear, every mistake brings you one step closer to being fired or moved back in a career.

The opposite is a safe workplace. Every challenge, even every mistake, is an opportunity to learn and contribute to a project. People share information and talk regularly. We acknowledge that we each have something different to contribute; we contribute when we can and learn the rest of the time.

The safe workplace is much more conducive to successful projects. People are happier, work harder, and make fewer mistakes. When I feel safe, I happily admit when there is something that I do not know yet. I say so before wasting time working in the wrong direction or building a product full of defects.

There are three magic words for a supervisor in a safe workplace. These are "up to now." When a person says, "I do not know how to write subroutines of type ABC," the supervisor replies, "You do not know how to do that up to now. You will learn today."

When a supervisor establishes a safe workplace with an "up to now" attitude, being supervised and supervising properly become much easier.

The Experiment Lab

Part of a safe workplace is an experiment lab. This lab can be real or virtual as the physical implementation is not as important as the concept and attitude. The experiment lab provides people with a chance to perform those experiments they are dying to do. As discussed earlier in the chapter, many people love to do experiments. A good supervisor will not fight that, but will work to allow such experiments in an open and safe manner.

Experiments can bring much good to a project and to a person. The supervisor should set aside reserve resources for people to conduct experiments that do not apply to today's project. These are like small and local research and development funds. They yield all the good of experiments, without hurting projects. The people who like to experiment know that they will have the opportunity to perform them. It is sort of like eating vegetables before dessert. Once the project work is finished, the experiments can happen.

An experiment lab makes supervision much easier. The person doing the experiment knows they are doing something that may not work. Failure to produce a product is acceptable. The main points of the experiment are to produce knowledge and boost the morale of the person. A big side benefit is that the supervisor is supervising and the person is being supervised. Each is doing their job without stress, strain, worry, and fear of stepping on the toes of the other.

This is what happened with the users who helped create a wireless interface for Delphi's system. They had an idea and they "knew" that the technology was out there to implement it. Their supervisor allowed them the resources to do some experiments. While they did not conduct the experiments efficiently, they did accomplish enough work to show that it was possible to implement their idea. A little supervision from us, some technical knowledge from the builder, and lots of enthusiasm from the user combined to create a useful interface.

Let's Talk

A large part of supervising is mentoring or teaching. Most engineers and scientist are not good teachers. We tackle a problem, solve it, and move on to the next one. Teaching is for schoolteachers, and coaching is for football.

Projects move much better if people who know something share that with people who do not know it (up to now). We advise engineers not to try to be teachers or mentors, but to help others solve problems just like they solve them.

In an effort to help fellow engineers, we offer a few things we have learned about how to talk when helping. All engineers are not completely insensitive. The words we use when talking to them make a difference.

First, speak for yourself. Speak in terms of "I" and in terms of your own experience. A classic "do not do" is to say something like, "That approach will not work." Who says it will not work? How do you know it will not work? Have you ever tried that approach? A better thing to say is, "I think this will not work. I say this because I once had a similar problem. I did something like this and I failed. I wasted a lot of time and energy and I suffered."

In this example, you are talking about your personal experience. It is not universal knowledge from an encyclopedia, but something learned from hard knocks.

Another piece of advice is to talk with questions. This may sound odd as most people think that mentors tell people the right answers. Mentoring, however, is much more effective when people realize that they already knew the right answer. The right questions merely pointed them to the answer.

The story about the wireless interface contained several samples. Others include, "What do we want to happen? Will what we are doing cause it to happen? What are three things wrong with this? What could we do to make this better? Given no constraints, what would we do? What are our current constraints? What have we not tried yet?"

The right questions also help pull information from people. A supervisor or helper needs to pull information instead of waiting for people to provide it. Remember that we are working with engineers and scientists. Many of us are introverted and do not volunteer information without prompting.

As part of the questions, we should use inclusive language. This means talking about "we" instead of "you." Examples of questions with inclusive language include, "What have we done so far on this problem?" and, "What should we do next on this?" In like manner, "I had a case like this before, tried that, and it did not work. We should try to be smarter than I was. What is something different that we can do?"

CONCLUSIONS ABOUT PROVIDING SUPERVISION

If you are reading this book, you are probably in a supervisory position like project manager, team lead, or head of some group of technical people. You, like the two authors, spend more time watching people do technical work than doing technical work. This is not how we started our careers, but somewhere through the years we became one of them instead of one of us.

Given that we are in a supervisory position and will be there for a while, we suggest the principle of supervision: Provide proper guidance to allow great ideas while still preventing waste on bad ideas.

Some warning signs we have (sometimes) heeded to keep out of trouble include:

- People hiding things.
- Unplanned work.
- Experiments.
- "I had to do it the hard way."
- "I'm not a mentor."

Some ways to make supervising and being supervised a little easier include:

- Talk to everyone everyday.
- Create a safe workplace.
- Provide a place for safe experiments.
- Practice helpful talk.

Supervising people and providing the benefit of experience is not easy. Nevertheless, it can be rewarding and satisfying. Watching a person do something today that he could not do up to now gives one a good feeling and provides the person doing the task much satisfaction, too. On top of those good feelings, projects benefit.

When I first entered the workplace after college, there was much that I did not know. One of the big things I did not know how to do was go to an experienced person and say, "I do not know this. I do not know how to do this. Would you please show me?" I remember that there were fundamental concepts that we were using that I did not understand. Nevertheless, I could not bring myself to ask my supervisor about them.

Some twenty-plus years later, I ask my supervisor about everything all the time. The ability to admit weakness and ask for supervision seems to be one of the things that comes with experience. Maybe this is the one thing we should concentrate on in all our supervision and coaching. It is okay not to have all the answers (we do not live that long), but still we should ask the questions.

Part 6

The next two chapters look at how we can misuse others and ourselves. Chapter 18 discusses how we sometimes approach a task with more confidence than experience. The task is much tougher than expected, so we consume far more resources than planned. Chapter 19 discusses how we often assume things about people when we assign them a task. We have one piece of information about the person, assume many implications of that information, and assign the wrong person to the wrong task.

It Sounded Good When We Started. By Dwayne Phillips and Roy O'Bryan
ISBN 0-471-48586-1 © 2004 by the Institute of Electrical and Electronics Engineers.

Chapter 18

Being Too Big for Your Britches: So Much Confidence with So Little Talent (Experience)

We are pretty smart and we work with builders that have plenty of smart people. We, our builders and ourselves, are accustomed to tackling problems with which we have little or no experience. These are not good situations, but our brains and determination often carry us through.

We build up confidence after working through enough of these new and difficult situations. Sometimes, though, we have too much confidence and not enough talent and experience. We get a little too big for our britches. This chapter is about how a lot of confidence combined with a little experience can cause us much grief.

THIS IS BUSINESS, NOT COLLEGE

Most of us have stories from our college days of working hard enough to overcome any challenge. In graduate school, I routinely devoted 70 hours a week to my studies. In addition, I was married and had a small child. I once saw a fellow graduate student work 28 hours straight to finish a project. He did not eat or sleep the entire time. He sat in a chair and banged out a program that worked.

Such stories are common. In college, in graduate school, and in our early lives we worked endless hours for months at a time. That was our life, and we did not think it was unusual or heroic. Those experiences taught us that, "we could do it." We could write a program that worked in a field at which we knew little. We could design and build a circuit even though we had never done so before. We had the resources to overcome almost any challenge.

The business world is different. First, most working engineers and programmers have distanced themselves from "college days" and have families and lives outside of work. These responsibilities weigh on our minds, and they should. We do not routinely concentrate on work for 10 to 14 hours straight. We do not work all day Saturday and Sunday. We do not neglect everything so we can complete a project.

Second, there are constraints in the business world. People are paid for the time they work. All companies do not pay all workers for all the hours they work. They do, however, pay most people for most of the hours they work. Program managers watch expenses and cannot afford to have people working 70 hours in one week, let alone 70 hours a week for several months.

Another business constraint is schedule. The consequences of not submitting your homework on time and not finishing a task as scheduled are different. Projects require that tasks finish on or near schedule. A project manager should not accept it when an engineer tells him, "I think maybe I'll finish this next week." Late tasks delay projects and cause cost overruns.

We had one instance on Delphi with a filter circuit that needed redesign. A young engineer was assigned the task. He was smart, confident, worked hard, and finished the task. The trouble was that the task did not fit in the constraints of business. The builder had estimated three days for the task. The young engineer finished the task in six weeks. These weeks included ten-hour weekdays, eight-hour Saturdays, and four-hour Sundays. A 24-hour task took 372 hours. The project paid dearly. We fell five and a half weeks behind schedule; we went thousands of dollars over budget on one task, and we lost a good engineer. He was exhausted, so he left the company for another job where he only had to work 45 or 50 hours a week.

WARNING SIGNS OF TIGHT BRITCHES

We work with smart people on our projects. Our source selection process (almost always) ensures that. Confidence usually follows smart, but being smart and confident do not always guarantee that the builder we select has the talent and experience to match the task at hand. The following sections discuss cases in which we had problems and the task was too difficult for our talent and experience. These cases had warning signs that indicated coming trouble. These warnings fall in the areas of sounds, sights, and other things.

"All I Have to Do Is..."

The phrases "Just watch this . . . ," "I'll just . . . ," and "All I have to do is . . ." have found their way into the hearts and minds of some really smart people who work on projects. These words are not uttered in a braggadocios fashion, but quietly and with confidence. These smart people are really, really confident. This type of confidence can lead you down the garden path.

The first confident sound bite we hear is, "I'll just (fill in the blank)." When hearing this, immediately replace the word "just" with "have great difficulty attempting to." For example, when someone says, "I'll just move this code to a new compiler", we should hear, "I'll have great difficulty attempting to move this code to a new compiler."

A similar confident statement is, "All I have to do is (fill in the blank)." When hearing this, immediately replace it with "I'll have great difficulty attempting to." For example, when someone says, "All I have to do is adjust the filters in this circuit," we should hear, "I'll have great difficulty attempting to adjust the filters in this circuit."

These statements ("just" and "all I have to do ") show that someone thinks a task will be easy. Most projects have few if any easy tasks. If the tasks were easy, we as buyers would do them ourselves in our spare time. They are difficult, so anyone thinking they are easy will probably stumble.

The buyer will hear these statements while listening to the builder talk at monthly reviews. The builder will show how things are not going well, but they are about to reverse the fortunes of the project. A few tasks are approaching with which the builder thinks he can regain lost time. They have looked at the tasks, and (here it comes), "all they have to do is . . ." and they will be done. They "just" have to do a couple of little, quick things and they will jump ahead of schedule.

Overconfidence most often occurs in less-experienced engineers. As described earlier, most engineers are smart and they worked through many challenges while in school. They did not, however, face the constraints of business in college projects. These constraints will usually overwhelm the less-experience engineer whereas technical problems will not.

The "just" and "all I have to do" statements will hurt the project in several ways. First, people are about to hurry. When I think a task will be quick and easy, I work on it quickly and easily. I do not take time to think, I do not have a peer review it, and I do not look up references that will help me do the task. It will be easy, so I do it quickly. I am about to trip and the project will fall with me.

The second way the "just" statement will hurt a project is that people are not addressing reality. The project is in trouble because up until now the tasks are more difficult than the builder estimated. If past tasks were difficult, future tasks are likely to be just as difficult. If the builder thinks the future will be easier than the past, they are deluding themselves and will try to delude the buyer as well.

Vive la Difference!

The second confident but chilling sound a buyer might hear is the builder saying, "this is a little different from what I've done before." The main words are "little" and "different." The word little is like the two overconfident phrases discussed above. The word different is the key here. Different means this is the first time the person has done this task. It is always difficult the first time someone does a task.

For example, I have traveled much in my career. I move through airports much easier than most people because I have done this so much. Driving also comes easier to me as I have to drive from airports to facilities of builders in many different cities. Regardless of my experience, I sometimes have problems. I have 90% of my traveling problems on my first trip to a different city.

Strictly speaking, all tasks are unique. We deal with degrees of similarity in tasks. The more similar a new task is to our experience, the easier it is. When someone admits the task is a "little different," they are admitting that this is not different because it is June instead of January, they are admitting that this is something new. What the buyer should be hearing is, "this is something that will be difficult." These tasks that are a little different will hurt your project. People will commit more mistakes than usual and consume extra resources as they ask colleagues for help.

This happened to us many times on Delphi. The situation that occurred frequently was working with different electronic parts. Companies that make electronic parts will make a part for a year, then drop it and issue a new and improved part. The new part does everything the previous one did, but the footprint is a little different, the power is a little different, and the function is a little different. Our builder's engineers commonly told us that they had a new part. They knew how to work with the old part, and since the new part was a "little different" from the old one, they did not expect any problems with it. This prediction was wrong most of the time.

School Days

The two situations discussed above illustrate that projects have many difficult tasks. The builder's people face things that they have not seen before, so they have to learn how to do them.

A confident warning sign the buyer often hears the builder say is, "We'll learn while doing." That statement might be fine had the builder planned for learning, as learning costs time and money. The problem is, builders rarely plan for learning.

One principle holds true for buyers; we do not want the engineers working for our builder to learn while doing. We want them to learn (on someone else's project) before coming on our project and work while on our project. It is unfortunate, but the knowing before starting does not happen often.

The builder often tries to comfort the buyer with, "It will not take us long. We'll have a short learning curve." The builder is trying to convince the buyer that people will learn quickly and inexpensively. There is another expression at work against this hope. That expression is, "You get what you pay for."

Things learned quickly and inexpensively are not worth much. If they are not worth much, they will not add much to the project. Most tasks add greatly to a project. Therefore, any task worth doing on a project will cost a lot to learn how to do.

Again, this cost is fine if the builder planned for it. The trouble arises when the builder planned for little or no expense in learning. This is what happened on Delphi with the filter circuit that needed redesign. The engineer learned much while doing this task. The builder, however, did not plan for learning. They planned for someone who had enough knowledge to do it in three days. The builder was wrong in both cases. They were wrong about how much time it would take irrespective of who did it, and they were wrong about how long it would take the junior engineer to learn how to build it. The cost of the unplanned learning was huge. In the end, the learning was lost. The filter was completed, but the engineer who learned to build it took that knowledge with him when he left the company.

Going Solo

Another thing we did in college was work alone. That was the way professors assigned tasks, and that was the way students performed them. Often, we needlessly carry this "I work alone" philosophy into the workplace.

Someone working solo is a problem for a project. The tasks in real projects are difficult, and struggle is normal. However, it is not necessary that a person work and struggle alone. A project does not have any professors tapping people on the shoulder and telling them to do their own work.

Working in pairs or seeking help from colleagues is a good practice when confronted with new and difficult tasks. The extra pair of eyes often see solutions to problems much faster. An added advantage is that the two people working together teach one another. "Thinking out loud" is one of the best methods of training. It is not always the less experienced person who learns from the senior person, as the teaching goes both ways.

The buyer does not like to see people working solo on a project. Because of this, the buyer needs to ask questions about the tasks that are taking longer than estimated. Good questions include, "Who is working on this? Who is the second person working on this? How much time is the second person spending with the first? Five percent of the time? Fifty-five percent of the time?"

The answers to these questions may provide a warning sign that the project is headed for trouble. If the second person is helping the first person less than fifty percent of the time, someone is going solo. It is time to intervene and do something different.

Working solo introduces difficulty into an already difficult project. As with most of the problems in projects, this will hurt the project now and in the future. The solo worker will take more time than estimated to complete the task and will make mistakes. The project team will catch some of these mistakes now, but will not discover the others until later, when the cost of repair will be much higher.

We had far too many instances of people working solo on Delphi. The engineer redesigning the filter was working solo. The builder made several attempts to bring in senior engineers to help. Fred was the project manager at this time (see the Chapter 11 for background). Fred was not receiving the support he needed from his managers. This was one situation when an outside consultant from one of the local universities could have helped immensely. The result was that the junior engineer toiled alone for weeks. We were fortunate that the design was free of errors. We were unfortunate that it took so long and cost us a good engineer.

HOW TO CREATE A GOOD SITUATION

We had plenty of difficulties in working through cases where people had less talent and experience than confidence. There are ways to create a situation in which people can succeed in such difficult circumstances. These fall into two areas. The first is to hire people who have talent and experience in the areas needed in the project. The second is to acknowledge the difficulties that lie ahead and plan ways that allow people to succeed in spite of the difficulties. The following describe some of these techniques.

Pick a Builder

The preceding stories and warning signs showed how it can be difficult to succeed in a project when talent and experience are lacking. There are some things we can do to make up for these shortcomings, and the following sections will discuss these. Regardless of the ways to make up for a shortcoming, the best thing to do is to have a project without such shortcomings.

Chapter 3 describes the steps that we as buyers take to hire a builder that has the experience and talent needed for the projects we undertake. Picking a good builder for a project is difficult, but not impossible. The key is high quality during the source selection process.

First, we as buyers must decide what we really want in the product. Our user may want everything in the world, but it is our task to remove all the gold plating. Building systems is difficult; building systems with extra features causes unnecessary difficulties. Second, we as buyers need to know what we want the builder to do. There are many things a builder can do in a project, and our Statement of Work (SOW) states the specific things. We should write the SOW in simple and straightforward terms and examine the tasks we request.

Good questions to ask ourselves include: "Can anyone do the tasks? Are we asking people to create new science? Are we asking people to perform unnecessary tasks? Are we being too specific and not giving the builder the room to decide what is best?"

Choosing a well-qualified builder helps reduce the number of problems. Notice how this reduces but does not eliminate problems. Projects will have problems; that is natural.

In any project, the builder's people will do tasks that they have never done before. With an experienced builder, however, they will be doing tasks that are similar to what they have done before. The learning curve will be shorter—not always short, but always shorter.

An experienced builder will have persons (plural not singular) who have done work like that found in the project. The persons will be able to help one another with the toughest tasks. This (almost) eliminates people working solo on tasks.

We experienced plenty of problems on Delphi. Some, like the story of the filter redesign, resulted because the builder had more confidence than ability. In retrospect, the Delphi builder did more right than wrong. The assembly workers made about 100,000 electrical connections while peering through microscopes. They made about one error for every 10,000 operations. The software people on the project performed in an exemplary fashion. Note the lack of software horror stories in this book. Finally, the builder's corporation applied enough competent people to complete the project and deliver good products.

Acknowledge that We've Never Done this Before

Our projects often build systems containing many disparate subsystems. We rarely find a builder with experience on all subsystems. The best way to work around this is to have the builder choose a subcontractor for those areas with which the builder has little experience. The subcontractor can work through the unusual area with fewer problems.

Some of our projects involve subsystems with which no one has any experience. This is the norm in government projects because governments often do things that no one else does. We have learned a few things to help in these situations. The first thing we as buyers should do is ask the builder if they have ever attempted like this something before. That question often startles people because they assume that all their tasks are supposed to be new. That is what they are paid to do—solve new problems. They do not think that this new problem will hamper the project.

Asking does no good if we do not make it safe to answer. One way to make the situation safer is to relate the problems we have had in the past with new challenges. Our college stories are humorous and our on-the-job stories are not so humorous. These stories, however, show the builder that we have experienced ups and downs. We are human and we know the builder's engineers are too. We do not expect superhuman triumphs, but we do expect honesty.

Good questions we have learned include, "What is your direct experience with such a task? What sources of knowledge will you use while doing this task? Who will you consult while doing this task?"

The builder should state plainly that, "My experience is X. This task is Y. They are similar in the following ways. They differ in the following ways. We think we can overcome the differences by doing such and such. Our helpers will be so and so."

These are honest and straightforward answers, and they show that the builder has thought about the tasks.

We have learned to watch out for hesitation in answers. Troubling answers include, "Well (long pause), I think we'll be fine on this. I'll just do such and such. All I'll have to do is such and such."

Delphi lacked honesty at the beginning (see Chapter 3). At times, people hid the truth, and at other times they lied. That is one type of honesty or lack of honesty. There is another type of honesty that can be just as important to a project. That type of honesty is when a person says something that they suspect or know to be true. They do not wait for a direct question to make a direct statement.

Delphi gained honesty as it progressed. Peter, a wonderful project manager (see Chapter 11), helped with this by practicing the basics of project management. He looked ahead and found things that might cause trouble. These things were coming all along, but Peter had the honesty to see that maybe the original planners had more confidence than talent and experience. Peter noted these, had his team admit they were true, and told us about them.

For our part, we helped create an environment in which people could talk about problems. We did not jump on people when they reported trouble. That helped them admit possible trouble on the way. Such admissions allowed managers on both sides to gather resources in advance to help the situation.

Plan for Learning

The prior section describes the first step in creating a good situation when confidence outweighs talent and experience. In it, we acknowledged that we could have a problem. Now it is time to do something about the problem and that something is learning. Earlier we stated that we want the builder to learn on his own time, but reality rarely permits this. Learning during a project can happen in many ways. One of the most effective and efficient ways is when the builder plans for learning.

Learning takes time. If an engineer lacks experience on a task, the project manager should allow 20% to 50% more time for that task. This gives the engineer a chance to perform experiments or build prototypes. After experimenting, the engineer can throw these away and do the task for real. Allowing throwaway prototypes relieves pressure. Working without pressure often makes the difference.

Learning takes money. The materials and test equipment needed for experiments and prototypes are not free. The time needed for such learning is not free either. The project manager needs to budget for these expenses. These resources pay for themselves when the engineer is able to complete the task on time.

Learning is not open-ended. As buyers, we must check with the project manager and engineer early and often. After one or two prototypes or experiments, it is time to reach closure. If the engineer is not finishing the task, we should bring in extra help.

Planning for learning is essential. At least it is essential if we want the person to learn without destroying the project. The resources needed for learning will not appear by accident. They only come when someone sees a need for them in advance and plans for them.

Delphi's third project manager, Peter, did a fine job of planning for learning. He looked ahead at coming tasks, saw the ones for which the people did not have the needed talent and experience, and planned for those coming situations.

Peter's actions showed that the cost of learning is not prohibitive if it is planned for. Peter was able to start people on the learning curve weeks before they needed the knowledge. The learning came in small pieces of a couple of hours here and there. Peter was able to bring in experienced people from outside Delphi. Those experienced people were in demand on other projects, but the builder saw that they could release someone for a few hours.

During the learning, the experienced people saw the need for and realized the benefit to the builder of their time spent teaching inexperienced engineers. As a result, they went a little farther than requested. They spent a little more time spreading their knowledge. This extra time came during lunches and those bits of time when they were unoccupied on other projects.

The result was that the inexperienced engineers on Delphi learned. They still were not as capable as some people in the builder's corporation, but they had a chance to do their tasks in the time allotted. The project benefited, the individuals benefited, and the builder's corporation benefited. We, the buyers, also benefited.

Risky Business

The prior two sections encourage two actions by managers. The first is admitting when there are gaps between confidence and the needed talent and experience. The second is planning to close these gaps. These tasks fall under the heading of risk management (see Chapter 10 for more details).

In risk management, the manager looks ahead for potential problems. The question is, "What could possibly go wrong?" The goal is to find the tasks that will probably have problems. Once the project manager identifies these tasks, it is time to arrange for extra resources. If the potential problem becomes a real problem, call in the extra resources. It is easier to find and bring in such resources if we have identified them ahead of time.

We did not do risk management well in the early phases of Delphi. The builder's early project managers did not identify the gaps between their confidence and their ability. The story of the young engineer who had to redesign a filter circuit is one example. The project manager at the time knew that the engineer would struggle with this task. Afterward, the project manager told us that he did not think the engineer could do the task. Regardless of these doubts, the project manager did not arrange for an experienced engineer to come in and teach the younger engineer. To our shame, we as buyers did not do anything to help either. We sat back and watched the problem grow.

The lack of risk management practices hurt Delphi. Neglecting this can hurt any project that faces challenges.

CONCLUSIONS

People attempt difficult projects. We sure did on Delphi. People who work on projects are usually smart and accomplished. They have tackled problems on which they should have failed, but their brains and determination carried them through. Such accomplishments build confidence.

These two factors—tough projects and confident people—sometimes collide in a bad way. Confident people can work their way through tough problems, but not always in the constraints of business. Working 24 hours straight may produce a good answer, but it is a failure in business if 4 hours were allocated.

These thoughts lead us to the principle of confidence and talent: Things are not as easy as they seem, especially within the constraints of business.

We urge you to watch for warning signs such as:

- "All I have to do is . . ."
- "This is a little different from what I did last time."
- "He'll learn while doing this."
- Going solo.

We have found ways to create a good situation in the face of more confidence than talent. These include:

- Pick a builder with care.
- Acknowledge it when you have never done something before.
- Plan for learning.
- Practice risk management.

We can succeed when we do not know everything we need to know. What we do need is humility, foresight, and planning.

In the summer of 2002, I moved away from Delphi to another job in another organization. By the spring of 2003, my new boss was assigning me projects in areas in which I had no experience. The assignments were a bit scary, but nothing as scary as I experienced at home at the same time. We were having people into our home for community activities, and a new family decided to join our group. This new family had a teenage son and two daughters age 5 and 8. My wife Karen and I have three sons who were teenagers themselves at this time. I had coached boys sports teams for ten years, so I had lots of experience with boys. These two little girls, however, were new to me.

I was able to follow the second bit of advice above, "Acknowledge it when you have never done something before." Little girls and little boys are different. I also planned for learning and practiced risk management. We all lived through the experience, and we had some fun at the same time. These practices worked in real life in my home.

Chapter 19

Appointed Experts:
Who Brings What to the Table

People bring talents and abilities with them when they come to work on projects. This is what they bring to the table. We have often been in situations where people assumed things about the talent and ability of others. They appointed someone an expert in a field and waited for them to do great things. The great things usually did not appear, and the person making the assumptions was disappointed. On top of the disappointment, the project languished because it did not have people with the expertise it needed.

Assuming that people have expertise is a mistake. Asking people what they bring to the table is wise. Something so simple has alluded us many times.

SETTING A FEW TABLES

The following are three stories in which people appointed others as experts. The appointing had little to do with what the people brought to the table. It is significant that this chapter has three stories whereas most of the chapters of this book have one. These stories came to mind quickly and flowed from the keyboard easily. We suppose that says something about the many mistakes we have made in this area.

The New Engineer—Dwayne's Story

When I started working after college, my colleagues assumed that I knew much more than I did. My college diploma said I was an electrical engineer,

It Sounded Good When We Started. By Dwayne Phillips and Roy O'Bryan
ISBN 0-471-48586-1 © 2004 by the Institute of Electrical and Electronics Engineers.

so everyone in my new job assumed I knew all sorts of things about RF communications. They talked to me without end about antennas, modulations, dB this and dB that (all RF engineers say dB or decibel in every other sentence), and lots of other jargon. I had no idea what they were saying.

They assumed I knew RF communications because that was their experience. All the electrical engineers they ever worked with knew RF communications, but I didn't. I was one of the new type of electrical engineers who knew much more about computer science than magnetic fields. I studied computers, digital logic, computer programming, and the like. Our electrical engineering department put people like me in the "computer option." Years later, they changed the degree name, but for us guinea pigs, they used the same degree title.

People kept putting me in situations in which I was supposed to use my knowledge of RF communications. I climbed antenna towers, connected banks of radios, ran electrical wire, and even tried to fix air conditioners. I tried in vain to tell people that I did not know what they assumed I knew. I was young, inexperienced, and did not speak well with people. I always had the fear of losing my job if people found out that I was unqualified. Besides, I was having so much fun on the job. This new field gave me the opportunity to learn every day.

I learned slowly and seemed to survive. This survival was literal as well as figurative. Some of that work can be dangerous, and a few jolts of 220 volts kept me on edge. I applied the basic principles of engineering that I did know, asked lots of questions, and tried hard. If you seem eager and jump on a task, people tend to forgive ignorance and mistakes.

My colleagues made assumptions about what I brought to the table. I failed to show them what I did bring with me. As usual, such false assumptions and failures to communicate hurt our projects.

Paul the Tester

Another story is about a test engineer on Delphi named Paul. Given a test procedure, Paul could run the most complicated set of tests. He paid attention to detail, conducted the tests exactly per the procedure, and recorded the test results in a manner that was easy for others to read.

On Delphi, people assumed that Paul would move from tester to lead test engineer and even to system engineer. Testers usually run so many tests that they soon see the patterns in tests. They learn the differences between high- and low-quality test procedures. After time, they can design tests and write the procedures themselves. Those are the tasks of the lead test engineer. That person knows test equipment, the types of equipment to test, and how to arrange tests that are effective and efficient. The step from tester to lead test engineer is a "natural" progression.

A step beyond lead test engineer is the system engineer. The system engineer knows all aspects of the system. He may not know every detail of every part of the system, but he knows the black box behavior of every part of the system. A person who has tested systems and designed tests for systems can step into the system engineer role because he understands the black box behavior of systems and subsystems.

Everyone assumed Paul would make that progression on Delphi, but it did not happen. Paul tried the system engineer job first. One of his early tasks was to choose the configuration and types of cables used to connect the pieces in the system. Paul really wanted to do a super good job and demonstrate to everyone that he could be the system engineer. Paul learned the properties of the basic interfaces among the system components. He also learned what types of cables the users wanted (there are many types available). This task should have taken about a week, but Paul took three months.

He went through the task over and over again. He would consult cable vendor catalogs, design a set of cables, and make detailed drawings of the set. When finished, he would think of a variation to the cabling and start over. He was reverting to the test performer role by testing every little detail of every possible cabling combination.

After a year of similar problems as the system engineer, the project manager reassigned Paul to be the lead test engineer. We were all certain that Paul would do well in this job, but he did not. Paul became entangled in details again. He laid out a test sequence, but instead of saying he was finished, he would test the sequence. He wrote a detailed test procedure, drew diagrams, specified test equipment and connections, and tested the test. He modified each test sequence a half dozen times.

We discovered that six months into the lead test engineer position, Paul had accomplished one month's work. The project manager made a brilliant decisions and made Paul the "Test Director."

At this time, we were convinced that Paul, although being a wonderful person, was possibly incompetent. It seemed that there was nothing he could do right. We were wrong again because Paul was a superb tester. We were shocked to see Paul walk into the test lab like Superman coming out of a phone booth. Paul grabbed cables, rolled test equipment into position, adjusted everything to his liking, and sped through the test procedures. He performed the tests faster and better than anyone on the project. We were testing 24 hours a day seven days a week. People called Paul at home during their shifts to ask him how to do things. Paul was the expert.

There is a problem with natural progressions like tester to lead test engineer to system engineer. There are no such things as natural progressions with people. There are only assumptions about what people will bring to the table. We assumed Paul would make this progression. This was our mistake, and we suffered for it with frustration, wasted resources, and a failing project.

Portable Production Units (PPU)

People make mistakes in assuming that they know what others bring to the table. Another mistaken assumption we make concerns the relationships that people bring to the table.

The relationships among the people on a project are important. It would be efficient if one person could place the result of their work in a bin, walk away, and have another person go to the bin, take the work result, do their work, and place their result in another bin. That is the way things happen on mass production lines.

We do not work on mass production lines. Engineering and IT work involves knowledge, not materials. People produce ideas and they hand those ideas to other people. This handoff is a complex relationship, not a simple bin. Relationships among different people are not equal. Some people work better together than others. Simply put, they "get along."

We see relationships in professional sports. Young men and women make their way up the ranks to the top professional leagues. There is no question about their individual abilities. Many, however, do not work well together and their teams perform poorly. This is because the relationships are poor. Immaturity, outside pressures, poor leadership, and other factors contribute to these poor relationships.

We see these poor relationships because professional sports team play in public. They work on television, are interviewed after their games, and commentators highlight and explain their faults at length. Most of us do not earn our salaries in front of the public. Our working relationships, however, are as important to our projects as the relationships among athletes are to the success of their teams.

When I first started working, I was on a project in which teams of two people traveled together through foreign countries for two months at a time. Our project paired an engineer with an operations person. I worked with half a dozen different partners in three years. Some of the partnerships were great. Several times I worked with a gentleman named Rod whose values and interests were similar to my own. We both liked sports and felt that living quietly with our families was important to a happy life. Our trips were fun and we did a good job.

Some of the other partnerships were not so good. One of these was when I was teamed with a gentleman named Mel. I did not drink alcohol, and Mel was an alcoholic. His constant drinking wore on my nerves, so I avoided him as much as I could. Avoiding your partner neither helps your partner nor accomplishes much work. That trip was the longest two months of my life.

The partnership of Mel and me was bad, but then there was another duo of two men named Ricky and Don. These two men had a genuine dislike for one another. A conversation with one of them was nothing but a stream of curses on the other. When I talked to the other, the situation was the same. They accomplished nothing on their trips and everyone suffered.

These bad examples of partnerships come from the mistaken theory of portable production units or PPUs. The theory holds that all engineers are alike and all operations people are alike. Any mixture of one engineer and one operations person will work.

Many of us have seen the PPU theory in action. One type of person is mixed with a few other types of people. The mixture should work as these are all adults and professionals. People will "act right," right?

People are neither production units nor portable. People are people, and some people have a difficult time working with other people. Such difficulty is not desired, but it is natural. Mel and I were a bad team, and so were Ricky and Don. Those were simple two-man teams. Most projects use teams of at least six or seven people. The PPU theory really falls apart in those situations.

WARNING SIGNS OF TROUBLE SETTING THE TABLE

The preceding stories were about occasions when some people appointed others to be experts. They did this without considering what people brought with them to the table. In retrospect, there were signs that could have warned us about what we were doing and the trouble that was coming. We did not notice those warning signs at the time. Below, we discuss a few of those signs, and we hope you notice them and take action soon enough to avoid trouble in your projects.

Assumptions

The first thing to watch is making assumptions in mistakenly appointing people as experts. We all make assumptions because they save us time. The problem is when we make assumptions about people. We assume they meet some stereotype we have such as, "All engineers know the same things. All testers make a natural progression, and all people bring the same abilities and desires to the table."

One assumption about people is that they know what we know. A common question I have heard countless times is, "Doesn't he realize such and such?"

Examples include, "Doesn't he realize that we need this product this week? Doesn't he realize that running a test in that way will give misleading results? Doesn't he realize that he is making me angry?"

The answer to these and other "doesn't he realize" questions is almost always no. If people are acting like they do not realize something it is because they do not realize something. All the assuming in the world will not help them realize it.

The "doesn't he realize" question is a warning sign for coming trouble on a project. I often hear this warning sign coming from my own mouth. On

Delphi, I asked this "doesn't he realize" question a dozen times about Paul the tester. I would ask the other members of the buyer's team, "Doesn't Paul realize he needs to stop fiddling with cables and move on with his job?" These team members would then ask me, "Doesn't Paul realize he is wasting time and falling behind schedule?" We even asked one another, "Doesn't Paul realize he looks incompetent?"

The trouble with these "doesn't he realize" questions is that no one tries to answer them. We ask them out of frustration. If we would think a moment, the answers would be obvious and enlightening.

Instead of the "doesn't he realize" question, we should ask the other person the simple and polite question, "Do you realize such and such? Do you realize that we need this product this week? Do you realize that running a test in that way will give misleading results? Do you realize that I am becoming angry?"

Other ways to phrase these questions include, "I am concerned about the delivery schedule. I need this product this week. What do you think about this schedule?"

If only I had asked Paul, "Do you realize that you satisfied everyone with the first cable configuration you presented last month? Do you realize we are happy with your design and we want you to move on?"

The "doesn't he realize" question hurts projects in several ways. First, it is frustrating. I was frustrated every time I asked that question. That frustration quickened my heartbeat, shortened my breath, and reduced my thinking.

Another problem with that question is it breeds contempt among people who should be working together. A good exercise is to quietly append the words "and he's incompetent" to the end of each "does not he realize" question. For example, "Doesn't Paul realize he needs to stop fiddling with cables and move on with his job?" becomes, "Doesn't Paul realize he needs to stop fiddling with cables and move on with his job? And he's incompetent!"

No one mutters these extra words, but the question often carries the thought. Paul was not incompetent. He was trying to provide a superior product to his customer. He did not realize that he had already done that and needed to move on. We did not help him realize his success because we did not tell him. Instead, we made assumptions about Paul, and then made fun of him. None of these things helped the project.

We need to ask plain questions and accept the answers. Becoming angry when someone answers does not help the situation. When he came forth with the first set of cables, we should have said, "Paul, this is perfect."

"We'll Just Move Some People"

One of the more difficult tasks for a project manager is staffing a project. It seems that the people the project manager wants are working other projects, and the people who are available for this project do not have the desired qualifications. The project manager and the personnel manager end up moving people among projects like children move plastic pieces on a game board. The names and individual abilities melt away and become generic pieces like disks in a game of checkers.

Shuffling people among projects as if they were game pieces is a problem on projects. The shuffling usually carries with it many assumptions about the people. The managers doing the shuffling are thinking wishfully that the people will work fine on a project. The people are smart, they work hard, they have a fine employment record, so they can do the job.

The warning sign of treating people like game pieces is easy to hear. The project manager will say, "Let's move John over to these tasks and we'll move Jim over to these other tasks." No one hears, "John has three years experience with the X tool kit. Let's put him on the GUI series of tasks. Jim has been working with filters for ten years. He can do the filter redesign." No one hears these things because the managers do not know the experience and abilities of John and Jim.

Shuffling people like interchangeable game pieces will probably hurt a project. People are not pieces in a game—they are people. They bring their own expertise to the table instead of some standard set. Since they do not have the appointed abilities, they will not perform as planned. They will consume resources (time, money, equipment, etc.) and make mistakes.

Paul the tester was an individual. He brought the zeal and expertise for running tests to the table. Some of the managers of Delphi expected him to fit into some other slots. He did not, but his managers tried to squeeze him in for months. We helped with the vain attempt to squeeze him in. It did not matter how hard we all tried to squeeze and squish, Paul was not the expert we appointed him to be. He was himself, and a very good self at that. Our efforts hurt the project. It is a testament to Paul's character that we did not hurt him in the process.

An Engineer, a Tester, and a Partridge in a Pear Tree

A problem in staffing projects is that people talk in terms of occupations instead of individuals. Typical statements are, "We'll put an engineer here and a tester there." People are assuming that all engineers or members of any other profession know the same things. It is true that all people with degrees in engineering have some common background. They probably took calculus, chemistry, and physics in college. For those readers who took these classes, consider the following. Those classes comprise what percentage of your total life experiences? One percent? One half of one percent? Is it wise to assign someone to a task based on one percent of their life experiences?

Assigning occupations instead of people often occurs in teaming situations. A warning sign comes in statements like, "A team should have an engineer, two programmers, a tester, and a support person." This sounds pretty good on the surface. Someone is thinking about the skills needed on a team for a successful project. This, however, is a sign of approaching trouble.

Immediate questions to ask include, "What engineer did you find? What tester did you find? Have they ever worked together before? Have they ever met one another?"

The most important question is, "What have you seen in the two individuals that makes you believe they will have a good working relationship?"

In an ideal world, all people come to work, work together, and go home. We do not work in an ideal world and we do not work with ideal people. We work with real people, and some people do not work well together.

When people do not work together, the project becomes an afterthought. The primary thought is, "Why is that SOB trying to steal credit for the work I am doing? I'll fix him, I will not do any work. He'll catch all the blame."

The story of the portable production units taught me a big lesson early in my career. Each team comprised an engineer and an operations person. Some of the teams we had were good, but some of them were terrible. Mel and I were a poor team because I did not want to be near him. Ricky and Don were a poor team because they despised each other. All four of us were competent individuals. In theory, a manager should have been able to create several combinations of strong teams with the four individuals. Theory, however, does not consider what people bring to the table.

SETTING A GOOD TABLE

It is easy to appoint someone to be an expert. We have done it many times and been disappointed almost as many times. It is difficult but possible to set a good table—to place someone in a position that matches their talent and ability. We have observed a few patterns of behavior that accompany good table setting. The following describe some of these.

Learn the Abilities of Each Individual

An important task in working with people is to know what each individual brings to the table. Each individual is just that—an individual. They bring a unique combination of skills and personality to a project. If we understand what they bring, we can better arrange a team and help a project succeed.

Knowing people as individuals requires time and energy. Project managers may wonder why they should invest the time to learn so much about people. These people are paid well and should be able to do their jobs. The trouble is when project managers assign them to do someone else's job.

Putting a person in a job that matches their expertise helps a project succeed. They know what to do, how to do it, and they do it well. Such a person has little or no learning curve, they make few mistakes, and they consume few resources.

Paul the tester was a good example on Delphi. Peter was the project manager who assigned Paul back to the testing position. Peter did not try to squeeze Paul into an ill-fitting position on another project. Instead, Peter put Paul where he could use his talents.

Use a Skills Matrix

A useful tool in assigning people to the right job is a skills matrix. This is a table with columns labeled with the skills needed for the project and rows labeled with the names of the people on the project. Each box in the table has a check mark where a person has a skill needed on the project. The skills matrix helps show if the project has the skills it needs.

Although it is a useful tool, the skills matrix can take on the worst property of any tool. In this case, a project manager assumes that the tool is faultless and will do all the work. We cannot make the checks in the matrix without first talking with the individuals as individuals. The people who assumed I knew RF communications had read my file and saw that I was an electrical engineer. They assumed I had the RF communications skill, but they never talked with me about what I brought to the table.

Often, the skills matrix will show that a project does not have all the skills needed. Many people can expand their skills into new areas. Be careful here, as this assumes the natural progression of things. This is the mistake we made on Delphi with Paul the tester. Some people will learn new skills, and others will not.

It is simple to know if a person is willing to expand their skills. The key is to ask them. State, "I see you have been a tester for ten years. Do you want to move into a lead test engineer role? Do you think you can do that on this project? Would you like to try to learn the needed skills?"

It is important to accept their honest answers. If their answer differs from what we assume, our face drops in disappointment. It is difficult, but ask the question without hinting at the "desired answer" with a facial expression or tone of voice. Raising eyebrows and smiling widely while asking, "Do you want to try the lead tester job?" is a strong hint that we want the person to answer yes. People often answer the way we want them to because they do not want to disappoint us. They can become self-appointed experts, and self-appointed experts are just as bad to a project as appointed experts.

We did not have a skills matrix on Delphi for the first couple of years. The builder kept shuffling people, grabbing occupations, and making all sorts of assumptions about what people brought to the table. We as buyers did not help. We kept believing everything the builder's managers told us without asking questions about individuals. In retrospect, we were afraid to ask questions because we wanted to believe that all would be well.

Peter and Bruce (see Chapter 11) used a simple skills matrix during the final two years of the project. They looked at the skills matrix far enough in advance to acquire the people with the necessary skills and keep the project on schedule.

Work with Relationships

Projects require people to work in groups, and this means that project managers need to assign people to groups. We urge project managers to consider the relationships of the people they group.

We have found it best to talk with people about their work styles and about good and bad working relationships they have experienced. A goal is to understand what contributed to making the good ones good and the bad ones bad. In hindsight, were there things the person could have done differently to improve a bad situation?

It is helpful to look at the past teamwork experience of the person. What have other people said about working with this person? What types of people made what types of remarks? Even with this information, a project manager should take care in making group assignments. Opposites sometimes work best together. At other times, people who are similar work best together.

Information gathering is helpful, but it is only the beginning. We may assume that we bring more to the "making assignments table" than we do. Most of us are trained as engineers or programmers. Few of us are trained in the dynamics of relationships.

The best advice for a manager is to be a manager. Talk to people individually and in groups; monitor their work; help if you can, and change the assignments and mixture of people if you must.

Considering the relationships of people on a project is hard work. People who are at ease with one another spend their energy working the technical problems. People who are fighting with one another spend themselves in the fight. They have nothing left for the project, and the project usually fails.

Some of my biggest successes in grouping people have come in coaching kids in sports. In the older age groups, practice time is sparse, and the kids are less likely to know one another from previous years. I start by pairing kids on the field who have played together before. Once they have some success, I stretch them in their playing relationships little by little. I add a new person to a group of two. The group of three still succeeds, and the kids learn that they can play well with more than one friend.

We advise doing the same in projects. Group people who have had shared success in the past. Let them continue their success, and stretch them little by little by introducing other people. The project benefits in two ways. First, it benefits by a job well done by people with good relationships. Second, it benefits as the size and number of successful groups grows.

I worked well with Rod on projects (see the PPU story earlier). Rod was 20 years older than me; he was from Idaho, and I was from Louisiana. Our manager, however, saw that we valued many of the same things and created a successful pair.

My coauthor and myself worked well on Delphi for three years. No one made a decision to put us together. We fell together by default when other people left the project. Our relationship worked through some difficult circumstances on Delphi. We did more as a team than the sum of the two of us individually.

CONCLUSIONS

We have made more than our share of mistakes with people and what they know and can do. People are individuals with their own abilities and preferences. Individuals are not stereotypes of their profession and are not portable production units. This leads us to the principle of what people bring to the table: Different people bring different abilities to a project.

We have learned a few signs that warn of coming trouble. These include

- Assuming that people know things.
- Thinking of people as being interchangeable.
- Referring to people in terms of occupations instead of individuals.

It is possible to create a good situation with people in projects. We suggest:

- Learn the abilities of each individual.
- Use a skills matrix.
- Work with relationships

People usually differ from our expectations of them. That can be maddening, and if we ignore it, we can doom a project to failure. If we accept it and work with it, we can help people bring their talents to the right place at the table. The work they do in such places can be marvelous.

We learned a bit about what people bring to the table while writing this book. Early in our collaboration, we thought that we could write chapters side by side. That was not happening, and we were both concerned about it. While thinking about the topic of this chapter, it hit me that I brought the ability to draft chapters to the table. Roy brought the ability to transform our experiences into chapter titles and themes. We both brought something different yet valuable to this project. We decided to let Roy bring the chapter titles and themes and me type the words. Once we accepted that, we were fine.

Part 7

The next three chapters step back and look at bigger issues. These issues concern employing the right people in the right approach to do the right thing. Chapter 20 looks at using a big corporation to run a small project. A mismatch in size can often spell disaster. Chapter 21 discusses the perils of outsourcing instead of doing a project in-house. Chapter 22 discusses doing everything in a project the right way, but doing the wrong project.

It Sounded Good When We Started. By Dwayne Phillips and Roy O'Bryan
ISBN 0-471-48586-1 © 2004 by the Institute of Electrical and Electronics Engineers.

Chapter 20

The Shallow End of the Gene Pool: Small Projects and Large Corporations

There are large corporations and small companies available to bid on projects. Each of these have their advantages and disadvantages. Sometimes a buyer must go with a large corporation because of the special facilities that only large corporations can afford. Sometimes the buyer's project is relatively small for the large corporation. Therefore, the project does not warrant the attention of the corporation's top managers and the time of the corporation's top people. In these situations, the buyer does not realize the benefits of using a large corporation. Such was our predicament on Delphi.

THE SHALLOW END OF DELPHI

On Delphi, our builder was part of a large corporation. We saw both the good and bad of working with a large corporation. It was our misfortune to experience much of the bad and little of the good.

Large corporations experience averaging in their projects. This means there is a consistency in their results. They have a few wonderfully successful and a few miserably dismal projects, but most fall in a predictable and comfortable range. They may have 1,000 engineers, so odds are they have 100 exceptionally bright engineers, 100 poorly performing engineers, and 800 people in the middle. Their large number of engineers gives them plenty of average engineers and, hence, plenty of average projects.

It Sounded Good When We Started. By Dwayne Phillips and Roy O'Bryan   **245**
ISBN 0-471-48586-1 © 2004 by the Institute of Electrical and Electronics Engineers.

Large corporations have an infrastructure. Their engineers do not take time to order parts because they have a purchasing department. We had this on Delphi. The engineers did engineering work while other people did the logistics work.

Large corporations have standards. They have many projects, so they can spread the cost of creating standards over those projects. The standards guide people in their work and result in predictable projects. Our builder had this advantage on Delphi. Their assembly areas, where they built the electronic circuits under microscopes, were certified per accepted standards. Their test equipment was always kept in calibration per standards. They even had Software Engineering Institute process standards for their software work.

Large corporations have strength in numbers. In theory, if engineers are having trouble with a technical problem, the corporation can bring in senior engineers for a few days to help. The large corporation usually has senior people who have worked on similar problems in the past. Large corporations usually have special facilities (warehouses, test labs, conference centers, etc.). Like standards, the large corporation has enough projects to share the cost of these special facilities.

There are also disadvantages to having a large corporation as a builder. Large corporations can have large bureaucracies. Their purchasing departments can take weeks to order parts, and the logistics departments can take days to move a received part from the loading dock to the engineer.

We had a terrible experience with the purchasing bureaucracy of our builder on Delphi. In one case, the builder needed ten of a type of part. They said that their vendor could not sell less than 100 of that type of part, so the builder ordered 100. The vendor did not deliver on time. The builder's purchasing people called the vendor every week trying to bother them enough so they would deliver the part. Finally, the vendor told the builder that they did not have all 100 of the part that the builder ordered; they only had 80. They had these 80 ready for weeks, but since the order was for 100, they did not want to ship an incomplete order. We could not put much blame on the vendor because we learned later that the builder's receiving department would have sent the shipment of 80 parts back to the vendor. Their quality manual instructed them to never receive a shipment that did not match the order exactly.

Large corporations are slow to change direction. The software people on Delphi learned several new practices that would speed development and testing. Nevertheless, they could not use these. These practices would violate corporate software process standards. The corporation was considering adding these practices to their standards, but this would take another year for the change process. Our people used these new practices via guerrilla tactics. They used them, but did not tell their software managers.

As buyers, we chose a large corporation for our project. The corporation had the special labs and the strength in numbers we needed. We also wanted the safety of having a comfortable and predictable project. We were not trying for any tremendous breakthroughs in technology (at least we thought we weren't). We would be happy with an average project.

Delphi had a bad experience with the large corporation. It took us several years to work through the issues. We felt as if we had the disadvantages of a large corporation with few of the advantages. Sometimes we take the advantages for granted—we use them without noticing them. We did enjoy some of the advantages of a large corporation, like the certified assembly areas and test equipment. The disadvantages were in the area of bureaucracies. The purchasing incident discussed is but one example.

We missed many of the advantages of a large corporation. The advantages we missed the most were in personnel. We often had the "shallow end of the gene pool" working on our project. The corporation employed some of the top people in the country in the technology areas critical to our project. These people did not work on our project. Instead, the builder assigned junior engineers to Delphi. They were smart, conscientious, and hardworking, but they had neither the knowledge nor the experience we needed. We suffered through their learning curve.

We hired a large corporation that acted like a small company. Our problem was that Delphi was too small for this corporation. The builder assigned their top engineers to large projects—projects in the hundreds of millions of dollars—whereas Delphi was small potatoes to them (only $30M). There were some exceptions. We had a few excellent technical people working on Delphi. We did not, however, have access to the experts we wanted, and certainly not when we needed them.

One way to understand this is to think of profit margins. Assume that the corporation has a profit margin on any project of 10%. This means if the project goes well, the corporation can expect to earn 10% (the math is easier using 10%). If the corporation does well on a $900 million project, they earn $90 million in profit. If they do well on our $30 million project, they earn only $3 million. Given these numbers, it is easy to see which project gets management's attention and most of the best people.

WARNING SIGNS OF SWIMMING IN THE SHALLOW END OF THE GENE POOL

There are potential problems in having a small project with a large builder. It is possible to avoid such problems, as warning signs appear before the problems occur. The following discuss some of these warning signs.

"Those People Are Busy Right Now"

A distressing but common problem in projects is that people proposed for a project do not always work on it. Builders, especially large corporations, season their proposals with the names of their best people. This tactic wins contracts. As buyers, we want experts to work on our projects. We see the names and select the corporation to be our builder. It is legal to move people off a contract and replace them with someone else. A buyer cannot require a specific person to work on a contract as that would be a form of slavery. This person, as a free citizen, can quit the corporation on any day.

Buyers might notice that the experts are not working on their project when they visit the builder. We wrote "might notice" because it is possible to go for several months without knowing that the experts are not working on your project.

This is hard to see early in a project. At that time, there are only a few people analyzing requirements and doing preliminary design work. When we visit, we only talk to the project manager and one or two others. We learn to be pushy and insist on meeting the people working on the project. The builder's project manager could tell us that, "Those people are busy right now," or "Someone in another building asked them to walk over and help with something for a couple of hours, so they are not available today." Those statements are warning signs that the experts will not work on the project.

The replacement of experts with other people hurts a project now and in the future. The current harm occurs because the junior people are not finishing tasks as quickly as the experts would. The task durations were proposed with the experts in mind. The junior people cannot possibly do them as fast. The future harm occurs because the junior people are probably making mistakes. They do not know as much as the experts, so mistakes are expected. Other junior people review their work and do not find the mistakes. The project marches forward with problems hidden in the analysis and design. These problems will surface later as people start building the system.

This happened to us on Delphi. Several key engineers were proposed for Delphi, but did not work on it. There was a delay in starting Delphi, so these key people were assigned to other projects. This made sense, as they were capable people and the corporation was not going to have them sitting idle while other projects could use them. By the time Delphi began, these people were integral parts of other projects. The project managers for those other projects would not release them to Delphi. Besides, the other projects were larger than ours and held more potential profit for the corporation. It was good business to keep these people on these other projects.

Delphi struggled through a year or more with junior people. They took more time to complete tasks and their products were riddled with small mistakes. These mistakes surfaced months later in assembly and test. The project, already behind, fell farther behind while the cost rose far above estimates.

The La Brea Tar Pits

Engineers can become stuck on a problem. This is the nature of people when working on difficult tasks. The answer always seems to be five minutes away, but this is what we thought five minutes ago. The harder we concentrate, the harder the problem becomes. An engineer stuck in the tar pit of a problem needs some help. A little jiggle or a day or an hour of help from a more knowledgeable engineer will do it. The problem for the project comes when help does not come. The person stuck in a problem continues to struggle.

The warning sign of this problem is difficult for the buyer to see. The buyer usually visits monthly. It is rare that the buyer visits long enough to see someone working on anything, let alone stuck on a problem.

The project manager needs to notice the engineer stuck on a problem. This is difficult to notice because we do intellectual work in which we sit in front of a computer terminal for hours. Some people look the same whether they are making progress, struggling to pull out of a tar pit, or daydreaming about other things.

The warning sign is in the posture, expressions, and breathing of the engineers. Warning signs that people are stuck on a problem are when they slump over more than normal, let out long breaths more than normal, and walk more slowly than normal. We emphasize the "more than normal" phrase here. The only way to know if people are doing these things more than normal is to know their normal work habits. This means spending time around them every day.

The project manager can also see stuck people by managing per the schedule. People have tasks to do and time frames for those tasks. The project manager should ask for products when they are due. This is not a form of mistrust. The project manager should tell people what he is doing so they do not interpret it as mistrust. This is managing a project and seeing when people need help.

The project manager cannot allow a person to "go dark." This means they shut themselves away for days without speaking with other people about their work. People usually allow experts to go dark because they are afraid to ask the expert about their work. Who would dare question a wizard about his magic? Too often, the expert reappears after weeks with no product. The project loses these weeks of schedule because other people were afraid to hurt the expert's feelings by asking simple questions.

Projects that have people stuck on problems fall behind schedule. Like the situation discussed previously, they fall behind now because their task has taken longer than estimated. The project will also fall further behind in the future. Since the person struggled for so long on a task, the product probably has mistakes hidden in it. These mistakes will surface later and cost time and money to correct.

Delphi suffered through this problem many times. We had difficult problems, and the junior engineers became mired in them. Our biggest problem was that help did not come. Fred, a project manager in the early phases of the project, (see Chapter 11) was new to the corporation. He did not have the years with the corporation to build good relationships with other project and personnel managers. Hence, these other managers were not quick to lend an engineer, even for a couple of days. The resources of the large corporation were there, but Delphi received little benefit from them.

The builder was an "old line" company. They did not like to bring in outside help. The builder's facility was in an area with many universities less than an hour's drive away. So many, in fact, that the builder prided themselves in how many of their engineers were adjunct professors. These engineers knew experts, but the company policy did not use these professional acquaintances. We could not get the help we needed from inside the company, and company pride prevented us from getting help from the outside.

Time for a 'Do Over'

A costly problem on projects is redesign. The usual process in making a product is design, build, and test. If there is a problem in test, sometimes a person can make a small change and the product passes the test. Sometimes the test failure is serious, and the cycle must start again with redesign, then build and test.

On a large, complex project, some redesign is expected. There may be hundreds of product elements (circuits, components, subsystems, subroutines, etc.) in the system. It is common to have to redesign three or four of every hundred product elements. The warning sign is when there are ten or twelve redesigns needed for every hundred product elements.

A high rate of redesign indicates that the engineers working on the project do not have the expertise needed. The testing is catching some of their mistakes and triggering the redesign. This is bad, but what is over the horizon could be worse. If the engineers are making big mistakes, ones that cause test failures, they are probably also making small mistakes. These small mistakes may pass through the first round of testing. After these tests, the team will integrate the first-level components into the next level. Tests on these integrated components may uncover the small mistakes. Redesign at this later time is expensive.

We experienced this problem on Delphi, as we had a high number of redesigns. The builder did not assign enough experienced people at the start of the project. The less-experienced engineers worked hard and learned in time, but they made plenty of mistakes. The repeated cycles of test, build, and test cost the project dearly during its first 18 months. It also cost us in the second 18 months, as the first round of build and test did not catch the small design mistakes. The second and third rounds of integrate and test did find these.

Fixing things this late in the project were expensive in time and money. They were more expensive in emotional energy. We felt as if we were past our problems and were going to roll through to the end of the project. The team felt good about itself, the project, and the systems they were building. These late problems brought us all crashing back to earth. We all had a difficult time recovering from the disappointment.

Corporate Policy

Large corporations have policies. This is natural, as they try to have the different departments work together for the good of the corporation. Sometimes, the policies intended to benefit the corporation and its employees have unintended side effects. The side effects can contradict common sense. Someone could call a friend in purchasing and make a suggestion, but that is not a valid line of communication. The receiving department could accept an incomplete order if that order had all the parts a project needs. This, however, would violate corporate policy.

Corporate policies can hurt projects, especially relatively small projects. Smaller projects have shorter durations. This means that builders need to react quickly when a change is required. Corporate policies usually prohibit quick change, because reacting quickly means circumventing the "needed" coordination and oversight. This "needed" coordination and oversight can take weeks.

As a buyer, we have collided with corporate policies several times. The usual case is when we suggest an idea that will save time and money. The warning sign of trouble is when the builder replies with, "We cannot do that as it goes against corporate policy."

One of the problems we had on Delphi was with corporate policy regarding the interface between the engineering and assembly departments. The builder had an excellent record in assembling tiny electronic components. This is one of the major reasons we selected them. The builder often assembled a thousand copies of a circuit. Their policies were written with this situation in mind. We were building nine copies of circuits. For Delphi to be efficient, we needed to have an engineer test an assembled circuit, take it back to assembly for small changes, test it, take it back, test it, and so on. These iterations would allow us to complete the design of the circuit rapidly.

These quick iterations contradicted corporate policy. Although they worked well for us, they would wreak havoc in a project that was trying to build a thousand copies of a circuit. The engineers constantly told us, "If I could run back and forth to assembly a couple of times in a day, I could have this finished in two days, but assembly will not allow that because it breaks all the rules."

We were frustrated by this policy. Our project was a legitimate one; we were a paying customer, and it was best for the corporation to have a successful project. We were not trying to change their policies; we just wanted them to work around roadblocks for the good of our project.

In the end, we were able to work through this situation. The engineers met with the chief of the assembly area many times. They found ways to abide by the spirit of the corporate policy while not quite abiding by the letter. They made some informal exceptions to the rule. This was only possible because the chiefs of the different departments wanted to please us as their customer.

CREATING A GOOD SITUATION IN THE SHALLOW END OF THE GENE POOL

Our experience with a small project in a large corporation was painful but educational. We learned that there are several things that will help avoid the disadvantages of large corporations.

Check Before Buying

Chapter 3 discussed the process of receiving proposals from different builders and selecting one for a project. This source selection process considers many elements. One element rarely considered is the size of the project and how it relates to the builder's other projects. The buyer should consider the size of the builder's typical project. Watch out for statistics like size of the average project. Averages can be misleading, so look at the typical project instead. A project that is one-tenth the typical size could be in big trouble.

A project that is the typical or even 10% bigger than typical for a builder will receive their full attention. Such projects make profits for the builder and keep their company going. This type of project is their specialty—their niche in the marketplace. Their people are accustomed to working in teams of this size, and their managers are accustomed to managing teams, budgets, and systems of this size. Stretching a company into new capabilities can be a good thing, but do you want a company to go through a learning curve on your dollar?

In retrospect, it is hard to imagine how our organization could have selected the builder we did based on project size. The simple answer was that we did not consider the depth of the gene pool, where we would swim, and if we were a big fish or a tadpole. Ours was a $30M project. We knew of a project next door to ours that was a $200M project. The expected profit from the next-door project was $22M—almost two-thirds the total size of our project. Several good people left Delphi in its second year to work on a project down the hall. This was a $500M project with expected profits of $60M. Its profits were to be twice our total budget.

Delphi was tiny compared to others at this builder, and we suffered because of our relative size. It is possible for a small project to thrive in a large corporation, but this requires special action and attention. The next sections discuss these.

Promises, Promises

There are occasions when using a large corporation for a small project is appropriate. Builders will seek small and unusual projects for various reasons. They may want to move into a new business area, and a small project is a good test of that area. They may also want to work a small project because the customer holds a special place in their heart. This may sound silly in the heartless business world, but it does happen. Senior business managers do have customers that mean something special to them.

Before starting a small project with a large corporation, obtain specific commitments from corporate managers. The buyer should address the issue of small projects in a large corporation directly and in specific terms in a meeting with the builder's managers. Clear communication is key in this meeting. The buyer cannot leave this meeting without a signed memorandum from the builder. The buyer needs commitments for the project's critical resources, including names of people, facilities, test equipment, exceptions to corporation policy, and anything else the builder has and the project needs.

Commitments obtained in this manner help create a good situation for a project. The buyer knows that the builder will come through when needed on the project. The builder's project manager also knows this. The project manager will be able to make calls and obtain resources. The project manager should use the commitments wisely. The project manager works for the builder and probably has aspirations for a career. If the project manager must choose between satisfying a customer on a small project and keeping his paycheck, he will choose his paycheck.

The buyer should follow up on these commitments and not allow them to fade away. The buyer should also take care in invoking these commitments. Ask to see the corporation's CEO only when necessary. Corporations have a chain of managers and they like people to use that chain. The buyer should be assertive and protect his organization's interest, but be assertive wisely.

We tried to obtain such commitments on Delphi. Ours was a special project to Art, one of the builder's senior managers. Art had a long history of working with our organization and believed in what we were trying to accomplish. He was committed to delivering what we needed. Art had the best of intentions, but was not able to meet his commitments.

This was because Art's organization was sold from one large corporation to another even larger corporation after Delphi began. These types of sales often mean closing facilities to save money for the buying corporation. Art was occupied with keeping his business unit solvent. He made the right decision for his organization and its employees. Unfortunately, he could not devote the attention to our small project that he wished.

The warnings to the buyer and builder to use commitments wisely are important. The next two sections offer advice on how to do so.

Let's Do Lunch

Once the project begins, the buyer should meet with the builder's senior managers. These meetings should be one of the commitments the buyer obtains before the project begins. These need not be long meetings. Half an hour at the most will suffice as long as the meetings are held as scheduled.

The regular meetings keep the relationship established earlier in a healthy state. There will be problems on the project, as all projects have problems. This situation with a small project in a large corporation presents extra opportunities for problems. The meetings allow both sides to anticipate and prevent problems.

We did not do this on Delphi. We met with the builder's senior managers occasionally, but not on a regular basis. Remember from above, these senior managers were distracted trying to keep their business unit operating. When we did meet, problems had already occurred and we were trying to save a troubled project. By the time we met, we were left with choices between something bad and something worse. We rarely had good choices and we often concluded that had we done something sooner, we would have been in better shape.

Looking Ahead

Part of a project manager's job is to manage risk on a project (Chapter 10 discussed risk management at length). Risk management belongs to both the builder's project manager and the buyer's lead. They should look ahead on the project to anticipate when problems might occur. Whereas risk management is a normal part of any project, it is a special part of a small project at a large corporation. As we have discussed in this chapter, small projects in large corporations have trouble acquiring extra resources in times of trouble. Small projects also have shorter schedules, so acquiring extra resources quickly is important.

All projects have critical products and points in time. Analysis of a product, a project, and a plan will reveal these critical points. Junior people, typically employed on small projects, will probably not be able to carry a project at these critical points. The buyer and builder's project manager should discuss these critical points with the builder's senior managers in advance. Talking in advance allows the senior managers to arrange for the needed resources. The regular meetings with managers discussed earlier are the time for these discussions.

We did not look ahead during the first couple of years of Delphi. The first project managers were buried under details and were short of resources. They were not able to see problems coming and garner resources from their senior managers. We suffered and the project fell further behind each day.

We learned our lesson and were proactive in the final two years of the project. The final two project managers had the resources and opportunities to manage risks. They took on this challenge and did a fine job. We were able to anticipate problems and obtain commitments for resources should the potential problems become real. The final two years of the project had many successes. We attribute these to proactive management at all levels.

CONCLUSIONS

One area of concern with builders is the size of the project compared to the builder's typical project. If a buyer's project is small, it may not receive the needed attention and resources. This leads us to the principle of small projects and large corporations: It is hard to have the full attention and resources of a large corporation when your project is small.

Watch out for:

- The people named in the proposal are not appearing in the project.
- Engineers become stuck on a problem and no help arrives.
- Frequent redesign.
- "We cannot do such and such because it goes against corporate policy."

How to create a good situation:

- Check on the size of projects of builders before selecting the builder.
- Obtain specific commitments from senior managers.
- Hold regular meetings with senior managers.
- Look ahead.

Working with a large corporation can be a great experience, as they have things to offer that are found nowhere else. Nevertheless, we should acknowledge the potential problems of being a small fish in the shallow end of the gene pool.

In the summer of 2002, I changed jobs within the government. My new job was with an organization that ran large projects ranging from $500M to $1B. I was now in the deep end of the pool where resources were plentiful and life would be grand. After a couple of weeks, however, I discovered that it was not so easy to swim in the deep end of the pool. Every time we wanted to do something, we had to form an interdepartmental team of 30 people. Forming the team took a month, and since the team could only meet one hour each week, accomplishing anything took at least six months. It was like swimming in mud, and I longed for the days of shallow water where Roy and I did everything by ourselves. Maybe one day I will master the art of finding the shallow part of deep water and the deep part of shallow water.

Chapter 21

Telling Your Customer What You Think He Wants to Hear and Believing It: Outsourcing

Outsourcing is more prevalent today than ever before. Firms do not have or do not want to have all the resources to do every task on a project. Instead of paying for these resources full-time and only using them part-time, firms pay for them only when they need them—via outsourcing.

There is, however, a problem-plagued part of outsourcing. In an outsourcing situation, there is a user, a builder, and someone in the middle. For much of our careers, we have played the part of the person in the middle—the buyer. The buyer is responsible for what the builder does, but the buyer does not have complete control over what the builder does. Delphi was an outsourced project, and we suffered through the agony of many outsourcing problems. Our builder also suffered through our frustrated attempts to help them.

THE AGE OF DELUSION

During a one-year period on Delphi, the builder accomplished two months worth of planned work. We discussed this back in Chapter 9. In that chapter, we looked at problems with producing parts and tracking schedules. In this chapter, we discuss the problem we had when the builder had trouble obtaining parts from vendors. The builder needed to buy some circuit boards for the project. These circuit boards were unusual and difficult to make, so our builder outsourced this task to vendors. The builder had problems with the vendors they hired to make these circuit boards.

It Sounded Good When We Started. By Dwayne Phillips and Roy O'Bryan
ISBN 0-471-48586-1 © 2004 by the Institute of Electrical and Electronics Engineers.

We, the buyer, were frustrated because we were not controlling what the builder was doing. The builder's project manager had that control. The builder contracted with one vendor to build the circuit boards. This vendor worked hard for six weeks, but quit because they could not build the circuit boards to specification. The builder went to another vendor to try to build the circuit boards. The second vendor failed as well. The builder went to a third vendor with the same result. They went to a fourth vendor, and this fourth vendor was able to deliver the circuit boards to specification.

We were going crazy while the builder was floundering with these vendors. This project was spending $40K a day on engineering and production labor. The circuit boards were to cost about $20K. We felt that the builder's project manager should have contracted with at least two different vendors at the same time. If one failed, maybe another one would succeed, and the project could move forward. The project manager did not want to "waste" $20K or $40K by hiring multiple vendors.

This disagreement caused trouble on the project. We lost confidence in the builder's project manager's ability to manage the project. If we had control, we would have made the "right" decision. At least we felt we would have done so.

When it became clear to us that the project was in trouble, we started visiting the builder twice a month instead of once a month. One problem with outsourced projects is that the buyer has a limited view of what is happening. We wanted more visibility into the project. Perhaps if we knew more, we could help. The builder gave us a full-day briefing on status during one visit, and we had informal discussions during the second visit. We were seeing information, but we still were not seeing the status we wanted. We felt this way because the project was still in trouble. We believed that if we saw more status more often the project would right itself.

We were victim to a common occurrence on outsourced projects. We did not understand everything that was happening, so we felt that the builder was disorganized. Things were happening daily, the builder's people found problems, told the project manager, and the project manager shuffled resources to address the problems. Since we only saw every third or fourth piece of information, we were confused and frustrated.

We, as is common among buyers in outsourced projects, interfered. The theory was simple. The builder was in trouble, they needed advice (do not people in trouble need advice?), and we were just the people to give advice. We second-guessed the builder's every move. We were trying to be helpful, so we offered alternative ideas. The trouble was that these did not sound like ideas to the project manager. He had plenty of ideas of his own. He also had plenty of problems and not enough resources. Our helpful ideas sounded like criticisms, and criticisms only burdened the project manager more.

Another form of our interfering was talking to the builder's engineers on the side. We would tell them what they should really be doing. We were only offering advice and not direction. The trouble was the engineers saw us as the customer, and the customer is always right. They wanted to please the customer, so they did much of what we suggested. Unfortunately, some people were going in one direction while others were going in another.

About this time, we stopped trusting the builder and they stopped trusting us. We would visit the builder, hear about the problems, and hear the direction the project manager gave the team. We agreed with that direction. A few weeks later we would visit again and expect to see people working per the direction the project manager gave during our previous visit. This was rarely the case. Instead, the builder's team was doing something different. We felt the builder had lied to us about what they were going to do. We were wrong. They had changed direction because the situation had changed between our visits, and we did not realize that. We compounded our error by acting as if the builder was lying. The builder became angry with us. They were justified in their anger as we were falsely accusing them of lying. The mistrust grew each day.

WARNING SIGNS OF OUTSOURCING TROUBLE

We and our builder had many problems with outsourcing. In retrospect, there were signs that should have warned us of trouble. We discuss some of these signs below in hopes that you will recognize them sooner than we did and avoid trouble.

What's Your Name?

IT and engineering projects are mostly mental work. People think about problems, create solutions in their minds, and describe these solutions in software source code or engineering drawings. People should have a purpose to their work. What they are doing is important to many other people. We should work toward satisfying those people.

One problem that can occur in an outsourcing situation is that people become disconnected. Their work is just work. It does not mean much to them because they do it in isolation. They do not see a person waiting for the product.

A warning sign of the builder's people being disconnected is that they do not know your (the buyer's) name. You are the buyer—their client. It is their job to build a system that satisfies you. If the builder's people do not know your name, they are probably not connected to you, the product, and the project.

The first type of trouble is when the people are disconnected or disengaged from the project. It is just a job. They work on the task their boss assigns them and then go back for another task. Each task is something done in isolation. There is nothing relating the tasks, so they cannot see how to better the output of one task to improve the next task.

The second type of disconnection is a separation between the buyer and the user. We try to build systems that improve people's work. Once disconnected, we do not have any idea what these people desire from us. If we do not know the users, we are building a product for a nameless and faceless organization. Such an exercise has little meaning for people. This leads to another problem. The builder's people have no sense of urgency. A sense of urgency is important because we do mental work, and much of it is invisible. A sense of urgency, the urge to do something productive for the project, keeps people thinking and moving forward.

The builder on Delphi was a large corporation. People would come on the project for a while, do a few tasks, and leave. We felt comfortable with this flow of people on and off the project but we were wrong. One case involved the people who did the outsourcing for the circuit boards we needed on the project. We could not name any of the builder's people who worked with the circuit board vendors. We did not know them, and they did not know us. We were disconnected, and the results showed it.

Please Call Back

Organizing people, schedules, tasks, and other resources is not easy in the best of circumstances. Outsourcing involves trying to organize and coordinate people in different locations. Sometimes it never happens and outsourced projects fail.

A warning sign of a disorganized outsourced project is when the builder does not return the buyer's phone calls. As the buyer, we are the paying client and must oversee the project. This is our responsibility to the people who are funding the project. We have a right to information, and the builder has a responsibility to provide it. One explanation for not connecting on the phone is poor organization. This is a problem with both buyer and builder. It is possible to arrange schedules so the two parties can talk on the phone.

There were times on Delphi when we did not connect with the builder on the phone. We always had a "good" reason for missing one another. It seemed that talking was not as important as other things. The project suffered during these uncoordinated periods. We did not know what was happening, so we could not help. The builder was not sure what we wanted, so they made assumptions and moved on.

Visiting Hours Are Over

Outsourced projects involve two sets of project managers. The first is the real project manager who works for the builder and manages the people building the product. The second project manager is the lead person on the buyer's side (this was me on Delphi). The buyer's lead usually has much training and experience as a project manager. The buyer's lead is often a frustrated project manager. We think we know more about project management than anyone else and are happy to lend our expertise. It is easy for the lead person on the buyer's side to wander into the project manager role for the builder. We did this on many occasions on Delphi.

A warning sign that a buyer is stepping outside a role is when the builder does not like the buyer to visit. Visits by the buyer mean it is time to tell the status of the project. When things are going well on the project, it is easy to deliver the good news. When things are going poorly, it is not so easy. It is at these bad times that the buyer is apt to wander into the project manager's role.

The builder's project manager does not want someone else to tell him how to do his or her job. Stepping outside our role means we are being a bad guest (also known as a pest). Cries of, "It is our right to visit and gather information," do not justify being a bad guest.

We were often bad guests during Delphi. This was especially true during the age of delusion described earlier. We interfered, second-guessed the project manager, meddled with engineers, and did other things. In hindsight, it easy to understand why the builder was not thrilled with our visits. As a buyer, we were responsible for visiting and gathering information. We could not do that if we were not welcome to visit. There is a fine line between gathering information and meddling. Meddling in the project manager's job made us unwelcome. This meddling led to bad feelings, poor exchange of information, and more trouble for a troubled project.

Hard Labor

Outsourced projects have plenty of technical problems. This is why we hire a builder that employs plenty of smart people. We want them to solve these problems and deliver a product. There are times, however, when there are lots of problems with no solutions in sight. The project, like Delphi, is failing and no one can foresee a time when it will turn around.

A warning sign of this type of trouble is when the builder says, "Everyone is working really hard." At first, this seems to be a good sign. We want people to work hard. This shows they are dedicated and committed to the project. It can also be a cry of hopelessness. During the age of delusion, the builder's managers constantly told us that people were working hard. They were falling farther and farther behind schedule, but they were working hard.

The builder did not want to tell us the bad news. They did not want to say that the situation looked hopeless. Maybe if they worked enough long days and weekends they could catch up. This was the hope, but it was not realized.

"Working really hard" is something many people do to lessen criticism and relieve guilt. We heard, "Yes we are behind schedule, but everyone is working long days and Saturdays. (This should make you feel better, does not it?)" It did not make us feel better. We felt worse. The project was in big trouble, and people ruining their family lives only saddened us. We did not want people to work really hard. What we wanted was results borne of clear thinking. We wanted the builder to change the fortunes of the project by understanding the problems and moving in a different direction. Working long hours only meant going farther in the same direction.

This Is a Little Different

Everyone has a first time to do something. This first time usually takes a long time and involves many mistakes, and the resulting product is less than what people desire. In short, the first time follows a learning curve. Many people enjoy learning in an environment designed for learning. A project, however, is not such an environment. Learning while trying to build a product can be frustrating and infuriating. Frustrated and angry people usually build an error-filled product.

An unplanned learning curve may mean disaster for a project. If the builder admitted that parts of the product were new to them and planned for a learning curve, the project would survive. In our experience, builders rarely do these things. They often approach a project with great confidence that can come crashing down when the unplanned learning squashes their schedule and budget.

A warning sign of this learning often comes from the engineers (not project managers) in side conversations. They admit things like, "This is a really interesting project, I've learned so many new things working on this area," and, "Well, I'm not sure how this work will turn out, this is the first time I've used this tool in this way."

A variation on the problem is that the area is familiar to the builder, but they have not done anything quite this difficult. For example, they have built networks of 100 computers, but not networks of 1,000 computers. Another example is they have built user interfaces for workstations, but not user interfaces for the Internet.

A good question that comes to mind in these situations is, "Why did we hire a builder if this a new area for them?" There are many legitimate answers to this. This builder may have been the best available for the project. We often attempt to build products that no one has ever built before. We find the builder that has the closest capabilities and experiences.

We had many unplanned learning curves on Delphi. The circuit board vendors mentioned earlier were one example. Our builder eventually found a vendor that could work through the curve, but only after trying a few that couldn't. The learning curves cost us time and money that we did not have.

For Sale by Owner

Change during a project is almost a certainty. The requirements usually change, people often change, and sometimes the circumstances of a project change (it may be canceled, even when things are going well).

One of the biggest changes that can happen to a project is in the builder's organization. It is rare that a single person will remain the project manager for an entire project on the builder's side. This is our experience, as most of our projects run three to four years, and builders move their project managers for promotions and other reasons. If the project manager changes and the managers above the project manager also change, the project may not have any chance of success.

A warning sign of coming change in a builder is when another company buys the builder. Sometimes someone buys your builder and little happens because the new owner allows the builder to operate as an independent subsidiary. Often, however, being bought out means changes are on the way. In all likelihood, the new owners will send in new people to manage your builder. This may extend to sending in a new person to be the project manager for your project.

The new owners usually have new priorities. They may want to shift the focus of the builder. For example, the type of technology you are using may be obsolete. The new owner may also want to shift the top people off your project onto new projects they deem more profitable. This happened to us on Delphi when our builder was bought. The team remained together, but they became a division in one of the largest corporations in America. This had a bad affect on Delphi.

During the age of delusion, we did not have the attention of the upper managers at our builder. The project manager was struggling, and his immediate supervisor was not providing resources as needed. We tried to speak with the managers above that level, but were unsuccessful. The reason was that they were working to keep the doors open at the builder's facility. The large corporation that had bought them planned on closing the doors and moving the engineers to other projects. The local managers felt that was a poor strategy for the corporation, the community, and the employees. They spent their time working on that issue instead of overseeing our project. Delphi suffered as our project manager did not receive the help he needed.

TIPS FOR OUTSOURCING SUCCESS

The above story and problems show that outsourcing can be difficult. Despite the problems, outsourced projects can work and many people have used them successfully over the years. We have found a few techniques that create an environment for outsourcing success. The following sections relate some of these techniques.

Only When Necessary

The first tip for outsourcing success is not to outsource unless necessary. This sounds too obvious, but it has happened to us more times than we want to admit. Outsourcing introduces a new set of people into a project and brings a loss of control and visibility. With outsourcing, the project depends on someone else. We have a contract, and the builder is obligated by that legal contract. Law, however, does not build systems. People build systems, and sometimes outsourced people do not deliver as we would like.

It is best to find ways to do all the work on our project in our own shop. This does not guarantee success, but it does give us the possibility of control and visibility. We can see what is happening and can take action immediately when resources should be shifted. We may not always do the right thing, but we will have the choice available.

The Three Musketeers

If outsourcing is necessary, a prudent step is to always find three builders. Multiple sources give the buyer choices. The first choice is in awarding the contract. We can consider the three proposals and choose the builder that we feel has the best chance of success. Another choice is using different builders for different phases or parts of building the product. We may use one builder to build the hardware while another does the software. We may use one builder to design and build the systems while a second builder tests them.

These choices add responsibility to the buyer. We must manage more resources and make more decisions. These choices may save or doom the project.

We had few choices on Delphi. As related in the first chapter of the book, the builder had completed a four-year, $40M project that built two systems. They had the experience and knowledge for a production run of nine systems. Our builder did not use multiple outsourcing choices for parts vendors. In the age of delusion, the builder insisted on hiring one source for the circuit boards. Each source failed in turn until the builder found one that succeeded. It seems that few choices and many failures were frequent companions for our builder and us.

Triggers

As related above, it is prudent to have multiple sources in outsourcing because this bring choices. To assist in deciding among these choices, we advise setting triggers. Each trigger acts as a threshold. If things go bad and reach a threshold, call in help from other sources.

The key to these triggers being effective is to set them at the start of the project before work begins. We can think better before a project starts. The phones are not ringing, the customer is not asking, "is it done yet?" and the builder is not reporting troubles without solutions. We are better able to consider all the factors and make some good decisions. Waiting until the project is in trouble is the worst time to set such triggers. Few people make good decisions when everyone around them is screaming for attention. Things become tight, it is hard to breathe, and judgment degrades.

We tried to have the builder set triggers with the vendors they had chosen. We wanted the builder to monitor a circuit board vendor and call in another if the first did not make progress per schedule. These attempts were in vain. The project manager was too busy trying to do too many things to think ahead. The result was the builder stayed with a circuit board vendor until they called and quit.

We as buyers did not do much better at setting triggers. We held a major design review nine months into Delphi (that review was three months behind schedule). The builder was supposed to show us their finished designs for the system. In addition, they were to have detailed cost and schedule estimates for the remainder of the project. The builder had not completed any of these tasks satisfactorily. We should have stopped the project and directed the builder to complete these estimates. We failed to do so because we had not set a trigger before the project began. Instead, we held a 15-minute meeting at the end of the review and made a quick decision that allowed the builder to charge ahead.

'I'll See You Next Week'

A bad part of outsourcing is that the buyer does not see what is happening on the project day by day. This means the buyer does not know the builder's people well. In such situations, it is easy to become disconnected and the project suffers.

One way to help keep everyone and everything connected is to visit the builder frequently. The previous section discussed some of the pitfalls of the buyer visiting. We were bad guests as we often interfered, but we learned. It is important to arrange the visits so the builder is happy to see you. The first thing to do is to impose as little as possible. The visit will be an imposition, as the mere presence of the buyer causes the builder to change their normal schedule. Visit them during their normal work hours. If this means flying at odd hours or staying an extra night in a hotel, do it. Do not make the builder work long hours during the visit. This imposes on their families as well as on their work.

Try to be helpful during visits. The builder will have plenty of problems during a project. They may not state it aloud, but they appreciate helpful ideas. If necessary, bring a consultant or other expert along to work with the builder's engineers in their workspace. This is not the interference discussed earlier. This is real technical help.

It is also helpful to do nice things for the builder. We always brought in donuts or bagels when we visited. This cost us $5 a day, but was well worth it. The builder's engineers knew we were in town when they walked in and found donuts. Bring flowers for the secretary; bring flowers for the engineers to take home to their spouses; bring in whatever works well for the situation.

With some effort, we changed from being bad guests to being good ones. Good visits meant a good exchange of information that helped the project change from a disaster to a success. Buying donuts did not save the project, but it did help.

Visit Us

One of the hallmarks of a successful project is when the builder delivers a product that delights the user. Doing so is difficult with outsourcing. One thing that creates an environment where delighting the customer is more likely is to invite the builder to visit the offices of the buyer and user. This gives them a chance to see our environment and our work. It also gives them a chance to see the users at work. After all, the builder's job is to improve the user's work.

The visits also help to establish a relationship between the builder and user. Users who do not know the builder find it easy to complain and sling mud. Those things do not happen as much when the users realize that the builder is much like themselves. When the user knows the builder, they will tell them things about their work. The familiarity helps them to be assertive and state what they want and what would delight them. Often, these wishes are easy and inexpensive to put into the product.

When the builder visits, treat them like royalty. Meet them at the door, escort them around, treat them to refreshments, take them to lunch, etc. The builder is doing something for the user that you cannot do, so be grateful and express that gratitude. It is true that the buyer's organization is paying them money for their product, but money alone is often not enough. Builders are people, too. They appreciate the little things that people on the buyer's side do for them.

The Healthy Skeptic

A final tip to help in outsourcing is that the buyer should be a healthy skeptic. If I am not skeptical, I can get burned. If I am not healthy, I will burn everyone else and myself.

In the late 1990s, I was burned on two different projects. The first was a relatively small effort in which a couple of people were updating a system for Y2K. The builder had plenty of time to meet a deadline. I did not pay much attention because I assumed all would go well. All did not go well. The deadline came and went and the work was not finished. We had to scramble to avoid disaster. No one felt much pain, but we were all embarrassed.

The second case was Delphi, as related earlier in this chapter. I knew the project was behind (for many reasons). I assumed the builder was keeping track of the delays and knew when they would finish. I was very wrong, as we were surprised to learn that we were a year behind. This caused great pain for everyone.

In neither project was I skeptical. I had developed a trust in the project teams—too much trust. These were "my teams." I did not hold them and myself to good project tracking and oversight standards. I felt we were different; we could skip steps and succeed anyway. I was wrong.

The buyer must be a skeptic. We must always ask for the fundamental project information. This includes a project plan full of short tasks, status of accomplishments, data on expected and actual time, manpower, and cost, etc. Everyone must know what has been accomplished, what is left to do, when the project will end, the quality of the product, and what the project will cost.

The buyer must be healthy while being skeptical. This means being healthy in relations with the project team as well as being healthy yourself. First, constantly asking the team for status can become unhealthy. People who perform well feel they earn the privilege not to report fundamental project information regularly. The buyer, however, cannot grant this privilege. This would erase all the necessary skepticism.

The team will cry, "Don't you trust us? We are wasting time telling you that we are on time." Being skeptical has nothing to do with trust. The buyer must be respectful, helpful, and yet skeptical. The best thing to do is to explain the difference between skepticism and distrust.

Next, as a buyer I must care for my own health. Gathering project data is tiresome and not interesting. Part of my failures was that I, like many project managers on many projects, was tired, busy, and (a little) lazy. I was traveling too much, was given an extra five-week assignment, and squeezed in a week-long vacation with the family. I did not have the required physical and emotional energy to do what I needed to do.

SOME CONCLUSIONS ABOUT OUTSOURCING

Outsourcing happens more today than ever before. Outsourcing is full of potential problems because we spend a lot of time trying to communicate. We know what we want, but the builder does not. Once the builder starts working, they know what they are doing, but we do not.

This brings us to the principle of outsourcing: A danger in outsourcing, especially if you have only one source, is the builder can have problems that can ruin your project.

Watch out for:

- People at the vendor do not know you by name.
- The vendor does not return your calls.

- The vendor does not like you to visit.
- "The vendor is working really hard."
- "The vendor has never done anything quite like this before."
- "The vendor was just bought by another company."

How to create a good situation:

- Always find three vendors.
- Have a trigger set ahead of time that will cause you to turn to a second source.
- Visit the vendor frequently.
- Invite the vendor to visit you.
- Do not outsource if at all possible.
- Be a healthy skeptic

We have had the pleasure of many successful outsourcing projects. These projects involved good, smart people building state-of-the-art products for our users. We have also had the pain of outsourcing projects that ended in disaster. As with similar situations, great challenges also bring great satisfaction. We hope you can use some of our lessons to gain satisfaction.

The first few years of my career I worked with outsourcing. We were the buyers in a typical user–buyer–builder arrangement. I learned of a sister organization at which government employees built systems by hand for their users. Ah, they did the things that we learned how to do in college. I wanted to work there and build systems myself.

It took me a couple of years, but I was finally able to transfer to that other organization. Now I would be able to build systems. Since I had experience in outsourcing, the management at this new job put me right to work as the buyer in the only outsourced project they had. It seems I was the only person they had who knew how to be a buyer and work with outside builders. They were thrilled, and I was frustrated.

My entire career has been similar. Except for a couple of short years, I have always worked as a buyer in outsourcing situations. To compensate, I started writing software at home. This led to writing magazine articles and then books. I suppose I have found a way to be in control of a few projects while living in an outsourcing world.

Chapter 22

Going Where Angels Fear to Tread: There Is No Right Way to Do the Wrong Thing

There are times in projects when we set off on a path, work hard, do all the right things, and finish. After we finish, nothing happens. No one uses the product because no one wanted the product. We did the wrong thing the right way. This has happened to us many times. We are pretty good at building products, but we have not always been good at selecting the products to build. Sometimes we were able to catch ourselves before setting off down the wrong path. Sometimes we weren't.

THE GREAT WORKFORCE RETOOLING PROJECT

I once worked on a project known as "Workforce Retooling." The concept was simple (how many times have you heard that?). We wanted to answer a couple of fundamental questions: (1) How do we prepare our workforce for the future? (2) What should a person do to advance through their career?

Someone (we cannot recall who) decided that the final product would be a 50-page document full of many tables with lots of rows and columns and tiny print. This document would be the all-encompassing career guide. It would tell everything for everyone and cover all situations. Building this document would not be easy, but we were determined to do it the right way. Therefore, we stated with a preliminary study that lasted a year. This led to another study which led to an implementation. This all took three years. The work really was not that involved, but it was all part-time work done by people with full-time jobs.

It Sounded Good When We Started. By Dwayne Phillips and Roy O'Bryan
ISBN 0-471-48586-1 © 2004 by the Institute of Electrical and Electronics Engineers.

As we neared the completion of the document, the Internet became popular. We needed to turn our document into an interactive Web page. Such a worthy product deserved our best efforts. We did this part right, too. We called in some local Web page creators, had meetings about the look and feel of the page, went through prototypes, and even filmed an introductory speech and attached a video to the Web page.

Once we finished the product, we held training sessions. Hundreds of people attended half-day sessions to learn about this wonderful career advisory tool. We even held an open house day complete with door prizes and little give-away things advertising the product. We showed everyone the product and emphasized its importance. We did everything the right way.

Six months later, no one even remembered the tool.

It seemed that no one wanted this product. Maybe a more worthwhile product would have been a five-page brochure. Maybe people would have used that. The little brochure could have contained tips for different career paths. We could have created it by having six people spend two days with a facilitator. A little product from a little project might have worked. We certainly learned too late that no one in the workforce wanted a big product from a big project.

We built the wrong product. We did it the right way, but we did the wrong thing.

THE SUPERCOMPUTER

I worked in a signal analysis lab in the early 1990s. We had four sections of people in our lab. Three were composed of people working as signal processors, and the fourth was an R&D section. One of the three regular sections, we will call it the T-section, had a supercomputer. At that time, such a supercomputer cost about $4M. This was a lot of money, but they used this machine 16 hours a day to work their normal problems. The R&D section also had a supercomputer. The senior analysts used the speed of the machine to run many experiments in a day. It paid for itself by speeding the development of new techniques.

Another of the three regular sections, the E-section, decided that they too should have a supercomputer, so they found a problem that needed a supercomputer. They studied the problem, modeled the computing power needed, modeled how much time minicomputers would take to do the problem, and modeled the same for the supercomputer. They were able to convince lab's managers to buy the supercomputer for them. This cost about $4M to purchase plus about $250K a year for maintenance.

The purchase and maintenance costs were only one part of the financial situation. The users needed software to run on the supercomputer. They had been using desktop workstations, so we ported workstation software to the supercomputer. We ensured computation accuracy and did all the configuration management correctly. When a user moved from the workstation to the supercomputer, everything was the same. The files were in the same locations, the commands were the same, the environment was the same, etc. We did all this just right.

People started using the supercomputer, and all was well. Six months later, no one was using the supercomputer. We proved that rather easily. UNIX-type machines like this supercomputer have accounting tools that show who used the computer, how much they used it, CPU time used, etc. A group of ten people in the E-section used this supercomputer. Their usage amounted to about one-tenth as much as the three senior people in R&D section. What was more embarrassing was that the E-section's usage was about one-twentieth as much as the T-section's use of their supercomputer.

The people in the E-section were using their original workstations instead of the supercomputer. This was easier because they did not have to remote login to the supercomputer. The problems they were running were faster on the supercomputer, but the problems were small enough that the time saved was not worth the effort. The E-section really did not need the supercomputer. It would have been much wiser to use the money to buy faster workstations for their desktops. The problem that required a supercomputer went away quietly. In the end, buying the supercomputer was the wrong thing to do.

Once again, we did the wrong thing, but we did it right. We were trying to solve a problem that was not in our mission. It was a good problem, and it deserved a supercomputer, but it was not what the users would work on every day.

The two stories above illustrate cases in which we charged off and did a great job of doing the wrong thing. Below we relate a few stories in which we were able to stop ourselves.

FIXING A DEMODULATOR

On Delphi, we had a situation in which a demodulator was not working. Our builder investigated this situation diligently and after a couple of months of study presented their findings to us. There were some timing problems in the demodulator. Because of these problems, the demodulator was not performing up to specification. The question was what should we do with the demodulator to remedy this situation?

The builder's recommendation was to redesign the demodulator. They wanted to add more taps and feedback and feedforward circuitry. If you do not understand what that means, you are not alone. I did not understand it at the time and still do not. I did understand that this recommendation was challenging to the builder's engineers. It meant a lot of study, design and redesign, test, and hard work. Those are the kinds of meaty things that really good engineers enjoy.

We as buyers felt there was another solution. We felt that the electrical grounding was the root cause of the problem. Roy had seen this type of situation before. If we were to ground the components in the demodulator better, the timing problem would go away and the demodulator would perform up to specification. This was a mundane solution. It did not have the excitement and technical challenge of redesigning the circuit. The builder's engineers wanted to do the new design. After all, they are engineers, and engineers design things.

The mundane approach—grounding instead of redesign—held the day. The improved grounding worked. In fact, after we improved the grounding, the demodulator performed better than the specification. These results led us to improve the grounding in several other circuits of the system. These, too, performed beyond specification. This idea of better grounding turned out to be a significant event in Delphi.

This was not an easy situation. The builder's engineers had spent about a hundred man-hours of effort thinking about the redesign. It cost money to discard these hours. There was an emotional cost as well. The engineers had a hundred hours of emotion invested in their idea. It is always difficult to throw away such emotion.

THE FREQUENCY SYNTHESIZER MODULE

Another part of Delphi's system was a frequency synthesizer module or FSM. This FSM generated frequencies that were used throughout the system. At the beginning of the project, the builder's engineers designed a circuit for the FSM. It was a good design that comprised 70 individual components. Building the circuit would be difficult, but not impossible. The design, however, was sound and this was a tough project, so having one more tough circuit did not seem to make that much difference.

Before the builder ordered the parts, one of the builder's engineers found a single integrated circuit (a chip) that would replace the 70-component circuit. Some of us thought this was a great idea. The builder, however, did not want to use the single chip. Their engineers had already designed a circuit, and we had already approved their design. They did not want to throw away the hundreds of engineering hours they had consumed on the design. They were behind schedule and over cost. Throwing away those hours would put them farther behind.

Using the original design was the wrong approach. One part verses 70 components meant lots of extra work required to buy parts, build the circuit, and test it. We convinced the builder to discard their design and use the chip. This was a correct decision. The chip went into place and worked well. Later developments showed us that building the circuit as designed with the 70 components would have been plagued with problems. In the end, we saved far more time and money than we "wasted" by throwing away the original design.

Again, this was not an easy decision. We were throwing out an expensive design that we had already bought. As buyers, we would not receive a refund on this discarded work. This also carried an emotional as well as financial cost. The engineers had put a few months of their lives into this design. Throwing it away hurt (for a while), and it took time to move past that hurt.

WARNING SIGNS OF DOING THE WRONG THING REALLY WELL

The stories above show that it is easy for well-meaning people to do the wrong thing the right way. It is difficult to stop from doing the wrong thing and go in the right direction instead. These statements tend to run opposite to what we would expect. No one would want to go in the wrong direction, and everyone would want to go in the right direction. This, however, is not the case. We have noticed a few things that indicate trouble coming with this situation. The following discusses some of these warning signs.

"We Must"

A major problem in projects is when people try to make decisions while under duress. Chapter 24 discusses this topic at length. When in trouble, we stop breathing properly. We make decisions that seem good, but this is because our brains are short of oxygen and everything is fuzzy.

People making decisions under duress cause two problems. The first is that they make bad decisions. They go down the wrong road, attempt to build the wrong product, and take the wrong approach to a situation. The second problem with people making decisions under duress is that it is hard to have them understand that they are making bad decisions. They should stop, take more time, and make a well-considered decision. They, however, cannot seem to do that. They are already on negative time, and you do not realize their situation. They see you as trying to heal their wounds by killing them.

The warning sign that people are succumbing to the pressure is in the words they use. Watch out for "must" and "cannot" as in, "We must go in this direction," and "We cannot go in that direction."

The story of the FSM is one such example. The builder had spent hours designing the FSM circuit. They were already behind schedule and over budget in their project. We heard the key words, "We must use the design we have. We cannot throw away the money we spent on that design."

We Know

We always have choices. A problem that plagues projects is that people sometimes do not consider their choices. This can manifest itself in several ways.

One warning sign of not considering choices is in the statement, "We know just what we need." We might welcome such a statement of knowledge and confidence. Our experiences, however, indicate otherwise. Often, confident people are confident because they have not looked for problems. One thing to do when hearing, "We know just what we need" is to replace it with, "We are not sure what we need."

When people are certain of something, they have either spent thousands of hours researching, studying, and modeling or they have spent far less time and energy. They next time someone states, "We know just what we need," we need to find out which group they are in. Have they spent the thousands of hours researching, studying, and modeling or have they spent far less and are only certain of being tired?

The Workforce Retooling Project was an example of this. Someone knew just what the workforce needed—a 50-page book that explained everything. They did not spend five minutes studying different choices for how to provide career advice to people. The idea came to them, they said it aloud, and they had the authority to send the project in that direction. The project was a success in that we did everything right. The product was a failure as it was the wrong thing.

No Choice

People on projects can become tired. If the project is in trouble, the fatigue leads to frustration and being demoralized. This all leads to an attitude of defeat. People in such situations often go in the wrong direction and spend resources doing the wrong thing. They cannot find the energy they need to see the choices in front of them. Their pride and professionalism, however, keep them doing things right. This often fools them into thinking that they are doing the right thing.

A warning sign of a defeated attitude is when people say, "We have no choice." As stated already, there are always choices. We need to understand that when someone says, "We have no choice," they are telling the truth. They cannot see any choices for themselves. Someone else needs to help them see the choices.

This happened to us on Delphi in the story of the demodulator. The engineers who recommended a redesign saw that as the only choice. These engineers were tired. They had been working long days and weekends for months and felt like they would be doing that for many more months in the future. Despair led them to the automatic answer for any engineer—design. It is fortunate that we were able to help them see another answer. We were not smarter than they were, but we were not as tired. We had the energy to see other choices and encourage them to consider them.

The Universal Approach

One of the tools we use in projects is a basic problem-solving approach or the scientific method. People have been using this to solve problems for centuries. It works well, but sometimes we forget that there is much room for thought in the method. Instead, we fall into the trap of doing the same thing regardless of the situation. This same thing means that thinking has almost or completely stopped.

A sign that thinking is dwindling is the phrase, "We solve all problems using this approach." This is what happened to us in the Workforce Retooling Project. We had a problem—people did not know how to progress in their careers. We did what we always did—we had a project. The project did what all projects did—produce a big document. The process was what all our projects used—have a preliminary study, have a full study, have a committee work, etc. This consumed three years and thousands of man-hours, only to produce something that no one used.

Our problem in "doing what we always did" is that we forgot how much thinking we always did on projects. Workforce retooling was not like our usual engineering and operations projects. It was a personnel or human resources project. We thought it was easy and that since we were engineers, we did not have to think much about it. We were wrong. We chose the wrong path and did the wrong thing.

TIPS TO HELP FIND THE RIGHT WAY

The previous material shows how we can easily do the wrong thing. Doing that wrong thing in the right way can fool us into thinking all is well. We have learned a few things that help create an environment in which we are more likely to do the right thing. The following describes some of these ideas.

Mark Twain Was Wrong

We begin our techniques by asking people to remember the air conditioner. This may sound strange, but consider the old saying (attributed to Mark Twain), "Everyone talks about the weather, but no one does anything about it."

We talk about the weather because it affects our lives. We did not change the weather, but we did the next best thing. We built weatherproof buildings and conditioned the temperature and humidity inside them. We have refuted the old saying and done something about the weather.

Often in projects, we let our statements control our thoughts. Some of these statements from this chapter's stories are, "We are engineers, so we design things. We have already done some work, and we cannot throw that away." The first part of each of these statements was correct. The second part was an incorrect conclusion we drew from the situation.

Much has been made in the last 20 years about "thinking outside the box" and "changing the paradigm." People say these things so often that some have become cynical about them. They do hold some truth, as people have changed situations drastically by thinking, creating choices, and doing something out of the ordinary. To help create an environment in which people do the right thing, remember the air conditioner. Ask, "What is a fundamental thing that if we changed it would change our situation?"

Your Mission, Should You Choose to Accept It

Organizations exist for a reason. In government, it is to serve part of the public. The Department of Highways oversees the construction and maintenance of roads so the public can travel safely. The Department of Defense defends the nation against those who wish to do the nation harm. One way to create an environment in which people do the right thing is to examine the mission of the organization. Three useful questions are: Why does the organization exist? What is its primary product? Who are its primary customers? The answers to these questions help us determine if we are doing the right thing and heading down the right path.

Let us first look at the reason for existing. Recall the story of the supercomputer. The signal processing lab existed to process signals. The people in the lab were processing all the signals they had in the time they had. A supercomputer would enable them to process their signals in half a day. They would have had nothing to do the rest of the day but drink coffee. Drinking coffee was nice, but not why the organization existed.

Organizations have a primary product. Too often, we find ourselves trying to build other products. It is good for an organization to explore and open new markets. This, however, is the reason why R&D groups exist. In the FSM story, the builder was trying to build a system. This system was the main product of Delphi. The builder was wandering off trying to show how well it could build a complicated circuit when a simple one would do just as well.

Finally, organizations have a primary customer. They should do all they can to serve this customer. Bigger, older organizations wander into serving themselves instead of their customers. The Workforce Retooling story was an instance of this. We spent thousands of man-hours building a product. The problem was the product was for ourselves instead of for our customer. We did not know how to build a product for ourselves and we did not have any justification for doing so.

Three's a (Necessary) Crowd

In all our years of working with people and systems, we have yet to see an approach that was faultless. This is because we as people create the approaches and we have faults. Systems and approaches are optimized for one attribute, not all attributes. A technique to avoid taking the wrong approach is to ask one question about the approach we choose. The question is, "What three things are wrong with this?"

There is nothing wrong with finding things that are wrong. As discussed above, all systems are optimized for one attribute, and we let the other attributes falter. It is enlightening to learn what we have allowed to falter. It is a good exercise to write these weak points on the whiteboard and allow everyone to read them. This exercise often uncovers more faults than we anticipated.

Recall the FSM story. Using a 70-component circuit had its faults. These included (1) harder to document, (2) harder to build, (3) harder to test, (4) harder to purchase the parts, (5) harder to stock replacement parts, and (6) more chance that parts would become obsolete. We thought of these six things in 30 seconds.

Finding what is wrong with an approach is not an exercise in finding fault with the people who created it. It is an exercise in improving the product. Take great care in separating the product from the people. Admitting that we have faults and that our approaches may have (at least) three things wrong with them is a big step in humility. It is also a big step in avoiding doing the wrong thing.

The Big Picture

People working in a situation often become engrossed in the details of that situation. We lose sight of much by becoming expert in little. This concentration on details can lead us into doing the wrong thing. One way to avoid this is to heed the old saying, "Get off the dance floor and get on the balcony."

There are several ways to get off the dance floor and gain perspective. One is with time. A few extra days to think about something can produce many new ideas. Time is also helpful when we spend a few days thinking about something else. After that time, we can come back to the original situation to find that its appearance has changed.

Another way to gain a better perspective is with physical distance. Go away somewhere else and then come back to the situation. Distance changes the weather, the people, the culture, etc. In Delphi, we as buyers were three thousand miles away from our builder. This distance allowed us to see the big picture and suggest new approaches. Sometimes our suggestions actually helped.

Having an outsider look in is another way to gain a better perspective. There are several types of outsiders we can invite in. One is an outsider from another profession. Invite an accountant or nurse to look at what a group of engineers have decided. They may not understand any of the technical details, but they may catch key thoughts. Pay close attention when they say something like, "I do not understand why you are doing such and such." Also watch if they keep asking questions about one particular area of an approach. This area may have problems. A good choice for an outsider is a person from another culture. Invite a European, Asian, or African to come in a look at work done by Americans. People from other cultures use different language and see things differently. Pay attention to what catches their attention and to their words. Do not dismiss anything as ignorance or lack of familiarity.

Another type of outsider is a person who has a different amount of emotional involvement. We invest our emotions in our work. This investment blinds us from seeing things about our work. Bring in a consultant as they have no emotion invested in the approach. If a consultant is too costly, bring in someone from your organization who is not working on the project. They too have little invested and can see the project with fresh eyes.

Live a Little, Learn a Little

The techniques discussed above are not free. Thinking requires time and bringing in outsiders costs money. These are easier to afford if we plan for them. Sometimes, we need to try something before we can see that it is the wrong thing. It may help to head down a path for a while to see if it is a good one. This requires resources so we can stop, back up, and try another path. These walks down paths cost something. This something would not be on hand if we did not plan ahead.

This is not a plea to be fat and happy and hack away for months. The idea is to plan for learning. We have intelligent people and tough problems. Rarely is the first idea the right idea, but intelligent people can learn. Plan to give them a chance to choose the right thing.

SOME CONCLUSIONS ABOUT DOING THE WRONG THING THE RIGHT WAY

There is no right way to do the wrong thing. Part of our job is to be sure of our destination before we start down a path. If we win the rat race, we are still a rat. Instead, we need to step out of the rat race and run with some other more desirable species.

This brings us to the principle of doing the right thing: Find ways to choose the right thing for the product and the people creating it.

Watch out for:

- "We must."
- "We know just what we need."
- "We have no choice."
- "We solve all our problems using this approach."

Helping to create a good environment:

- Remember the air conditioner.
- Remember your reason for existing.

- Ask, "What three things are wrong with this?"
- Look at the big picture.
- Have a reserve for experiments and learning.

People work in chosen professions. Those professions are known for the things they do. Sometimes, however, those things are not the right ones for a given situation.

We have often charged down the wrong path because a manager sent us there. A typical case is when a manager says, "We develop architectures here, but we do not have a management plan that states how we do it. We need one of those." We charge off and spend three days a week for a month writing a management plan. Once finished, we proudly bring it back to the manager and explain it to him. His eyes glaze over and he mumbles, "This is nice. What is it? Why did you write it?" We did the wrong thing the right way.

A couple of years ago we learned an excellent tip from consultant and author Jerry Weinberg.* His advice is, "Test, not detest." The "detest" part refers to what we did above. We charged down a path, did a lot of work, and finished our work by detesting a manager who told us to do the wrong thing. Instead, Weinberg urges testing the manager first. We should take a few small steps down the path and show the manager the results. If he is still interested, we take a few more steps and show the manager the results again. Only after we have tested him a few times do we go all the way down the path. These three words have kept us from wasting resources doing the wrong thing the right way many times.

*www.geraldmweinberg.com.

Part 8

The final three chapters discuss ways that we fool ourselves while working on projects. Chapter 23 is about how we sometimes think we know something when we really do not. We allow the circumstances to distort our view of things and lead us astray. Chapter 24 discusses the bad decisions we often make when we are behind schedule, over cost, and under pressure. Chapter 25 ends this book with a discussion of our desire to be "out of the woods" and coast to the end of a project. We are never out of the woods until the customer has the product in their hands. When we think otherwise, we have problems.

It Sounded Good When We Started. By Dwayne Phillips and Roy O'Bryan
ISBN 0-471-48586-1 © 2004 by the Institute of Electrical and Electronics Engineers.

Chapter 23

Not Knowing What You Know: Are You Really Getting the Desired Results?

Engineering and other types of technical work often deal with gathering and interpreting data. People gather data, people interpret data, and people make mistakes. Sometimes, our mistakes are that we interpret data the way we want to and often ignore the real meaning. We know things from the data. Sometimes, however, we do not know what we know.

DRIVING IN FAIRFAX COUNTY, VIRGINIA

We both live in Fairfax County, Virginia, a suburb of Washington D.C. Fairfax is growing rapidly as developers knock down trees and build roads, houses, and shopping centers. The people who make maps for the county are unable to keep pace with the builders. There are many roads that are not on the maps.

My sons play soccer, and their teams play around the far reaches of the county. We often have to look on the map to find our way to a new soccer field. The map contains data. There is little chance that I misinterpret the map data, so I know what I know. I often tell myself, "This must be the place because that is what the map says."

With the growth, however, the map may not be correct. I act as if I have no other choice. I really do not know what I know. I tell my sons, "I think we will turn right up here and be at the field." While driving by map in Fairfax County, we know what we do not know. We know that although the maps are pret-

It Sounded Good When We Started. By Dwayne Phillips and Roy O'Bryan   **281**
ISBN 0-471-48586-1 © 2004 by the Institute of Electrical and Electronics Engineers.

ty dependable they do not contain all the roads. These new roads are troublesome, but we can work around this trouble.

REPAIRING A SYSTEM

During Delphi, we sent one of the first systems back to the builder for repair. There were hardware problems, and the builder required eight weeks to find and fix them.

The system had "clock jitter." This was because the circuitry was generating unwanted electromagnetic energy. This indicated that something was broken or loose. All the builder had to do was locate the defective circuit and replace it. The builder's engineers found the clock jitter at the output of the system. They traced back one circuit at a time until they found a circuit that did not have clock jitter. This meant that this circuit was the culprit. The builder was certain of this, but further investigation showed that it was not the culprit. They did not know what they knew.

The engineers thought about this a day and changed their test equipment. They went to another test setup that gave them a much better view of the unwanted energy. They found clock jitter in circuits farther back in the chain. They were back on track. One problem, however, with the better test setup was that now they were not sure of the clock jitter they had seen with the previous test setup, so they had to start over.

The engineers traced back from the system output one circuit at a time. They finally found a circuit with no clock jitter at its output. The previous circuit had to be the one that generated the clock jitter. All they had to do now was replace this circuit. This was not exactly the case because they could not replace the entire circuit. They needed to find the specific components in this circuit that were causing the problem. They would replace those components. What they knew before, replace the entire circuit, was incorrect. Again, they did not know what they knew

Now they were looking for the individual components that caused the problem. The test setup failed at this point. It sensed clock jitter throughout the circuit, but could not isolate it to individual components. They did not know what they knew. They needed yet another test setup that would help isolate the bad components.

The builder switched from an electrical test to an optical one. The builder's engineers examined the circuit with a microscope because this technique had worked before on other problems. They peered through a microscope for a day but found nothing. Again, they did not know what they knew.

The builder's engineers eventually found the problem components. They did this by pressing down on a tiny component with the point of a pencil. When they pressed on the component, their test setup sensed clock jitter. When they relieved the pressure, the clock jitter was gone. They removed the component and found that a tiny amount of solder had flowed under the component. This solder shorted the circuit and caused the clock jitter. They finally knew what they knew.

After the builder removed the clock jitter, they had another problem. Another part of the system would not work. It worked at room temperature, but it would not work at 40°F. The builder's engineers ran the built-in test, and it failed. They worked on this for a week. Upon further discussion, one of the engineers admitted that the system did not fail the complete built-in test, but a shortened version of the built-in test. The engineers doing the troubleshooting were working with partial information. They did not know what they knew so they started over.

The builder now knew the precise test that the system failed at 40°F. The builder's engineers worked on this for a week. Upon further discussion, one of the engineers admitted that the outside of the system was at 40°F. The inside of the system, where the components were, was at an unknown temperature. It took a long time for the inside of the system to cool down to 40°F when placed in the cooling chamber. The engineers did not want to wait that long, as they were in a hurry to find and fix the problem. So once again, they did not know what they knew.

At this time, one of the engineers decided to try a radical procedure. The software engineers were working on an upgrade to the software. The software upgrade was in the area of the system that was failing at 40°F. Just as an experiment, the hardware engineer loaded the as yet to be completed software upgrade. The system started working. It worked 100 times in a row whereas previously it had failed 100 times in a row. This was remarkable. How could anyone explain this dramatic change? There was some hardware in the system that the upgraded software did not use but the original software did use. This hardware was broken. If only the software engineers could find that hardware.

Upon further discussion, an engineer confided that the system might have been closer to room temperature than 40°F when it worked 100 times in a row. Maybe the temperature and not the new software was the cause of the remarkable change in performance. Again, they did not know what they knew.

After a few more weeks of work, the builder repaired the system and returned it to us. I honestly do not know the final resolution because I lost myself in the chain of knowing and not knowing. Now I did not know what I knew.

WARNING SIGNS OF NOT KNOWING WHAT YOU KNOW

The above stories relate out experiences in situations in which we were confused about what we knew and what we did not know. We think we are not alone in this, as colleagues have related similar situations to us. There are signs that warn of such uncertainty.

In the Eye of the Beholder

The following three sections describe problems that we experience in our mind. Sometimes we are overconfident, sometimes less than confident, and sometimes impatient. These cases have nothing to do with the systems being built or the data. They are all in our minds, so they are some of the toughest problems of all.

It Is Obvious to the Casual Observer

The first problem we have with ourselves is being too confident. We think we know something when we do not. A warning sign of this is when someone says, "It's obvious from the data that. . . ." Data are rarely obvious. They may lead us to conclude something, but the conclusions mean we still need to check a few things.

At different times in my career, I worked in jobs where I had to repair systems. Some of these were software, some hardware, and some combinations. Troubleshooting a defective hardware system involves running tests and taking data. The data point me to where the problem may lie. The point of failure, however, is obvious only on rare occasions. Debugging defective software is similar. The test data indicate possibilities that I follow to an area of source code. Debuggers help, but I need to look at the code, work with it, and fix it.

Overconfidence is often wasteful. When I "know" something is obvious, I hurry to that point. Hurrying means that I skip steps, do not record data properly, and miss other fundamentals.

The story of Delphi included many times when the data seemed obvious to the builder's engineers. Further investigation often showed that they were too confident in their conclusions. Their early conclusions often led them to hurry down a path that led nowhere. Such hurrying wasted time and frustrated people.

Analysis Paralysis

The opposite of being too confident is having no confidence. In this case, the person looks at the data endlessly without creating any possible explanations. A sign of this is when people say, "I'm not sure about this, so I want to run a few more tests." This is analysis paralysis. The data are inconclusive, so we think and think and think. Something happens in analysis paralysis. People become afraid to do anything so they sit and worry.

When stuck in analysis, people do not realize how much they know. We always know what tests we have run, the data that the tests produced, and, most important, we always know that we are good people working on a difficult problem. We can use what we know and take the next step. In analysis paralysis, we tend to forget what we know and dwell obsessively on what we do not know.

Projects conducted in an environment of fear often have analysis paralysis. People have been hammered for taking an idea and exploring it. It is true that we should not spend large resources on a whim. We must, however, remember that large and whim are subjective.

The story of driving in Fairfax County is an example of avoiding analysis paralysis. When the map and terrain do not agree, I do not know what I know. It is easy to pull over and study the map and the nearby street signs. I could sit for hours hoping that somehow that map would change or that someone would drive up and change the street signs. I do, however, know that I have been in this situation before. I stop and ask for directions because I know that the map and terrain often do not agree in a fast-growing area.

Inconclusive Conclusions

The third problem that exists in our minds is impatience. We tire of looking at data and feel the urge for action. A warning sign of impatience is when someone says, "The data are inconclusive, so we will go ahead and do X." People who say this want to plunge ahead. They know that there are things they do not know, but they feel certain they can overcome that ignorance with action. This problem occurs more frequently when people are behind schedule. Every moment they sit and think, they fall farther behind. Action seems to be the only way to catch up, so they act.

The problem with impatience is that we waste resources. People lurch off in a direction and spend large amounts of resources on a whim. Again, "large" and "whim" are subjective. In this case, the whim is too whimsical and the large is too large.

The builder did this several times in the system repair story. The builder never seemed to run a full set of tests before reaching a conclusion and starting on a course of action. A quick test indicated something; the builder jumped on that indication, and set off in a direction. A week later the builder learned that the first indication came from a partial instead of a full test. They had to retrace their steps.

Looking Wrong

Part of the problem with not knowing what we know is how we look for or sense data. The following three sections discuss different mistakes we have made while looking for data. Sometimes we look in the wrong place, sometimes at the wrong time, and sometimes with the wrong tools. These mistakes in looking often lead us in the wrong direction.

Looking for Love in All the Wrong Places

Engineering and IT projects involve intellectual work. This means that people spend much of their time thinking. Sometimes we forget that. We become nervous if we are not doing something physically. This desire to be doing something can be a big problem on projects.

A warning sign of this is when someone says, "Joe is an expert in area X, so he will start looking at X." For example, "Joe knows maps and map reading, so he will study the maps." It seems that this is a good thing for Joe to be doing. He is working in his area of expertise. The problem is that no one has determined that the trouble is with the maps. Joe is charging off spending time doing what he knows, but will that exercise help us know what we need to know?

People tend to look in familiar places. Programmers look in software, and hardware designers look in the hardware. If the system has a problem, we can convince ourselves that there is a problem where we are looking. Now, if the hardware designer and software designer are working together, the hardware person will be convinced that it is a software problem and vice versa.

The desire to do something may cause us to try changing something in our area. Maybe that will do the trick. The keyword here is "trick." There is no real reason why doing something here will lead to a good result. We do know that we can do something, but we do not know that the something will help us.

The story of driving in Fairfax County is an example of this. I often find myself where the map and the street signs do not agree. My first reaction is to study the map, as that is what I have in my hand at the time. The trouble is, looking at the map will not help me. The street signs disagree with the map because they are newer than the map. Looking at the map is looking in the wrong place.

Time Is (Not) on Our Side

Related to the problem of wanting to do something whether it is right or not is the problem of wanting to do something now whether now is the right time or not. This often occurs when a project is behind. People want to do something today, right now.

A sign of this is when people talk of problem solving with an emphasis on near-term time. One example is, "We can take measurements in the next 15 minutes, so let's do that now and not waste any more time."

Will taking those measurements in the next 15 minutes help us know anything, or is it looking for data at the wrong time? Maybe the best time for taking measurements is eight hours from now. Maybe waiting is the best way to spend those eight hours.

The story of the builder repairing a system is a case in which we were looking at the wrong time. The system was not working at cold temperatures. At one time, the builder thought they had found a remedy to the problem. They had run a set of tests that the system passed at cold temperature. They were mistaken because the outside of the system was cold, but the inside of the system, where the components are located, was not cold. The builder wanted to take measurements now instead of waiting for the inside of the system to cool down to 40°F. The engineers were collecting data at the wrong time. Once they allowed time for the system to cool, they could take meaningful data. The answer was bad news (the system was not working), but it was a good answer.

If I Had a Hammer...

A major problem in troubled projects is a lack of resources. Sometimes, what people lack are the right tools needed to do the job. Often someone will say, "We will investigate the problem using tool X."

The warning sign of trouble is the answer to, "Is that the right tool?" Now come the flashing red lights. Trouble is looming if the answer is either, "I do not know," or "No, but that is all we have."

The story of the builder attempting to repair a system is a case in which we used the wrong tools. The builder was looking for clock jitter. Two weeks of troubleshooting were thrown away because they were using the wrong tools. Their first tool showed them some but not all of the clock jitter. These inadequate tools convinced the builder that they knew something when the reality was they did not know much of anything.

The builder switched tools used to gather data. The new tools showed them clock jitter with much greater accuracy and reliability. Now the builder's engineers knew what they knew. They could see the data, draw conclusions, and locate the problem. The builder found the cause of the clock jitter problem by switching tools altogether. Someone picked up a pencil and pressed on the top of a chip. This was the right tool for this case. It showed the location of the physical problem.

PROBLEMS WITH DATA

Sometimes our problem on projects is how we treat data. Data are facts, plain and simple. Sometimes, however, we give data power over ourselves so that we fear and avoid them. Sometimes, the opposite is true in that we give ourselves power over the data. We are powerful enough to manipulate the data to our advantage.

General Terms

Data are important in engineering and IT projects. The data indicate what is happening with the system we are trying to build. The data are our window into the system's world.

One problem people sometimes have in projects is they avoid data. It is as if the data were poisoned or unsanitary so they walk out of the room when data are present. A warning sign of avoiding data is when people speak in general terms. They say things like, "We did some testing," and "They showed me some test data." Data are specific—"27.4 volts DC" instead of "some voltage." Tests are specific—"section 3.2 of the acceptance test procedure" instead of "some final tests."

Avoiding data may mean that people do not know what they know. Sometimes, people do not know what tests someone else conducted. They were told, "I did some tests and the system has some problems." They stopped the conversation at the point and reported the general results to others. They did not pull information by asking, "Which test? Which part of which test? Which steps in the test procedure? In what way did the system fail? What were the results supposed to be? What were the actual results?"

Avoiding data may also mean that people do not want to talk about what they know. We know we are in trouble, but admitting trouble is a sign of weakness. Instead of admitting we have problems, we talk around problems using general terms. Maybe something will happen while we are talking. Someone else will find a solution and burst into the room while we are mumbling generalities.

People avoided data in the story of Delphi presented earlier. The first data avoidance was when the engineers used a test that showed them little information. They seemed to deny that the test setup was faulty. Another case was when the engineers forgot that just because the skin of a metal box was at 40°F, the inside of the box was not necessarily at the same temperature. Finally, they avoided the data that said the successful tests were run at room temperature instead of a cold temperature. All this avoiding of data wasted time and money. People stumbled from one test to another. Their stumbling produced fatigue, which brought on more stumbling.

Great Expectations

Data are important on projects. We can, however, believe in that statement too much. In such cases, we manipulate data to our advantage. One warning sign of manipulating data is when someone says, "We'll run test X and we expect it to show us Y."

The problem with expecting an answer is when we want a test to produce an answer. We have been working on a problem too long and we want to move on to something else. If the test will produce the desired answer, we prove our theory, fix the system, and move on. The desire to see the right answer can cloud judgment. We run a test and interpret the data to fit our theory. Everything in our train of thought works but the system. We are out of ideas, out of energy, and we want someone else to walk in with the answer.

The builder on Delphi did this several times while trying to repair the system in the story presented earlier. Their engineers were tired of working on the system. If only the data would point to something they could repair, they could fix the system and move on. We were fortunate in that someone was available to play the role of the naysayer. This person kept the rest of the team grounded in reality instead of expectations.

Another warning sign of manipulating data is when someone says, "We expect to see Y, so we created a test to show us Y." This warns us that the person expects an answer so much that they are creating a special test to find it. They work hard to create the test, run the test, and the data show what they expected. We now know that we can create a test that will give a result we want it to give. The trouble is, we do not know any more about the real situation at hand. The most harm comes if we mistake this meaningless test data as real knowledge. We think we know something about the system when what we really know is that we can create meaningless tests.

TECHNIQUES THAT HELP PEOPLE KNOW WHAT THEY KNOW

It is difficult to know what we know when working with complex technical systems. As the story of navigating Fairfax County shows, it is difficult to know what we know in some common, everyday, easy situations. We have learned of a few techniques that create a situation in which it is easier to know what we know.

Three Interpretations

One way to create a good environment is to write three possible interpretations of the data. If I can only think of one interpretation, I have not devoted enough time and energy to the data. Writing the interpretations is important to me. They physical act of writing and then seeing my interpretations helps me to think. It also helps others to consider my thoughts and help me.

The story of driving in Fairfax County serves as an example of this. When the map and streets disagree, I can decide that the street signs are wrong and start driving in some unknown direction. The rule of three interpretations gives me alternatives. Three possible interpretations of these data are: (1) someone did not yet put up the street sign, (2) someone moved the street sign, and (3) the map is not up-to-date. Given my experience, I almost always choose (3) and ask for directions.

The rule of three interpretations helps us to avoid hasty actions. We admit to ourselves that maybe we do not know what we know. There could be something else that we have not considered yet. Now is the chance to use time and energy and consider three alternatives.

Outsiders

Part of the struggle with knowing what we know is that we tire of looking at a problem. One way to improve this situation is to bring in an outsider to view the data. The outsider has different expectations, familiarity with different things, and new energy. The different expectations offer interpretations of data that are different from the team's. These interpretations may not be correct, but they may help the team understand and refine their own interpretations. As discussed earlier, we often look for data in familiar places. The outsider is familiar with different things, so this person will look in different places. This increases the chances that we will find something that we have missed. The outsider usually brings new energy to the situation. In many cases that we have discussed, people were tired. Their judgment was less than their potential. The outsider is not tired with the situation. It is new to him, and this new energy often infects the team.

The builder on Delphi often did this. They had a senior engineer named Ray who was a key designer on the system. He left the project after it moved from the design phase to the build phase. He was knowledgeable and he became an outsider by spending months working on other projects.

Ray came in and had to ask questions to refresh himself. Those questions often gave the other engineers the insight they needed. They saw areas to explore that they had not considered. Ray was fresh and brought new energy along with a positive personality. People were happy to see Ray and his smile. He infected them with his energy and hope.

Private Eyes

A technique that helps us know what we know involves a facilitator and private interpretations of data. This is a group technique that begins with each person writing their interpretation privately on a blank piece of paper. No one writes their name on their paper as this is an anonymous exercise. The facilitator collects the papers, shuffles them, and hands them out to the people in the room. Each person now reads someone else's interpretation, thinks for a few moments, and writes their interpretation on the same piece of paper. The person can write the same interpretation they wrote the first time, or the may write something different—something that was influenced by what they read.

The facilitator repeats this process. He collects the papers, shuffles them, and hands them out to the people in the room. Each person now reads the interpretations of two other people. After reading and thinking about these two interpretations, the person writes their interpretation on the same paper. Again, they can write exactly what they have written before, or they can write something that shows the influence of the interpretations of two other people. The facilitator repeats this process until everyone has read the interpretations of three or four other people.

The facilitator then writes each interpretation on a large piece of paper and places them on the walls of the room. The facilitator leads the group in a discussion of each interpretation on the wall.

This technique helps us know what we know in several ways. First, data usually reinforce our beliefs and expectations. This technique allows each person to see what others expect and how they interpret the data. Second, this technique prevents flocking, whereby one person states their interpretation and this colors what everyone thinks. All the other people state ideas that follow the theme of the first interpretation. In flocking, the first person to speak dominates the discussion. This technique prevents flocking by allowing each person to see the interpretation of one person, then of another person, and so on. No one person is able to dominate the group.

Vive la Difference

A key to knowing what we know is finding the difference that makes a difference. Everything we do is different from everything we have done before. If we run one test on Monday and repeat it on Tuesday, we have done something different by running the same test on two different days of the week. Does the different day of the week make a difference? Probably not, but maybe it does.

An example can be seen in the system our builder made for us. We had the builder paint the system black. The builder did not paint the system until late in the integration of hardware and software.

What difference did it make what color we painted the system and when we painted it? I kept asking that question as a joke until I met the engineer who did the thermal modeling for the system. The paint acted as a thermal sink. It pulled heat away from the components inside the system and sent that heat out into the surrounding air. The system was cooler on the inside when it was painted and thus it performed better. In addition, each color of paint has different thermal properties. The black paint pulled heat away from the components better than any other color paint. The paint and color of the paint made a difference.

Other differences in our project made a difference. We learned that the date a component was attached to a circuit board could make a difference in the circuit's performance. The humidity in the builder's facility varied through the seasons of the year. The epoxy used to bond components to boards did not work as well when the facility was dry. We were fortunate to learn this early in the project. As a result, we closely monitored the humidity in the facility. When needed, we brought in extra humidifiers, and when necessary we stopped assembling circuits.

Yankee Doodle

A technique that I have used often that helps me know what I know is the "yank a wire" test. I perform this test when everything in a system appears to be working. The key word is "appears." We often think things are fine, but we do not know that. When a system is performing well, I yank a wire out. The system should stop performing well because I just broke it.

I learned this technique from an older engineer while we were testing a large switch matrix. This system had a hundred inputs and a hundred outputs and could connect any input to any output. The system occupied five boxes mounted in one rack. The builder was demonstrating how well the system was working by running test signals through every possible path in the matrix. The older engineer turned off the power to one of the boxes in the center of the switch matrix. This blocked the signal paths through the system. The system test, however, kept indicating that all was well. We then knew that the system test was faulty.

A couple of years later I used this test while we were learning how to use a communications system. A common test in communications is the "loop back" test. This is where you loop the output of the communications system back into its input—like pointing a transmitter back at a receiver. We had the system looped back into itself and were learning how to send messages of different formats. Everything was working well as every message we typed went out and came back to us. Something puzzled me, so I removed a wire in the path of the signal and sent another message. The message came back to us just as before. I now knew that we did not know what we were doing. Our tests and our messages were faulty.

Applying the yank a wire test is a little tougher when testing software. There are no wires in software, just lines of code. One equivalent here is to use input data that does not make any sense. For example, in testing Y2K modifications, input dates such as January 34th, 1776 or February 40th, 9764. The system should break or indicate that the input is broken. If it works fine with this yanked wire, you now know what you know—this system is not working.

CONCLUSIONS ABOUT NOT KNOWING WHAT YOU KNOW

People run tests, people interpret the results, and people make mistakes. Hence, we could be all wrong in how we collect and interpret data. This is one of the great challenges in working with systems.

This leads us to the principle of knowing what we know: People interpret data, and people make mistakes.

Watch out for:

- "It's obvious from that data that X. . . ."
- Analysis paralysis.

- "The data are inconclusive, so we will go ahead and do X."
- Looking for data in the wrong place.
- Looking for data at the wrong time.
- Looking for data with the wrong tools.
- Speaking in general terms.
- Expectations.

How to create a good situation:

- Write three possible interpretations of the data.
- Conduct independent reviews.
- Keep interpretations private.
- Find the difference that makes a difference.
- Run the yank a wire test.

One of the great challenges on projects is to remember the fallibility of people in interpreting data. It is easy to assume too much as well as admit too little.

One morning Roy and his wife Lynda awoke to find that their home air conditioner had quit working. Roy relates the following story (I means Roy).

I had an early morning staff meeting and could not stay home to work on the problem, so we called in the AC repairman. The repairmen came out 9:30 and spent a considerable amount of time going from inside the house to the outside and back.

At about 11:10, Lynda gave me a panic call saying, "The @#$%&$# repairman is not any closer to a solution than when he arrived. He made at least six calls back to his office explaining what he had done. He continued to go back and forth from inside to outside and from outside to inside. Could you please come home?"

Since I was just five minutes away and most of my problems at the office were under control, I went home. I asked the repairman, "What's the problem?" He said that "we" had a broken control wire, but he had been unable to find out which one it was. I glanced at the control box on the compressor (the outside unit) and noted four things: (1) All of the wires were color-coded, some with solid colors and some with different color stripes. (2) There were about 12 wires attached to terminals. (3) The terminals to which the wires were attached were annotated with numbers and letters. (4) There were four unattached wires—spares.

I asked the repairman if the wires were attached to a similar terminal block on the condenser (the inside unit). He said "yes" or at least "he thought so." We went inside and confirmed the situation. I pulled a 3" × 5" card out of my shirt pocket and jotted down the terminal's letter or number and the color of the attached wire. We went back outside to determine if, in fact, there was correlation between color of the wires and the terminal to which they were attached, and there was.

At that point I said to the repairman, "So you think we have a broken wire?" He reaffirmed that he was sure. Since I really did not want to pay $75 per hour for him to ponder how to find out which wire was broken, I casually asked, "How long have you been convinced that the problem is a broken wire?"

He said what I wanted to hear, "I knew it was a broken wire within the first 15 minutes after I arrived." He, however, had not been able to find out which one.

I said, "If it is a broken wire, we will find it in just a few minutes."

He was skeptical. I took all the wires off of the terminal block and twisted them together.

He asked, "what are you doing?"

I said, "We are about to discover which one is the broken wire."

His next question was of course, "How are you going to do that?"

I said, "With your ohm-meter"

We went back inside. I placed one lead of the ohm-meter on the bottom terminal (with the wires still attached) then I went down each terminal until I found the open circuit.

I said, "The broken wire is the orange and red wire on terminal J."

He was almost dumbfounded. He could not believe I had found the broken wire so simply without any analysis. We simply twisted the wires together and found the open circuit in less than 10 minutes. In another 5 minutes we had the compressor up and running.

Needless to say, the company wanted to charge me $225 for the repair job. I told them I would pay for a half an hour and no more. I related what happened and explained that it was better for them if I paid them for a half hour of labor rather than if they paid me for training their repairman how to isolate a broken wire. My rates were considerably higher than theirs. We settled on $48.

Chapter 24

Don't Forget to Breathe: What People Often Do Wrong When Behind Schedule

When we are behind schedule and under pressure, we stop breathing. We are in a hurry and we try to do things faster than we are able. The result of this physical and emotional lack of oxygen is we do stupid things instead of smart things. We feel like we are behind schedule because of fate or something. Since the unexplained caused our problem, the illogical will solve it.

THE BIG BANG

Before Delphi, we had a project with the same builder to create two fieldable prototype systems. It was a four-year $40M effort to develop a system with all new capabilities. (It was supposed to be a three-year $30M effort.) The requirements and design phases of the project were more difficult than expected, so the project was behind schedule and over budget.

The hardware portion of the system had 50 sections. The builder had tested each section a little, but performed nothing more than a smoke test (turn on the power and see if any smoke comes out). The system also had a complex software portion to control the hardware and perform digital signal processing.

The builder had an idea to save time. They wanted to use a big bang integration and test approach. A traditional bottom-up approach tests each section thoroughly to determine that they perform as expected. The next step is to combine the sections into one of nine modules and test each module individually. This process of combining and testing continues by combining the

It Sounded Good When We Started. By Dwayne Phillips and Roy O'Bryan
ISBN 0-471-48586-1 © 2004 by the Institute of Electrical and Electronics Engineers.

nine modules into a system and testing the system. The builder's idea was to skip all the low-level testing. They wanted to combine the sections into a system and test it all at once. The builder was confident of their design and construction. They expected to have a few problems in the system test, but they could find and fix the defects. The builder convinced the buyer to try it.

The big bang approach did not work. The builder would start the test and hit a wall of defects. It took forever to find and fix the errors because no one was sure of the location of each defect. The defect could be in one of 50 sections or it could be in software. Often, there were multiple causes of a defect. The builder would find and fix a cause, run the test again, and still see an error. They were not sure if they fixed something, or if that something was a cause of something else, or if the something else caused that, or if that cause of something else caused them to fix something that was broken but was not the cause of that something. Confused? So was everyone else.

The acceptance test took nine months instead of six weeks. The builder saved neither time nor money with the big bang approach. Instead, the project fell farther behind schedule and went farther over budget.

The big bang approach was a bad idea. This approach is almost always a bad idea, especially with a complex system like the one the builder was making. The builder, however, was behind and under pressure, and in that state the big bang seemed like a good idea. It was the the one miraculous event that could save the project.

SINGLE-SOURCE VENDORS

Several years later on Delphi, the builder needed parts from vendors. (We discussed this in Chapter 21 with the emphasis on the perils of outsourcing.) These parts were out of the ordinary and more difficult to build than the parts vendors usually supplied.

Our builder went to a vendor to buy a $20K part. The vendor had six weeks to deliver this part. The vendor tried but failed to meet the specifications. The vendor told the builder that they were quitting, and the project lost six weeks. The builder went to another vendor to try again for another six weeks. We, the buyer, recommended that we go to two or more vendors at the same time. The builder would not do that. Multiple vendors would cost too much money and time, and they were already behind schedule and over cost.

At this point in the project, we were spending $40K a day on the project. If we took another six-week hit in the schedule, that would cost us 30 days times $40K per day. This was a lot of money. It was obvious to us that multiple vendors would be worth the cost. Spending $60K for a $20K part could save us $1.2M.

The builder did not use multiple vendors. They made the wrong decision, and the project suffered. The overriding factor to the builder was that they were already over budget. They could not spend extra money on multiple vendors. The builder wanted to believe that the vendor they chose would come through, so they believed that.

It was a mistake to not use multiple vendors. The second vendor could not build the part either, and the project lost another six weeks. The builder went to a third vendor who was able to build the part. The project, however, had lost 12 weeks at $40K a day.

THE 0.1% NEGOTIATION

Another Delphi story involved another part of the system. Our builder was to buy this part from a vendor. This part was relatively easy to build and buy. The part vendor wanted $20K for the part times nine parts. The builder wanted to buy the nine parts for $15K each. The negotiations went on for six months. The builder was very concerned about the $45K ($5K difference in price times nine) because they were over budget.

This was a $33M project. The $45K difference in price was about 0.1% of the total project cost. Why would anyone care about that? The negotiations went on and on and on.

The builder put more time and energy into the negotiation than anyone could justify. While they were occupied with this negotiation, other needed parts were not ordered on time; designs were behind schedule, and engineers were quitting and leaving the company from frustration. The project manager did not attend to these other matters because he was busy with the negotiation. The pressure of the budget clouded the builder's judgment, and the project suffered. After six months, the builder bought the part at the vendor's price.

THE RACK FANS

After Delphi ended, I was assigned to help with another project that was struggling. This was a complex and difficult project (the Gamma project discussed in Chapter 5) that had large political as well as technical problems. This project had several major false starts that consumed several years. The project was off on another fresh start, but about a year into the fresh start, things started falling apart.

The project required more resources than management had allocated. The project manager needed to stop work and replan. If he understood the places in the project where resources were inadequate, he could present this information to management and request what was needed.

Instead, the project manager spent time working on technical details. We discussed whether a rack of equipment should have four or five little fans to move air. We discussed the optimum place to put the rack fans. We debated if we needed an internal heat sink, external heat sink, or no heat sink for the rack. We discussed many other little details at length. We did not replan the project to obtain the resources we needed, and the project continued to fall farther behind.

Why did the project manager dive into technical details instead of working on high-level issues? He realized that the high-level issues would bring him resources and help the project dig out of trouble. He, however, did not work on those issues. The pressure was on him, he was nervous, and people revert to what they know best when pressured and nervous. In this case, the project manager's background took him to rack fans instead of project resources. In the big picture, this did not make sense.

WARNING SIGNS OF LACK OF OXYGEN

The above stories relate how people stop breathing when under cost and schedule pressure. This lack of oxygen often leads to bad decisions that put projects in greater trouble than before. The following relate some warning signs of people not breathing properly.

The Quick Brown Fox

We hire builders because our users want products that we cannot build ourselves. Often, we cannot build the products because they are difficult to build. We frequently see this situation when people are attempting to build products that are complex and difficult. Sometimes people have the mistaken belief that their product is simple to build. This fallacy is often explained by a lack of oxygen.

A warning sign that people believe they are attempting to build a simple product is when they suggest quick fixes. People say things like, "If we just did this, we would get back on track." We have found that "doing this" usually means skipping steps. Our builder wanted to use the big bang approach. This would be a quick fix to the schedule and cost problems. They felt they could just slap the system together, run the tests, and be finished. Their designs were good, their assemblers were good, their test procedures were good, and it would all work out fine. The technical problem facing them was not that tough.

They were wrong, and the buyers were wrong to let them try the quick fix. Skipping steps caused a nightmare of testing, troubleshooting, fixing, testing, and so on. There are no easy answers that fix things quickly in hard projects. If we had easy answers and quick fixes, we would not be under pressure.

The Sands of Time

Projects have schedules. The user or marketplace wants a product on a certain date, and the builder strives to meet that date. Sometimes, the builder concentrates on that date too much. They let the calendar rule their lives and all their decisions. People in these situations may be lacking oxygen. A warning sign of lacking oxygen and bowing to the calendar is when people say, "We do not have time to (anything)." Anything can be talk, plan, organize, think, and so on. Let us look at each of these "anythings."

"We do not have time to talk." Talking with a coworker does not take much time. When compared to a six-month project, a five or ten-minute discussion is trivial. There are few things more valuable than talking with a coworker.

"We do not have time to plan." A project in trouble usually experienced troubles during planning. We thought we could do tasks faster than we could; we thought things would come together better than they have, and we were mistaken. Taking time to plan again armed with the knowledge of our mistakes is the best way to correct those mistakes.

"We do not have time to organize." People work through projects with some sort of organization. If we were not organized, everyone would be doing the same task at the same time. This duplication of effort would be chaotic and catastrophic. Organizing is not just for bureaucrats. It is what we all do when we breathe properly.

"We do not have time to think." Let us state the obvious one more time—we do intellectual work. If we do not think, we do not accomplish anything. We can fall into "analysis paralysis" and spend all day worrying about something so that we do not have time to do anything. This is the extreme. A few good hours of thinking, however, is usually the best thing we can do for a project.

The key words, "We don't have time to . . ." are a cry of desperation. They are telling us that we are in trouble. Do not listen to the "we don't . . ." part; listen to the cry of desperation.

This is what happened in the rack fan story above. The project manager was working hard on the project details. People kept suggesting to him that we stop and plan our way out of our troubles. We had to talk, think, and discuss our situation. He did not have the time to do such things. Someone really needed to finish the detailed design of the rack ventilation system. This other stuff might have merit, but there was no time for it. He was making a mistake induced by a lack of oxygen.

Pretty Sure

People have feelings and emotions. These are important parts of our lives and professions, and denying them is a mistake. Feelings, however, do not move electrons through circuits and do not repair faulty logic in software. We have seen people under pressure and lacking oxygen who feel that they can bring a project back on schedule.

A warning sign of placing a project in the hands of a feeling is when people say, "I'm pretty sure this will work, so let's move on."

Aha, some confidence! The project is in trouble and, finally, someone sounds like they know what they are doing. Most people are happy to pick up on that confidence and follow. Nevertheless, what does "pretty sure" mean? It means that the idea has some merit, but people have not examined it closely. In projects, it is rare that we are absolutely sure of an approach. Pretty sure, however, is not good enough. It means that we have not yet found the problems and the solutions.

In the story of single-source vendors, the builder was pretty sure that the chosen vendor could deliver the parts in six weeks. The builder had not thought enough about the vendor. Hindsight showed that the vendors who failed had problems in their parts-building processes. Their chance of success was about 50%. Going to multiple vendors at the same time would have increased the chance of the project succeeding.

The Expert

People are important to projects. Project managers, however, can put too much emphasis on people when they believe in the power of a single person to change a project. We have seen cases in which one person with the right knowledge solved many problems in a short period of time. Those cases, however, were rare and they did not make up for months of problems.

Sometimes, people believe that a senior expert will walk in and solve all the problems. This usually happens with people who are lacking oxygen. A warning sign of this is when they say, "Good news. John is coming on the project next week. He'll bring us back on track." They see nothing else that can save them from many more weeks of long days and weekends of vain attempts to rectify the project. They are lacking oxygen and hope, so they applaud the senior expert's arrival.

The senior expert often comes in with a loud sure voice. Some people ask a few questions, but the senior expert quickly and confidently quiets the questions. The problem here is not the senior expert. The problem is that people are putting all their trust in the senior expert. They believe the senior expert has a unique insight into the situation. They take the senior expert's word as irrefutable and they follow blindly.

The rack fans story is a case of the senior expert. In that story, the project manager also served as the system engineer. Upper management had labeled him as the expert on this project. He felt that working on the technical details was the right approach. If we would just give him a little support, he would knock off all the details one at a time. One day we would all awaken to find that the project had been finished by the senior expert. It did not happen.

TIPS TO RESTORE HEALTHY BREATHING

The above stories related how people under schedule and cost pressure often stop breathing. We have learned of a few techniques to create an environment in which people breathe better. The following describe some of these techniques.

One Step Ahead

The first way to avoid bad decisions while under schedule and cost pressure is to stay on schedule and budget. This means we need to manage the project well. This begins with better planning at the start of the project (Chapter 6 discusses this). We should track progress closely and act early when we start to slip (Chapter 9 discusses this). If all else fails, we should call time out and change the situation (see later).

These are fundamentals. The stories about the single-source vendor and the 0.1% negotiation are from a troubled project. Much of this book tells horrific stories of that project. We fell behind at the start and it was two years before we stopped the project and regrouped. We suffered through two years and more of oxygen-deprived decisions. This was a terrible situation, and we do not wish to see anyone suffer through a similar one.

Check, Please

While it is difficult to make good decisions under pressure, one way to improve our chances is to use a checklist. The checklist reminds us of things that have worked in the past. It does not rule our lives, but it helps us.

Some people avoid checklists. The reason is that checklists represent standard processes to many people. As with many things, some people have gone overboard with standard processes. Others have reacted to this extreme by going to the opposite extreme and banning anything that smells of a rigid process. We do not care what end of the process spectrum you favor. We encourage people to have a process that works for their situation and a checklist that reminds them of their process. Use this checklist when under pressure. If there is nothing to serve as a guide, it is easy to forget what has worked in the past.

The story of the single-source vendor resulted when the builder did not use a checklist. The builder had to decide to go with a single vendor or multiple vendors—a basic business decision. The builder should have looked at the probability of success of a single vendor, the cost of multiple vendors, and the cost to the project if a single vendor failed. All these steps could have been in a checklist. The builder forgot the steps because they were under pressure and not breathing properly.

The same is true of the story of the big bang integration and test. There are various integration and test strategies available, and each has its own advantages and disadvantages. The builder should have looked at the different strategies and picked the one that fit their situation. The steps for such an analysis could have been in a checklist. Once again, the builder forgot the steps because they were under pressure and not breathing properly.

Change, Change, Change

People create schedules and people have the power to change schedules. One way to avoid making bad decisions while behind schedule is to relieve the pressure by changing the schedule.

The first step in change is to acknowledge that the current schedule is incorrect. We thought we could do tasks in a given time period and the system would come together, but we were wrong. Things are more difficult than we expected, and it is time to stop fooling ourselves. Some organizations do not allow people to admit mistakes. They operate as if all their employees are perfect. Mistakes by employees mean that the managers made mistakes when hiring these less-than-perfect people. The managers never make mistakes, so the people they hire never make mistakes, either.

The first way to change the schedule is to do so officially. Convince management that we overestimated productivity and underestimated the difficulty. We are behind and bad things happen when under the pressure of being behind. (This chapter should provide plenty of horror stories.)

We have seen several cases in which buyers did not want the builder to change schedules. Changing the schedule is called "rebaselining," and many buyers see it as a way for the builder to clear their name of any wrongdoing. They want the builder to keep the original, failed schedule in place. They want the builder to suffer for their mistakes. This approach is along the lines of "misery loves company." The buyer is miserable because the builder is behind schedule and over budget. The buyer typically has to pay these bills and suffer these consequences. Some buyers feel that the builder made the mistakes and the builder should be miserable. This misery will spur the builder on to better performance.

We have never seen miserable people work better than happy people. If you are a buyer or a manager, be miserable for a while, then get over it. The object is to finish the project and deliver a product. Allowing a new schedule helps us towards those ends in many ways.

If people will not allow changing the schedule officially, another technique is to change it unofficially. Create a second, unofficial schedule that we think we can meet. An unofficial schedule is a schedule that we create and use just like any other schedule. The difference is that we still have the official schedule on the wall and we use it to brief progress to managers. We no longer use the official schedule with our team; we use the unofficial one.

Meeting the unofficial schedule has several benefits. First, the team is out from under the pressure of the official schedule and can breathe. They usually build a good product in such a situation. Second, success breeds success. The team meets its weekly goals and goes home on Friday happy. A good weekend follows the week's success, and the team returns to work on Monday refreshed and ready to work.

We have used this approach on several projects. What usually happens is that the unofficial schedule becomes the official schedule, as people see the unofficial schedule working and they stop looking at the official schedule. The official schedule disappears quietly. This is a good outcome for bad things—disappearing quietly.

A third way to change the schedule is to change it emotionally. Do not make a new, official schedule, and do not make a second, unofficial schedule. Instead, change your attitude about the schedule. The project manager acts like the project is on schedule and tries to convince the team to act like the project is on schedule. People think, talk, and make good decisions. The main idea is to avoid the bad behavior common to people who are under pressure. Try to forget the pressure of schedule and cost; relax and do the things you know to be right.

Convincing the team that all is well may be difficult. The best tactic is to lead by example. For example, if the team exclaims, "We do not have time for a systematic integration and test. Let's try the big bang approach!"

The project manager can say, "We know the big bang approach will not work in this situation. We will do what experience has shown us is best."

"But," replies the team, "we know the systematic approach will not get us to the end on time."

"I know," concludes the project manager, "and we know that the big bang approach will only bring us more headaches."

Quick Without Hurry

Finally, projects and people under pressure should heed the advice of former UCLA basketball coach John Wooden, "Be quick, but do not hurry."

We should do everything as quickly as we can on projects. We should not, however, try to do things quicker than our quickest. This is hurrying, and that is when we make mistakes. The pressure of being behind schedule and over budget pushes people to hurry. This is when we skip steps, try quick fixes, listen to the senior expert without question, and so on.

We need to watch ourselves and everyone else on the project. Are people who always eat lunch skipping it? Are people who always go home on time staying late? Are people who always talk to you before making a big decision making them without the talk? Those people are hurrying. They are trying to go faster than they can, and they are about to make some big mistakes.

SOME CONCLUSIONS ABOUT BREATHING

Good breathing leads to a clear mind, which leads to better decisions. Sometimes, things do not go well on projects, and we fall behind our schedule and overrun our cost estimates. The pressure is on, pressure inhibits our breathing, and we do not think well. This often means that we make mistakes and fall farther behind.

This leads us to the principle of remembering to breathe: Being behind leads to all sorts of harmful activities.

Watch out for:

- Quick fixes.
- "We do not have time to (anything)."
- "I'm pretty sure this will work, so let's move on."
- The expert.

How to create a good situation:

- Stay on schedule.
- Use a checklist.
- Watch everything.
- Change the schedule.
- Ask for help.
- Be quick, but do not hurry.

About two weeks before I did the final edit on this chapter, I underwent double hernia surgery. I did not breathe well for several weeks. I am happy to report that I was aware my shortage of oxygen and avoided important decisions for several weeks. When I had to make such a decision, I used checklists and the advice of trusted friends and colleagues. I think I did fine until my breathing returned to normal.

The surgery and its affect on my breathing were obvious to me and everyone around me, so we compensated. Pressure on projects is not so obvious, so the desire to compensate is much weaker. When behind schedule or over budget, go find someone who has had double hernia surgery and talk to them about how hard it was to breathe properly while they were recuperating.

Chapter 25

We're Almost Out of the Woods: You Aren't Finished Until You Are Finished

Most of us like to coast. We work hard, move through a project, and look forward to completing some critical tasks so we will be "out of the woods." Ah, to be out of the woods in that wonderful place where the project is practically finished! Nothing can go wrong once we are out of the woods and into the clear.

One thing about projects, however, is that we are never out of the woods. Something can happen in the final week that dooms the project. We can fail at that point and never recover because the last month is where everything is supposed to come together. If everything does not come together, the project falls apart.

We have worked on a few projects where we felt we were out of the woods. The tough things were behind us, and we could coast to the end of the project. Sometimes this worked, but usually it didn't.

A Y2K STORY

Like many, I was involved with several projects that updated systems to make them compliant with Y2K. I was the lead buyer for a system that scheduled resources. The builder could remedy most of the Y2K problems by updating to newer versions of the operating system and a database system. In addition, the builder needed to make three or four changes in the software they wrote.

This was going to be easy. Our upper managers had taxed all the offices to create a pool of money for Y2K issues. We were to receive funds from this pool to pay for the Y2K fixes. The minimum amount we could receive was $100K, and that was much more money than we needed. I was out of the woods and coasting before we started! I did not have the builder create plans for this effort and I did not monitor their progress. I did few of the things a conscientious buyer should do.

We had problems. First, we updated the operating system for the computer only to learn that the compiler would not run under the new version of the operating system. The compiler company quit selling compilers for that line of operating systems. We tried to make an old compiler fit a new operating system. This sort of worked, but we were not sure of it. Second, we were short of good programmers. All we had to do was replace some commercial products, change a few lines of code, and we were finished. We did not think we would need good programmers for this project. We were coasting along only to be surprised that the people we had could not do the job. We hired several consultants who brought us through, but that cost more money than we planned for.

As the months dragged on, we ran into some unexpected tasks. One was that we had to update a personal computer that was a distant part of a communications system. This was not a hard task, but it was an extra task that required extra people working and also included some travel.

The travel led to another incident that can happen when you think you are out of the woods and not paying attention. One of the builder's engineers needed to visit another office to install a new PC. This office, a four-hour flight away, was tightening its security for the impending Y2K. They required a picture ID for admittance. The engineer forgot his driver's license and the office's security people would not let him in. We were able to fax a picture ID to the office, but we had to scramble for half a day and that was yet another headache for all of us.

As if these difficulties were not enough, the free money stopped being free. People from the office that supplied the Y2K funds started calling us They were running the great Y2K project and had to report progress on all the little projects. These people wanted us to finish our project early so they could gain some credit. We, however, could not finish early. We were dependent on the group of people in another city finishing their new facility so we could install our system and declare victory. We had no influence on the time that this other facility finished. The phone kept ringing, and I started to be sick.

This project was a success (we updated everything and were operational before 1 January 2000), but it came down to the Y2K wire. I found myself sitting in front of the workstation with the builder's chief engineer trying to have it pass the final test the week before Christmas of 1999. The system was not dialing the phone correctly to communicate with the PC we had installed in another city. We had made a simple mistake in how we entered the phone number in a field. We found and corrected the error. I was really sick, though. I could not believe how such a simple project was coming to a close.

CUTTING THE BURN RATE

At one point in the Delphi project, things were going well. The builder had delivered five good systems on time, and had four to go. They suggested that we could save money by lowering the "burn rate" or the amount of money we were spending each month. We could do this by moving senior people off the project and replacing them with junior engineers. The junior engineers could do the remaining work and they would cost the project less money.

This was a good idea. The builder had delivered five good systems and had proved they could build them well. We were out of the woods and did not need experts to guide us every step of the way.

This strategy worked for about a month, but then we encountered technical problems. The junior engineers could not solve them. We were spinning in circles. We were lost in the woods. This was not the fault of the junior engineers. They were doing their jobs well, but the problems were beyond their expertise. We needed to bring the senior engineers back on the project. This was hard to do as they had become fully occupied on other projects. We retrieved them one by one, but slowly.

Once back on board, these senior engineers also struggled with the problems. We were looking for solutions to several problems in the system at the same time. Such multiple-problem situations are horrid. When a system has two problems, finding and fixing them are five times harder than finding one problem. Such was our plight, and we struggled.

We eventually solved the problems, but fell behind schedule—eight weeks behind. Everything on the project went well after the builder delivered system number six. The project, however, never recovered these eight weeks.

WARNING SIGNS OF BEING OUT OF THE WOODS

The above stories relate how thinking we were out of the woods caused us problems on several projects. It seems that when we believe we are out of the woods we stop paying attention to things. This lack of attention leads to problems. In hindsight, we have learned that there were things that pointed to our lack of attention. The following relate some of these pointers to coming trouble.

I've Got a Feeling

Emotions and feelings are an important part of us. We cannot deny them just because "we are working on an important project." Our feelings, however, can cause us problems such as when we assign an emotional value to tasks in projects.

One warning sign that people are assigning value to a task is when they say, "This isn't that important." If something is a part of a project, it is important to that project. If we can find a task that has no bearing on the success of the project, we should delete it. Assigning a low value to a task is a way of saying, "We are out of the woods. This task is unimportant, so we will coast on it."

An opposite, but equally important, warning sign that people are assigning value to a task is when they say, "This is the most important thing in the project." It may seem that placing high importance on a task has nothing to do with coasting. Once, however, this "most important thing" passes, people will believe they are out of the woods. Overemphasizing something sets up an opportunity to fall off afterwards.

Looking back at the story of the Y2K project, we kept telling ourselves that the Y2K issue was not important. All we had to do was update a few products, change a few lines of code, and be finished. We had important things we really wanted to do with that system. Sitting here writing this a couple of years after the fact, I cannot remember what these other important things were. I do, however, remember how we coasted on the Y2K issues and created a terrible mess.

A Day Late, A Dollar Short

An extension of the above problem is when people neglect overhead or background tasks. These do not directly add to the value of the product, but they do help us manage the project. "Managing the project" does not seem exciting to most engineers we have known. Nevertheless, most engineers we have known agree that bad management can overshadow lots of good technical work.

A warning sign that people are not giving management its due is when regular, short-term products are not turned in on time. These include things like metrics, time cards, and weekly reports. As with all other tasks on a project, these are important. Time cards and other time-accounting systems are important for tracking the cost and effort on a project. They tell managers when tasks are harder than planned and need more attention. When people turn them in a couple of days late, they are saying that these things are not worthy of attention.

One of the things we always do when working with a builder is have regular phone conversations. These occur on regular days like every Tuesday and Thursday. I skipped a number of these on the Y2K project. I did not think they were necessary as this was going to be really easy.

Another little regular task is a monthly review. This builder and I were in buildings about ten miles apart. It was easy to hold a two-hour review of status each month. It was also easy to skip a few of these. The builder would simply fax me the financial sheets with a couple of lines of explanation. This would suffice on this easy project. Again, I was wrong.

Out to Lunch

Projects are marathons, not sprints. It does not matter if a project is scheduled for three months or three years. Anything over three days is a marathon. Someone may be able to work 72 hours straight, but we have never met anyone who can work 24 hours a day for 90 days. People need to pace themselves when working on projects. When they do not, they work extra hard for periods of time and then crash when fatigue catches them. They are working in sprint–coast–sprint cycles.

A warning sign that people are not pacing themselves is when they take longer lunches. The key is not the length of the lunch, but its relative length. If people normally take 20 minutes for lunch, watch out if they start taking 30 minutes. If people normally take 45 minutes for lunch, watch out if they start taking 60 minutes.

People take longer lunches when they are coasting. This usually comes after they have finished a sprint. They take a little longer for lunch, a little longer break at the coffee pot, come in a little later in the morning, and leave a little earlier in the evening. None of these little periods of time is very long, but they are just long enough to indicate that they think they are out of the woods.

This happened on the story about cutting the burn rate. The builder had delivered the first five systems in the project. By everyone's reckoning, these were the toughest systems. The rest would be easy. The builder's engineers started to take longer breaks because they had earned them. In retrospect, the engineers working for the builder had earned a little break. The break, however, should not have been longer lunches. One suggestion for the break is discussed in the last section of this chapter.

Contagious Diseases

Coasting can be contagious. When one person see another taking it easy, the first person often feels that coasting is appropriate. This can be a big problem on projects. One person feels that they are out of the woods, others get the same feeling, and before we know it, the entire team is coasting.

This happened to us in the story of cutting the burn rate. The builder was moving senior engineers off the project onto other projects. To the uninformed, it appeared that the senior engineers were working half time. This was because the project manager was moving them off in stages. They would work 40 hours this week, 32 hours the next week, 16 the next, and so on. People who did not know that thought that the entire project had permission to coast. They still came in to work, but maybe worked hard 7 hours instead of 8 or 9.

I did this when I was young and on my first project out of college. Our job involved traveling out of the country for 60 days at a time. I saw people readying themselves for these 60-day trips by taking off a few days. I had the impression that everyone was supposed to stay home a few days while preparing for a trip.

I was misinformed (there are always many misinformed people on projects). In retrospect, the actions of these people were normal for their situation. They were married, had wives, kids, houses, and many other responsibilities. They had the "Honey dos" (before you leave for two months, honey do this, honey do that, etc.). They also had seniority. In this case, that meant they had built up vacation days they could take and they were taking those days off appropriately. I was not in that situation. I had no seniority and no vacation days I could take, but I did not understand this.

But still, I saw people coasting in front of a big thing. I wanted to coast, too. I was fortunate in that someone noticed how I was watching these older people "coasting" and wanting to emulate them. People explained the situation to me, and I was able to do my part on the project.

TECHNIQUES THAT PREVENT PEOPLE FROM BEING OUT OF THE WOODS

Coasting is a real danger on projects. The previous material related how it hurts projects and how we can lapse into it easily. We have learned a few things that help create an environment where coasting is less likely. The following discuss a few of these techniques.

Everyone, Every Day

For one last time in this text, we discuss the tried and true practice of talking to everyone every day. The project manager should know what people are doing every day and compare these actions to the plan. If the people are done with their current task and not working on their next one, they are acting like they are out of the woods. Acting like being out of the woods is different from being stuck on a task. Being stuck shows itself when the person is working on a task, but has not delivered the product of the task. Being out of the woods is when the product of a task is in hand, but the person is not on the next task.

One instance of this occurred when the project manager was gone for a week of jury duty. The first task the project manager did upon his return was to hear everyone's status. He discovered that people were not on task. They had fallen a week behind during his one-week absence.

The people, most of them older and experienced professionals, had wandered around a bit. Some were helping others. Some were investigating interesting problems that might come up later in the project. Everyone was at work all day as expected. They, however, were not doing what they were supposed to do. The project manager learned this by talking to people. If he had let those conversations slide for another week, they would have fallen two weeks behind.

The people on the project assumed they were out of the woods because the project manager was gone. It seems strange that anyone would equate the project manager being on jury duty to the project being out of the woods. As people, we all have times when we are a bit fuzzy in our reasoning. The people inferred that if the project was in trouble, the project manager would not have gone on jury duty. Since the project manager left, the project must have been out of the woods.

Let's Talk About It

One way to create an environment in which coasting does not occur is to talk with people about coasting. One way to do this is to ask people, "Do you think we are out of the woods? Do you think we can start taking it easy and coasting a bit?"

People might consider these odd questions, and that is why we recommend asking them. This could lead to all sorts of conversations, and during these conversations the project manager could mention stories like those related earlier, in which projects nearly died because people acted like they were out of the woods. The project manager can also relate some of the warning signs discussed earlier. People who are aware might watch for the signs in themselves and others.

Once these conversations begin, another good question to ask people is, "What three things need to happen for us to be out of the woods?" There is a danger in asking this question. Once some people know the answers to this, they may complete those three tasks, be certain they are out of the woods, and start coasting.

Most of the time this will happen. Instead, people will think of answers. Some might be, "Number one, finish the design of the I/O system, second, make it through my sister's wedding in June, and finally, see the interface between the field and home offices working. Once these three are done, I'll be fine."

These answers provide useful information. Now the project manager knows to watch closely after we finish those three things, as there will be a great temptation to coast after these events. These answers also alert the project manager to what concerns people. The project manager can watch these tasks intently and plan around them.

Another good question to ask is, "What three things need to happen for us to be back in the woods?" Ask this question when the project is going well. The question is looking for anything that could trip us. Some answers might be, "If Tom catches a cold like he usually does in November," or "if Linda's fiancée backs out of their wedding plans."

The example of Linda's fiancée was a real one I encountered on a project. Linda, a system administrator, grew up in a large, traditional family. She wanted a traditional wedding and family more than anything in life. At age

30, she was engaged. If her fiancée backed out, it would have been devastating. I am happy to report that they were married as planned and she does have a large, traditional, and happy family of her own. We did, however, see this as something that would plunge us into deep, dark woods. We could not do much about Linda's fiancée, but we did find other system administrators that we could bring in on short notice.

I wish I had asked this question on the Y2K project. Answers could have been, "One of our commercial products will not update with the new operating system, one of our tools will not work with the new operating system, and one of our people will quit this stupid Y2K project and go work on something interesting." Those answers would have helped wake me and cause me to pay attention to what I thought was an easy project.

Thinking Versus Coasting

Being out of the woods is an attitude; it is something in the mind. A characteristic of engineering and information technology work is that people spend large parts of the day sitting at a desk or in front of a computer terminal. Little physical activity takes place so we do not know if they are daydreaming or thinking. One way to prevent coasting is to discern between it and thinking.

The only way we know if someone is coasting or thinking is to ask. Ask in simple, short questions like, "What are you thinking? What is on your mind today? Do you think we are out of the woods?"

In the story about cutting the burn rate, there was one senior engineer of whom we wished we had asked these questions. He always took a moment to think before answering. We can see him smiling while holding his chin between his thumb and first finger. We can hear him hesitating with a long, "Well." His next words would have been, "Things look pretty good, but I do not know if such and such will pop up and bite us on this next system." If only we had asked.

The Theory of Relativity

A final technique for avoiding the out of the woods attitude is to understand and use the relative importance among tasks. First, emphasize critical tasks—they do exist. As stated earlier, everything in a project is important or it would not be in the project. Some tasks, however, make and break projects. They should get extra attention and concentration. The project manager should schedule the critical tasks to occur early in the project. If these tasks encounter problems, there is more time available to work through the problems.

There were several of these critical tasks on the Y2K project. The new operating system had to run on the old computer. If it did not, nothing else mattered. We should have put the new operating system on the old computer as soon as possible. Another "must have" for that project was to have all the development tools running on the new operating system. We delayed this task too long. We were three months into a nine-month project before we saw this.

Second, celebrate when the team finishes a critical task. After all, this was a critical task that could have broken the project. Instead, the team put forward the extra concentration and effort needed and came through successfully. They should celebrate with an intensity that matches the importance of the task. A weak celebration or no celebration at all shows the team that the project manager was not sincere about the importance of the task. Insincerity on this task will lead to a "who cares?" attitude the next time the project manager tries to emphasize something.

After the celebration, take a day off. Do not let people come to work and coast for a couple of days. Remember how coasting is contagious. Instead, have them stay home. After the people have celebrated and stayed away from work a day (or two), have them come back to work and go on to the next important task.

We wish we had done this on the Delphi project. We should have celebrated and taken a day off after the delivery of each system. Instead, we kept pushing until we pushed people into fatigue.

CONCLUSIONS ABOUT BEING OUT OF THE WOODS

There comes a time on most projects when we think we have passed the last big hurdle. We are out of the woods and can relax a bit because we feel that the project should take care of itself for the rest of the way.

This leads us to the principle about coasting: People like to get ahead and then coast, which rarely works.

Watch out for:

- "It's not that important."
- "This is the most important thing in the world."
- Daily products are not turned in on time.
- Longer lunches.
- One person coasting.

How to create a good situation:

- Stay in touch with everyone on the project.
- Talk with people about being out of the woods.
- Discern between being out of the woods and thinking.
- Understand and use the relative importance of tasks.

This is the last section of the last chapter of this book. It would be easy to say that we are out of the woods on this book project. All we have to do is just wrap it up, send it in, and coast. We put as many warning signs from this and other chapters into that one sentence as we could. It would be so nice if those things were true, but they are not. This book is a two-person project, but there are at least a dozen things that could go wrong. Most projects involve many more than two people, so they have many more possible things that could trip someone who was coasting.

We are never out of the woods on a project. The project is over when the final little piece of the product is in hands of the user. If you are reading this in its finished form from the publisher, we are coasting. Thanks.

Index

It Sounded Good When We Started. By Dwayne Phillips and Roy O'Bryan
ISBN 0-471-48586-1 © 2004 by the Institute of Electrical and Electronics Engineers.